Information Technology and Globalisation

Information Technology and Globalisation

S. K. Bansal

A.P.H. PUBLISHING CORPORATION
5, ANSARI ROAD, DARYA GANJ
NEW DELHI - 110 002

Published by
S. B. Nangia
A.P.H. Publishing Corporation
5, Ansari Road, Darya Ganj
New Delhi-110 002
☎ 3274050

E-mail : aph@mantraonline.com
Website : www.aphbooksindia.com

ISBN 81-7648-253-6

2001

Typeset at
NEW APCON
25/2, Panchsheel Shopping Centre
New Delhi 110 017
☎ 6494336
6490802

Printed in India at
Efficient Offset Printers
New Delhi-110 035

Preface

Technology changes everything. With the ability to digitise any form of information, boundaries between the various form of surveillance are disappearing. Information technology is an enormously powerful tool. It has the capacity to record vast amount of data which might previously have been held only in some human memory, to process it in ways which would previously have been impracticable, to transmit and share information with other information technology systems and networks on a worldwide basis to retain the information for a potentially unlimited period of time. The benefits of information technology are, of course, immense and many facets of modern life are totally dependant upon technology.

Information technology plays a pervasive role not only in social mobility and nation building, but also in strengthening group consciousness. Nontechnical aspects of information technology plays a crucial role in coping with possible dysfunctioning processes of communication technology. Greater international understanding, therefore, is a direct or automatic result of the rapid expansion of international communication. Unless a reorientation of value systems takes place to bring about a corresponding change in the images and perceptions of communicators, the technological revolution in the machinery of international communication will be unlikely to result in an enhanced sharing of mutually recognised signs and meanings. Modern communication technology does not guarantee improved international understanding, but it does allow more possibility for it.

The rapid development of communications on the Internet constitutes an extraordinary collective resource for the international community. The Internet's international dimension, combined with the challenge represented by the globalisation of trade, naturally makes it imperative to develop appropriate international cooperation in order to ensure that the decentralisation of servers does not lead to national regulations being rendered null and void.

Many states envisage setting up a legal framework specific to the Internet which would be based on the adoption of an international convention to be applied by the competent authorities of each country and enshrining a minimum number of common principles that could serve as the basis for a code of conduct. That framework would include a set of ethical principles applicable to Internet services, under the joint responsibility of the publishers and host services, and, finally, governing legal cooperation between countries.

With the emergence of globalisation concept, the importance of information technology is increased at micro as well as macro level. This book brings valuable account on information technology in the era of globalisation. It will prove highly informative to all the media persons and general public alike.

Editor

Contents

1

Information Society

Information society" is clearly inappropriate as a societal label. The term "information society" has only been used for about a decade, superseding the less specific label "service society," and the even more ambiguous "post-industrial society." Information Society was apparently first used in Japan in the late 1960s, and was the focus of the *Plan for an Information Society.* When considering the future, there are of course no firm answers, but only rough estimates, probabilities, and speculations.

We should not be ashamed of such fuzziness and imperfection, nor should we turn away from questions about the future. It is natural and necessary to have visions of the future. But three types of preconception should be avoided. The first, and most widespread, is the uncritical, euphoric stance that is expressed by commercial interests, which invariably emphasize only the positive attributes of new technology. This same preconception is frequently found in the narrow world view of the technician (who cannot imagine any negative consequences), and in the Utopian passion of wanting to help people with this or that technology.

A second type of over simplified view is the opposite of the first: the hypercritical, pessimistic stance that perceives all modern technology as a human disaster, or focuses solely on growing corporate or government control of information systems. This pessimistic stance can bring forth some important truths, but it seldom offers guidance for positively shaping an Information Society.

The third over-simplified view acknowledges both of these positions, and concludes that there are opportunities for good and evil, centralization and decentralization, freedom and oppression, wealth and poverty. But this balanced view is often expressed superficially, merely concluding, for example, that we must choose between Computopia or a Big Brother society. The reality, however, is likely to be complex and ambiguous, requiring many critical choices over time and incorporating elements of simultaneous euphoria and gloom that fluctuate in their balance. Because ambiguity and uncertainty are highly probable, it is important that we continually ask the right questions, supply the best possible answers, and share these answers across national boundaries.

The following questions illustrate the type of concerns that ought to be addressed, and the type of answers that might follow. The first question will we live in an information society? is too often assumed as a given. It is now a fact that in the industrially developed nations of the world the bulk of the labour force is engaged in some manner of producing or disseminating information. Yet, ironically, these very nations are *underdeveloped* insofar as being information societies. Moreover, this dominant characteristic of the society and its labour force will not necessarily continue into the future.

But societal labels come and go, and hundreds have been proposed in recent years. Why should "information society" necessarily last to 2000, or even to 1990? A new variant might come into usage, such as "telematic society", or even "the age of infoglut," which focuses on the pervasive condition of information overload.

Unemployment caused by the automation of office work and other informational services may be extensive and, if not compensated by an equal number of new jobs in the information sector, could result in a labour force no longer dominated by information-related occupations. The major activity of society would then be some other occupation, or even involuntary idleness-the lack of any occupation-a condition that already characterizes some Third World nations. It should also be acknowledged that there are other concurrent technological revolutions that could have an even greater impact on society than the new information technologies.

The biological revolution could retard the aging process and lengthen human life spans so that we become, essentially, a "Society of Immortals" (albeit a crowded one). Advances in solar cell technology could bring a "soft path" revolution in energy use. The spread of armaments in general, and nuclear weapons in particular, could lead to a cataclysmic detonation of weapons, either through accident or design. (Either instance, ironically, could be seen as a profound failure of communication.) In fact, the EMP or electromagnetic pulse, of a single high-altitude nuclear blast could burn out a nation's electrical systems. In the wake of such a grim scenario, "information society" would seem in retrospect to be the ultimate illusion of modern man.

Although the nuclear threat is growing, most experts still think it unlikely that we will experience a nuclear Armageddon. Nevertheless, there is an increasing possibility of serious disruption by war or terrorism. If we survive, it is likely that we will have an information society of some sort, although we might not call it that. An intelligent approach to assessing the future would acknowledge the potential for changing images. We must consider the many ways in which we may not have an information society, as well as the many ways in which it may be realized, if we hope to shape such a society to the greatest benefit of the greatest number of people.

Will we experience a communications revolution?

The phrase "revolution" has been used promiscuously in recent years, even among those whose scientific training would seemingly inhibit rash statements about technical and social developments. Consider, for example, the proclamations in the late 1960s about the Green Revolution-new crops that would solve the world's hunger problems. Similar assertions were also made at that time about communications. In 1970, Isaac Asimov, the prolific author of science fiction and popularized science books, announced a Fourth Revolution of electronic communications (following speech, writing, and the printing press), which when truly established would bring worldwide electronic literacy, the library of mankind available to any person at any time, a personal immediacy to justify the sense of a global village, lessened differences among people, and cities spreading out and disappearing. Shortly thereafter, in 1972, the Carnegie Commission on Higher Education also proclaimed a Fourth Revolution brought on by' electronics.

A decade later, there are still intimations of such a revolution in higher education and the entire world. But one can hardly say that it has taken place. Remarkable developments have occurred in the cluster of technologies comprising the "communications revolution." These include not only the notable reductions in computer size and cost, combined with dramatically enhanced capability, but also the expanded use of satellies, cable television, home information services, and the many applications of microchips. The string of inventions has by no means run its course; in the words of Adam Osborne, an innovative designer and manufacturer of computers, these new technologies are "running wild." It is impossible to forecast the ultimate configuration of this rapidly evolving cluster of complementary and competing technologies, or to assess their multiple impacts on human life.

The best that can be done is to engage in systematic technology forecasting and assessment. Developments in technology can to some degree be anticipated, especially by procedures of collective thinking such as the Delphi method, which assembles expert forecasts, refining and revising them with two or more rounds of questioning.

The potential impacts of individual technologies can be assessed. The French government has sponsored a study of the impacts of computerization on society, and the Science Council of Canada has expressed concern about planning for an information society. Wilson Dizard has described what the us should do to understand and control the potentially dehumanizing and anti-democratic effects of this "massive technocratic drive." Unfortunately, no effort has been made to collect all of these forecasts, assessments, speculations, and warnings to determine what is known and not known, identify areas of agreement and disagreement, and establish the range of proven policies that might be pursued. Ironically, in the midst of an inchoate revolution in communications technology, this relatively simple act of communication between researchers and responsible policy-makers has not occurred.

A cautious approach to the "communications revolution" would be to withold such a label for the present. In contrast to the changes wrought by other technological revolutions in the past 200 years—railroads, the telegraph, telephones, electric power, automobiles, radio, and television-the new cluster of communications technologies has yet to shape the lives of most people profoundly. Still, these new technologies are likely to be immensely influential in the next few decades, if nuclear weapons have not obliterated much or all of humanity, and if a worldwide economic collapse (which would probably retard the development of the information society) is avoided. The development and dissemination of new technologies will probably not be as rapid or as widespread as many enthusiasts today believe. But the "revolution" will proceed, for there is little or no public opposition, and governments at best have only been able to influence-not control-it.

The nature of the revolution-how it affects the way we communicate and our lives in general-remains problematic. The question of whether we will communicate better and even whether we are *communicating better* today than we did in the recent past-appears obvious and simple. But it is a complex question with deep *significance, and* little or no attention has been paid to it.

The failure to consider this question may stem from the trained incapacity of communications experts to consider big questions, or from the twin assumptions that new technologies of communication will necessarily improve communication, and that all attempts to communicate are realized. Rather, it is important to recognize that, while error-free communication is an ideal, non-communication in modern society appears to be widespread. Examples include failed communications (important messages not sent or received), flawed communications (wrong messages sent as a result of unintentional error or intentional lying or distortion), miscommunication (messages not understood or believed, or resulting in an unintended effect), and junk communication (trivial messages that are received, but are of no importance).

The new communication technologies will greatly multiply capacities for storage, transmission, and manipulation of information. But will they improve human communication, or inadvertently make it more difficult? To sketch some tentative answers to this question, it is useful to briefly examine a few prospects in eight general situations in which people communicate.

Work

Major changes in the workplace are likely, with many jobs eliminated and new jobs created. Robots in factories will presumably perform many tasks that are dangerous or boring. Automation of office work will displace a large part of the female labour force, but, presumably, will also enable better communication within and among organizations, and allow some degree of decentralization of workplaces to rural areas and individual homes. Relationships between buyers and sellers may be improved with the advent of teleshopping (the display of wares on the home video screen), which would give consumers better information on alternative products.

Credit cards activated by thumbprints should be a further advance toward a cashless society. Computerized communications already offer physicians better access to medical knowledge, and the computerization of personal medical histories (with proper safeguards, one hopes) can supply valuable patient information. Individuals will also have much better access to medical information for their own self-care, with new devices to monitor body processes, worn on the wrist or implanted in the body. Microprocessor implants, for example, could detect the first sign of malignant cells being generated. New developments in microelectronics promise at least some degree of hearing for the deaf and sight for the blind, and computers might even act as psychotherapists.

Many people will surely have more electronic options for their pleasure, including videogames and simulated experiences, 100-channel cable television, cheap collector dishes enabling access to increasingly sophisticated communication satellites, and various videodisk and videocassette recordings. Some or all of these will be accompanied by greatly improved presentation in the home, such as wall-size television displays, improved high-definition pictures, and stereo sound. It remains to be seen, however, whether this will result in an abundance of high-quality options or merely a multiplication of banality, a vibrant free market between entertainers and audiences or cultural monopoly and control by governments and information conglomerates.

Any information utility will be a completely free service, as Utopians imagine. Nevertheless, the potential for electronic access to the world's knowledge and for computer programs of instruction, multiple cable television channels devoted to education, instructional videotapes and more, offer enticing possibilities for an education revolution, both within and outside of schools and colleges, that would affect the learning of both children and adults. But the general caveat for all aspects of the communication revolution-not as much, nor as soon-is especially applicable to education.

Educational institutions serve many functions other than learning, and they are difficult to change. Extensive self-directed adult learning is possible, but serious utilization of information abundance must compete with the many enticements of non-serious entertainment. Indeed, the mind-deadening influence of television is a major explanation for the steady decline in test scores among American high school students over the past 20 years.

Sober analysis of who is learning what as a result of the new technologies will be required. It may well be found that information technology will further widen existing divisions between the rich and poor, and create a new generation gap between the computer-literate young and their print-literate elders. Equal caution should be applied to predictions of enhancements in political communications.

The new communications technologies offer many promising ways to make societies more democratic: e.g., electronic plebiscites and opinion polls, teleconferencing with representatives, cable television channels devoted to legislative proceedings, and better voter information on candidates. But these possibilities will not necessarily be realized, and could be more than offset by a dossier society utilizing a centralized data bank, improved surveillance capabilities, new lie detector technology, and narrow-casting of political messages enabling candidates to say different things to different groups of voters. Automatic language translators might facilitate intercultural communication and lessen the tensions of world society, but Western and particularly American culture may very well increase its dominance over the Third World, leading to more angry but unheeded calls for a New World Information Order.

Both within and between nations, the new abundance of information, and its further fragmentation to meet the needs and interests of myriad racial, ethnic, religious, intellectual, political, commercial, and leisure interests, is unlikely to facilitate intergroup harmony and sharing. Mass broadcasting lacked diversity and generally aimed at the lowest common denominator; but it did at least provide a shared experience.

The de-massification of the media-enhances the virtue of greater variety, but the dark side of this trend is a chaos of specialized interests. And to the degree that one finds ample entertainment and education in the home, people will spend more time in their living rooms, and less time with their neighbours or in public places. Relations between men and women, husbands and wives, and parents and children may be enhanced by the imminent spread of mobile telephones and the possible development of two-way wrist video devices (popularized for many years in the "Dick Tracy" comic strip). But the multitude of specialized entertainments may nevertheless serve to strain these intimate relations.

Another important factor affecting communications within families will be the amount of leisure time available, which may or may not be improved by productivity increases at work and decentralization of workplaces (thus reducing commuting time or enabling more work at home). Involuntary leisure forced by unemployment often places a major strain on family relationships. To summarize this cursory survey of basic communication nexuses, it is difficult to say whether human communication has been improving or will improve in the future. It appears likely that the new communications technologies will produce overall improvements in work, commerce, health, and entertainment.

These technologies also offer considerable potential for improving education and politics, but we should be very cautious in making forecasts and assessments. Communications between groups and within families could improve, but are perhaps more likely to worsen. In all these areas, considerable monitoring will be required to provide a reasonably comprehensive answer to the question of whether we are communicating better.

The new information technologies lead to improvements in the quality of life? One must immediately ask, improvements for whom? There will surely be winners and losers, within and among nations. Economic abundance may result from the information revolution; Paul Hawken, for example, postulates that we are in the midst of a tumultuous transition from the mass economy of the industrial age to the "informative economy," where information increasingly replaces mass as a factor in production, resulting in better goods and services. But this does not necessarily lead to more equal sharing, or to enhancement of the *median* benefit. Will all nations benefit from an expanded economic pie (as some argue), or will rich nations increase their share of a relatively limited economic pie (as argued by others)? Will illiterate peasants of the Third World benefit in any way from the new abundance of information? Even within the richer nations, the unemployed and underemployed may not benefit, unless economies expand enough to fund a more generous welfare state.

One must also ask how "quality of life" is measured, which is no simple matter. There may be a growing maldistribution of work, with the current worldwide problem of surplus, unemployable populations aggravated by further advances in automation. The promise of many technologies, and information technology in particular, is that they will be labour-saving, allowing more people to have more leisure. But what is to be done with those who have involuntary leisure forced upon them? And among the employed, voluntary leisure in a technological age can prove illusory. Many professionals today find their workloads increasing, rather than decreasing. New ways to process information may only add to the chaos, much as superhighways have inadvertently led to more traffic congestion. Besides economic indicators of quality of life, one must also assess political and human indicators. Will information technologies increase or decrease the threat of nuclear war? Can we maintain and expand democratic forms of governance? Will non-democratic governments be strengthened by the new technologies (as now seems likely)? Will we spend more time in pleasant and productive interaction with people, or will our interaction with machines increase to the point where computers become our most important teachers and our best friends? Every society requires a minimum standard of competence for its members.

The information society will demand a new standard of literacy, well beyond merely knowing how to use a computer. To survive in any civilized fashion, we must learn to cope with what Alvin Toffler refers to as our "blip culture" of immense diversity, contradictory fragmented images, and shattered consensus.

The new literacy will require the ability to distinguish between knowledge and mere information, and to seek out wisdom amid abundant knowledge. Lifelong learning has been extolled for many years, but the new economic literacy will require an ability to learn, and a willingness to retrain for new occupations.

Finally, the new civic literacy must include an understanding of global affairs, for the new technologies of communications, combined with such problems as pollution, access to ocean resources, monetary chaos, and the arms race, are accelerating the process of globalization. But, in contrast to these needs, what do we in fact know? Victor Ferkiss asserts that technological man does not yet exist, and neoprimitive man continues to be trapped in a technological environment, in which things-not human beings-are in control. In introducing his notion of "meaning lag," Canadian sociologist Omin Klapp warns that meaning formation (the limited human capacity for processing information) is slow and inefficient, compared with the speed and amount of information now accumulating in society. We must recognize that we live in an age of ignorance, where the learning needs of all age groups are outracing their attainments. Our nation is indeed at risk.

However, the most important learning needs are not among children, but among adults-especially our political, intellectual, scientific, corporate, and religious leaders-the decision-makers who will be shaping the information society over the next two decades. Their decisions, for better or worse, will largely determine whether the information society is humane, just, productive, free, participatory, and safe, or whether it is a society characterized by greater inequalities, more centralization, accelerating dangers, and further alienation. Such a reorientation of educational priorities is unlikely, though-at least during the next few years.

We still fail to recognize our widespread ignorance and the need to focus on adult learning because the academic degrees that many of us hold convince us that we are well educated as individuals and as societies. We wish to appear knowledgeable and sophisticated, and this image is reinforced by the sophisticated technologies at our individual and collective command-tools such as computers and automobiles that many are able to use, although comparatively few really understand them very well.

The citizens of the industrialized countries live in a society that is *developed* in manufacturing era terms-but *overdeveloped* when assessed by humane and ecological measures, and *underdeveloped* as an information society. Our society is underdeveloped because of the gap between our present abilities and our need to learn new skills and shape new worldviews. This "ignorance gap" appears to be growing. As with the previous questions about the information society, this question also points to the need for empirical research-in this instance, research into what people in all age groups in all nations know.

And some global standard of information society literacy must emerge from this sobering assessment. The questions raised here are presumably of central importance to all individuals and nations. They could be considered as a matter of national security, deserving the funding equivalent that is now invested in a single battleship or aircraft, let alone the modern arsenals that every nation seems compelled to have. Worldwide, an estimated $650 billion was spent on military preparations during 1982. It is doubtful whether even 0.01 percent of this amount ($65 million) has been devoted worldwide to considering questions about the information society.

Annual spending on this aspect of national security is probably less than 0.001 percent ($6.5 million). Several hundred books have been published in recent years, dealing with some aspect of the information society. Yet there is little communication among those who address some aspect of this subject. This is largely due to our obsolete industrial era colleges and universities, which encourage attention to small and "manageable" questions, technical questions that result in "hard" answers, and questions that conform to the configurations of the established disciplines and professions.

The fragmentation of perspectives increasingly found in the wider society is reflected in the subject of communications itself, which is studied by the professions of journalism, education, and information science (formerly library science), and such cross-disciplinary areas as computer science, management science, behavioural science, language and area studies, and future studies. Adding to this intellectual tumult, researchers in the social sciences often specialise in the economics, politics, and sociology of information and communications.

2

Globalisation of Communication

The present chapter describes some of the cross-border TV channels, illustrating one form of communication globalization. The development in cross-border TV stations accelerated powerfully at the end of the 1980s. Some are privately owned general-interest channels (Super Channel, Star TV) or public service systems (TV5, BBC World Service), while others are specialized in newscasting (CNN, Euronews, etc.), sport (Eurosport, Screensport, etc.), leisure (Disney Channel) or music programmes (MTV, MCM).

They reach millions of homes around the world via cable networks or via collective or individual reception of satellite signals. In order to overcome language obstacles and increase their audience, cross-border stations are investing increasingly in national-language programmes (CNN, NBC, Star TV) or multiplex sound channels enabling televiewers to choose among several languages (Eurosport, Euronews). As a rule, TV stations are basically financed by revenue from commercials on the domestic market but are increasingly likely to target the international scene. In addition to commercials, some channels (CNN, Star TV) obtain a growing share of their revenue from pay-per-view systems via cable TV networks, as well as from hotel and individual subscribers. The success of cross-border television is due to a series of factors that are basically technological in nature: the boom in satellites, the proliferation of installed bases of dish antennae over vast regions of the world, progress in the miniaturization of TV control rooms, cameras and small-scale transmission stations which together have done away with distance and time.

Cable News Network (CNN)

CNN is the channel which best embodies the instant, global, worldwide status of television. The channel today can reach every region around the world via a network of satellites covering the whole planet. In 1995, the channel was distributed in more than 120 countries, beaming its programmes into more than a thousand hotels around the world and reaching more than 70 million homes. But it was the coverage of major events such as the abortive coup d'état in the former Soviet Union or the Gulf War that pushed the channel to the forefront of the planetary news system.

The aim to serve an international audience means that it repeats part of its newscasts every twenty-four hours to provide televiewers worldwide with a panorama of the main news at any time, hence the importance of CNN International, the version of the channel's news bulletin tailored for international audiences. It combines the international programme of CNN and televised newscasts from Headline News, the other non-stop news channel of the Turner empire that telecasts a summary of the day's events every halfhour. CNN and Headline News are the most profitable products of the Turner Broadcasting System (TBS), the mother company that also comprises Turner Network Television M and TBS Superstation. In recent years, the group has been putting into practice a diversification strategy by exporting its various models worldwide. In June 1997, CNN regionalized its news programmes aimed at North and South America, Asia and Europe.

The revised formula consists of adapting the editorial content to the targeted regions. Broadcasting is in Spanish for the South American market and English for the rest of the world. The channel operators have announced plans for alternative cultural and language versions, aimed in particular at the Arab, Indian, Japanese and Russian markets. This new policy does not rule out the extension of the TBS network round the world.

In Europe it has become the majority shareholder in the German non-stop news channel NTV and in the Russian station TV6 Moscow. Targeting the European, Caribbean and Central American regions, it has also recently launched two channels which are already highly prosperous in the United States, one specializing in animated cartoons. The Cartoon Network, and the other in films, Turner Network Television (TNT). The TBS group, with earnings in 1995 of $3,437 billion, has just merged with the Time Warner company to give birth to the largest global communication group in the world, ahead of Walt Disney-ABC. Observers expect the synergy generated by the two groups to buttress CNN's news potential, particularly in view of the journalistic input from the Time Warner group.

Notwithstanding this important influx, however, CNN has to contend with other competitors surfing in on the wave of satellites, players who have also become aware of the strategic power and potential of information.

BBC World Service

The BBC World Service ranks as a serious alternative to CNN. A subsidiary of the BBC, it covers practically all five continents. It broadcasts a non-stop news programme twenty-four hours a day. To cover its operating costs it receives neither licence fees nor state subsidies and strives to balance its accounts through sales.

In addition to its newscasts every hour, the BBC World Service adds news magazines and the best documentaries produced by the BBC. In recent years, it has improved its coverage through partnership agreements with regional or local channels such as the South African pay-TV network M-Net, and American and Japanese channels. While the BBC World Service seems to be the main rival for CNN, other news channels with specific linguistic or regional viewpoints are joining the throng.

Euronews

Euronews is the leading satellite-based multilingual European news channel, jointly set up by eleven European public service channels. Via the Eutelsat 11-Fl satellite, it covers all of Europe, including the central and eastern regions, as far as the Near and Middle East. Televiewers have access to programmes broadcast non-stop twenty-four hours a day on a separate frequency for each of the six languages available: Arabic, English, French, German, Italian and Spanish. The originality of the channel is that the news bulletins are image-only telecasts, with voice-over journalists simply commentating on the pictures, reports and magazines provided by members of the European Radio-Television Union (UER).

According to its proponents, by presenting a coverage of regional and world current events from a European point of view and in six different languages, Euronews can claim to be the European equivalent of the American channel CNN.

Other worldwide networks

Other networks have spread over all five continents. The largest of these today is that of the Rupert Murdoch News

Corp. group. It is the fourth largest communication empire in the world, with a 1995 sales figure of $9 billion (profits of $626 million from the press and $400 million from television). The Murdoch Group has a worldwide television network connected by satellite, notably comprising the fourth-ranking national American network FOX TV, the British encrypted BSkyB and the Star TV channel. After starting out as a small programming stream in Hong Kong, Star TV has grown to seven channels and is now the largest network in the Asia-Pacific region. It covers practically all of Asia, with a perimeter that includes Australia, China, Japan, Pakistan and even the Near and Middle East.

The network includes news, sport and music channels, and has seen spectacular growth, particularly in South-East Asia and in India. Finally, Rupert Murdoch has announced his arrival in the near future in Japan with JSkyB, the United States with AS-KyB, and the United Kingdom with the launching in 1998 of a digital stream of 200 theme channels and services.

The American operator Direct TV also has the same target, and is developing joint ventures with partners from different regions around the world. In Latin America, the company intends to launch a stream of 142 channels, telecast in Spanish and Portuguese. After consolidating its presence in Asia, the operator intends to target the Japanese market in 1997 by going on-air with Superbird C, a stream of a hundred specialized theme channels.

The company also intends to penetrate the African and Indian markets with the forthcoming launches of Direct TV India and Direct TV Africa. The French-language channel TV5 is also battling to gain planetary coverage by using four satellites: Eutelsat II-FI to cover the whole of the region from Helsinki to Casablanca, Statsionar 12 for the whole of the African continent, Anik El for North

America and finally PanAmSati to reach Latin America and the Caribbean. Since its start-up in January 1984, TV5 has operated continually in an associative French-language framework including the French-language Belgian Radio and Television Authority (RTBF), the Swiss Radio Broadcasting authority (SSR), France 2, France 3, the French National Audio-Visual Institute (INA), the Financial Broadcasting Authority (SOFIRAD) and the Canada Quebec Television Consortium (CTQC) comprising the main broadcasters and producers in Quebec and Canada.

The programmes on the channel basically comprise televised newscasts and magazines presented as the counterpoint to CNN, together with fiction, entertainment and theatrical and musical productions by the various French-language television channels. Another network with planetary status is the MTV music channel, which was launched in 1981 in the United States and has not ceased to expand since then It has consolidated its position in every region of the world with MTV Europe, MTV Asia, MTV Brazil, Mandarin MTV and MTV India.

This regional fragmentation is part of the new strategy of the channel, which consists in adapting to the cultural conditions of each region. Also worth noting is the arrival of new channels specializing in financial news such as CNBC, Dow Jones, Bloomberg and Reuters, which are vying for position on the world money market.

Newcomers

Although the international circulation of televised programmes has always been dominated by the developed countries, notably in North America and in Europe, major changes are taking shape. The trend is towards enhanced co-operation and a somewhat timid balancing of the flow of communication. The international circulation of programmes is becoming less of a mismatch as a growing number of Latin American, Arab and Asian broadcasters launch their own satellite TV channels. In this field, the conventional North-South cleavage appears somewhat narrower in relation to the other gaps between regions or major language communities. Asia, Latin America and the Middle East are asserting their presence and expressing a greater demand for news with a regional focus, while channels with international or regional status are developing and often competing with those of the Northern hemisphere. In Latin America, the Mexican broadcaster Televisa has invested more than $250 million in the Panamsat company to set up its own satellite TV channels. The Mexican operator provides a pay-per-view service in the United States and in Spain.

In Argentina, the Canal Sur channel telecasts a selection of news and entertainment programmes representative of South America over both American continents. For the Arab world, the Middle East Broadcasting Centre (MBC) channel telecasts from London via Arabsat to the whole of the region. Funded essentially by Saudi Arabian capital, it is picked up every day from Morocco to Iran with a programme featuring news, entertainment, cinema and religious broadcasts. News nevertheless remains the priority focus of the channel, with the recent acquisition of the UPI news agency networks and the modernization of the studios and the editorial department.

MBC today is fully equipped for digital broadcasting, but that eventuality will be possible only with the launch of Arabsat 2. Now that it has gone global, television displays whatever is happening around the planet, from the fall of the Berlin Wall to the massacre of Srebrenica or the genocide in Rwanda. It has become a bona fide worldwide counterculture that undermines totalitarian regimes and renders state control of content ever more difficult and illusory.

However, even if international television has enabled peoples that were previously deprived of images to open their windows onto the world, many feel concern about the power, the spirit of conquest and the scale of the networks, which have become nothing short of empires.

Regulation around the world

Regulation is a means of reconciling the economic interventionism of public authorities and the market forces in the audiovisual field. Domestic regulatory systems for the audiovisual sector feature a number of factors linked to the political, economic and cultural specifics of each country but also to economic and technological change around the world.

The radical technological upheavals of the 1980s, combined with the expansion in television stations broadcasting by satellite and their increasingly international nature and structure, have caused major changes in the audiovisual field in every country. First of all they attacked the monopolies held by national broadcasting authorities which traditionally have always controlled the various functions of programme production, programming and broadcasting.

Marketing and globalization have also brought the development of new markets with the emergence of private operators and that growth in their numbers, thereby undermining the conventional balance that existed between public and private sectors. These changes have been further amplified by the new possibilities of transmission opened up by digital broadcasting, as well as by the emergence of multimedia groups against a backdrop of internationalized markets, and finally by the growing importance of private interests in the audiovisual field. Faced with these new upheavals - which are likely to amplify during the course of the next few years - certain states have drafted a number of laws or taken decisions of a statutory nature. National contexts call for different strategies according to political traditions or patterns of media ownership. In countries where radio and television are a state monopoly, their management is generally controlled by the executive body, which governs the administration and guides decisions concerning the production and broadcasting of programmes. This structural concept tends to disappear as the democratic process evolves. A public broadcasting authority is distinct from a state-controlled television service in that it enjoys editorial independence guaranteed by law and operates in a highly competitive environment.

The state manages frequencies in order to prevent them from being used in an uncoordinated manner, and often supervises the financial management of the enterprise. On the other hand, regulation, wherever it exists, is controlled by independent authorities entrusted, according to the country in question, with regulating or supervising the programming activities of the private and public television operators. The authorities are generally placed outside the administrative hierarchy and are theoretically free from any judicial or political influence.

Some are endowed with decision-making powers enabling them to organize the domestic audiovisual market-place and to control the legality of the conditions in which programmes are broadcast by private and public operators, and are even authorized to sanction occasional breaches of the law. It would be difficult in a single chapter to quote all the texts issued by regulatory authorities or legislative bodies. It is possible, however, to highlight a number of systems and illustrate concerns common to them all.

Highly varied systems

Generally speaking, different countries have different approaches to the authority in charge of regulating the audiovisual and telecommunications industry. In some countries, there is a single statutory body. This is the case in the United States, where the 1934 Communication Act entrusted the regulation of the vast area of the telecommunications and audiovisual sectors to a single agency, the Federal Communication Commission (FCC). The FCC is responsible for frequency management, supervision of the telecommunication networks operators (prices, service quality, network interconnection, etc.) and regulation of international communications on behalf of the United States.

The organization of statutory authorities in Canada is quite similar to that in the United States. The regulatory body is the Canadian Radio-Television and Telecommunications Commission (CRTC), set up in 1961; its main assignment is to allocate radio and television frequencies and to define the operating conditions of each licence-holder, particularly with regard to the quotas of Canadian works broadcast and to the enhancement of domestic production.

Since 1976, the CRTC has also monitored the telecommunications market, in which it strives to maintain a balance among the different operators. In Japan, the Ministry of Post and Telecommunications (MPT) is responsible for communications in the broad sense of the term, including postal services, telecommunications and broadcasting. In Italy, the Bill presented by the Italian Government in July 1996 provided for the creation of a higher authority to supervise the audiovisual and telecommunications sectors.

In other countries, the two branches of communication are governed separately, for example by the Office of Telecommunications (Oftel) and the Independent Television Commission (ITC) in the United Kingdom, or the Autorité de Regulation des

Télécommunications (ART) and the Conseil Supérieur de l'Audiovisuel (CSA) in France. In practice, no country has a completely unified statutory structure, and it is only as a result of convergence pressures that attention is being brought to bear on the information and communication industry.

Effects of convergence

With the digital revolution and the convergence between the older industries such as the telephone and cable sectors, many conventional communication services, such as audiovisual services, can be routed through telecommunication networks. In some countries, cable operators can provide audiovisual and telephone services via the same physical medium. With the liberalization of telecommunications, new markets are developing and new operators are claiming the right to use competitor services on the same transmission system. The United States was the first country to take this change into account with the new telecommunications act adopted in February 1996, which completely opened up the communication industry to competition.

The act enables the three major operators - long-distance telephone companies, local telephone companies (the seven Baby Bells) and cable operators - to compete in a general free market system.

Anti-trust laws

Anti-trust laws have been introduced into national legislation. They usually place ceilings on shareholding in the capital of television channels. If a closer look is taken, however, and the legislation mentioned above is kept in mind; regulation in this area particularly in the United States and in Europe is more akin to deregulation than regulation of the audiovisual sector, a finding in keeping with the principle of liberalization which is characteristic of most countries nowadays. In the United States, the provisions of the 1984 Act on the concentration of operators on the American market have been slackened. The Act stipulated that no audiovisual consortium was allowed to reach more than 25 per cent of the American population, and it was out of the question to leave two stations on the same local market in the hands of a single owner. In the latest version of the law, the admissible percentage of the nationwide audience for all the stations controlled by a single owner was raised to 3 5 per cent (it is currently 25 per cent).

The networks today are also authorized to have their own cable companies. In the United Kingdom, the Bill to amend the 1990 law which was submitted to Parliament in July 1996 came into force on 1 November the same year. The new terms of the broadcasting Act relate to plurimedia ownership. They are intended to boost synergy between progress groups and local radio and television operations. Planned acquisitions have to be submitted for approval to the Radio Authority and the Independent Television Commission, whose task it is to see that the public interest rule is applied on the basis of diversity of opinions and programme content.

Broadcasting quotas

Many countries around the world have adopted rules that are both economic and cultural in their objective, forcing broadcasters to comply with quotas for programming and production of national works. By legislating on the quota question, states have sought to react to the consequences of the process of internationalization of the media on national television and film production and on the circulation of goods and services.

In Canada, the regulations stipulate that 60 per cent of all programmes broadcast annually must be Canadian in origin, and 50 per cent of those broadcasts must be during prime time. On Radio Canada stations, a 60 per cent minimum of Canadian programmes must also be broadcast during prime time. Canadian pay-TV stations have to allocate at least 20 per cent of their revenue to the production of Canadian programmes. In Lebanon, the audiovisual law adopted by the Lebanese Parliament in November 1994 stipulates that 40 per cent of all the programmes broadcast on national channels must be Lebanese in origin.

In France, statutory requirements include quotas for broadcasting films and audiovisual production, conditions for telecasting films, advertising rules and regulations, the protection of children and adolescents, and due regard for the French language. The effectiveness of these measures seems somewhat debatable, given the fact that viewers are free to watch other international channels if the domestic programmes do not suit their tastes, with the result that the ultimate effect of the measures may be diametrically opposed to their initial purpose. On the to allocate part of their resources to production may be a viable alternative to broadcasting quotas.

Europe and audiovisual regulations

European regulations for the audiovisual field are based on the celebrated 'Television without Frontiers' directive of 1989. The purpose of the document was to co-ordinate certain provisions laid down by law, regulation or administrative action in member states of the Union concerning the pursuit of television broadcasting activities. The most controversial aspect of the directive was the obligation for all European television channels to devote a majority of certain time-slots to broadcasting programmes of European origin.

The requirement resulted in considerable disagreement during the drafting of the directive and in the somewhat thorny dealings with the United States during there trade talks of the Uruguay cycle at year-end

1993. Compliance by TV channels with the abovementioned obligation has yet to become the subject of any systematic monitoring, and this feature of the directive remains one of the main concerns for the industry professionals and legislators alike.

The revision of the directive and its effects on the improvement of the circulation of European audiovisual works within member states of the European Union will be items on the agenda for the European Commission and Parliament in 1997. While the 'Television without Frontiers' directive remains the key document in the audiovisual policy of the European Union, another White Paper on *Strategic Options to Strengthen the European Broadcasting Industry* was published in April 1994.

3

Information Service

The community information service input is directed towards selecting appropriate materials, reprocessing information in a form that can be readily understood, packaging information, and arranging all these materials in a way that is easier for the customer to use. This kind of service is most suitable where there is insufficient staff or lack of trained staff to operate a personal enquiry service, such as a small branch or mobile library, or for deposit in an unmanned centre. It is usual for materials to be assembled, produced or packaged by a district or central office. *Support* for other information services or for groups of professional workers, etc. Where there are adequate information services for the public, the greater need may be for an information service to support the work of other agencies and workers in the field. This could take one or several of the following forms:

— selective dissemination of information (SDI) which, in essence, involves channelling information to meet the expressed subject interests of groups or individuals;

— current awareness services;

— press cuttings service;

— provision of loan collections of reference books;
— provision of publicity and educational materials;
— provision of local information.

Information giving, which can range from simple directional information to the complex, such as eligibility for housing benefit, and may involve *steering* an enquirer to an agency from whom further help or advice can be obtained, without the service making contact with that source of help or advice.

Referral, on the other hand, is a more active form of steering in which contact or an appointment is made for the enquirer with an agency who can help. In some cases, it may be necessary to *escort* the client to the agency if it is felt that they do not have sufficient confidence to make contact, may be intimidated by officials, or are likely to have difficulties in explaining their case.

Advice is information tailored to individual need. Giving advice can be a fairly neutral activity, such as setting out options from which the enquirer must make his or her choice, or it can involve evaluation of options with recommendations as to the best course of action.

Practical help with writing letters, form filling or making telephone calls.

Advocacy is needed where a client is not capable of obtaining the information, services, benefits or justice to which he or she is entitled. A positive identification is made with the client's case, which is then argued in front of officials, tribunals or courts on the client's behalf.

Community education, in the context of information and advice work, is a process of increasing the self-sufficiency of individuals or groups to manage their own affairs, obtain their rights, etc. or to improve their awareness and understanding of issues that affect them.

Community action involves the information service in playing an active role in precipitating change either by acting itself or by alerting other individuals and groups to campaign. Such action can arise out of an analysis of enquiries received, where it becomes apparent that there is a lack of a service or facility in the community or where a situation exists that is causing injustice or disadvantage to people.

Outreach is a means of providing information or a service to a clientele wider than that usually served by the community information service, in either geographical or sociological terms. It covers the use of extension bureaux, mobiles and deposit collections as well as the use of media, e.g. newspaper or magazine articles, radio, television, advertising or viewdata.

Counselling requires a greater commitment of time and level of training to help individuals with problems. At one extreme it can involve simply lending a sympathetic ear to clients who, in externalizing their problems, may thus be better able to face them and arrive at a solution.

On the other hand, counselling can lead on to diagnosis and analysis, with ultimate referral of clients to clinics for treatment. Counselling should not be undertaken without specialized training. Not all these activities will be appropriate to your organisation or the community it is intended to serve. Some organisations, for example, have to be impartial, and therefore are precluded from activities which might be construed as 'political' or partisan or from taking sides in a dispute. Although for the purposes of this book the different functions of an information service have been treated separately, in practice such clear distinctions can rarely be made.

The process of information-advice-advocacy is often

referred to as a 'continuum'. Boundaries are blurred and not generally recognized by users, even though, in setting up a service, limits have to be placed on its actions. Someone seeking information or help with a problem is not really interested in the philosophy of your organisation but in obtaining a satisfactory answer, or solution, irrespective of the means used to obtain it. Consequently, some people have argued that it is wrong to set up an information service and attempt to limit its functions to just giving information or advice but not advocacy, since users' expectations may be raised but not completely satisfied.

On the other hand, it can be argued that something is better than nothing. The decision must be yours but, in setting up a service, you must have a clear idea of what you expect it to achieve and, if it is necessary to set limits, how to deal satisfactorily with cases that need to be taken beyond those limits.

Management

An information service is set up to meet the needs of a given community and one of the best ways to ensure that the service meets its objectives is for the community to be represented on its management. A fairly common pattern is for a management committee to be made up of representatives from statutory bodies, the service itself, and from individuals and groups in the community. No one group should dominate the management committee and its chairperson should preferably be neutral.

An independent committee is particularly necessary where an information service works in the voluntary sector but receives most of its finding from a statutory body. This is in order to guarantee that undue pressure may not be exerted by the funding bodies on the way the service operates. It may be more difficult for a community information service belonging to a statutory organisation to have an independent management committee and, in those circumstances, an alternative would be to set up some form of advisory group representing users. The responsibilities of a management committee or advisory group might include some or all of the following:

— laying down rules for the use of the service;
— monitoring use and recommending changes;
— suggesting new strategies or areas of work;
— ironing-out trouble spots;
— taking community action where lack of provision or malpractice is identified by the information service;
— lobbying for funds or improved facilities;
— giving specialist advice and help on such matters as budgeting, publicity, law, etc.

What is needed to information service?

Establishing and operating a community information service requires certain resources:

— *finance:* capital and revenue;
— *facilities:* premises and equipment;
— *staff:* paid/voluntary, training, health and safety, etc.
– *a system:* for the collection, processing, storage, retrieval and dissemination of information.

Financial resources

Whether you are setting up a community information service from scratch or simply adding another function to an existing service, there are bound to be financial implications. Capital expenditure will most probably be required to provide premises, furniture and equipment. Revenue will be required to pay for such considerations as:

— staff salaries and travelling expenses;
— rent and rates;
— heating, lighting, water and telephones;
— insurances;
— stationery;
— publicity and promotion.

A non-statutory organisation setting up an information service for the first time has a number of possible sources of funding:

Local authorities. Counties, district councils, parish councils are all empowered to make grants for this purpose. They will be the most likely source of substantial continuous finding and the most problematical. Local authority funding is usually given in the form of a grant which usually has to be Applied for and agreed each year. Often the decision is made close to the end of the financial year and so an information service may find itself always existing on a financial knife-edge. Changes in the political control of a council can often spark off a reappraisal of support for services. Moreover, there is sometimes covert pressure by local authorities to influence the policies of organisations they fund, particularly those policies of which the authority disapproves.

Local authorities can also give grants for capital expenditure—premises, furniture and equipment. Some will use their lotteries fund for this kind of grant, but not for revenue funding. In recent years, the introduction of rate-capping and standard spending assessments (SSAs) has severely curtailed the amount of money that local authorities are able to commit to the support of non-statutory services. At the same time, other government legislation on, for example, compulsory competitive tendering is aimed at forcing local authorities to divest themselves of services that can, in the government's view, be better provided by the private or voluntary sectors. This may include local authority-run information and advice services. Where services are operated or taken over by voluntary organisations, there is a growing practice amongst local authorities to set down what is expected of the voluntary organisation in a contract which is signed by both parties and monitored. If you cannot get funding from the local authority, it may be prepared to give support in kind, such as the provision of premises (short-term accommodation) or shared accommodation in one of its own buildings, e.g. the library, or community centre.

The most likely local authority departments to approach are social services, leisure and amenities, libraries or education. Look out too for officers with titles like 'Community Development Officer', 'Youth and Community Officer', or 'Community Services Librarian', who may be able to advise you on what kinds of financial or other help are available. Your local Council for Voluntary Service (CVS) or Rural Community Council (RCC) may be able to advise you on the right approach to local authorities. In the London area responsibility for grant-aiding voluntary organisations has been vested in a separate body known as the London Boroughs Grants Scheme. They can be contacted at 5th Floor, Regal House, London Road, Twickenham TW1 3QS.

Government departments and agencies. There is no doubt that the voluntary sector's prospects of funding from central government are not rosy at this present time, particularly for new projects. Funds available are contracting and many of the government departments are now channelling their grants through other agencies, such as Training and Enterprise Councils. It would be advisable to consult your local Council for Voluntary

Service or any of the books listed at the end of this section for the latest position regarding grants. The following sources currently available may be of particular interest for a voluntary organisation wishing to set up an information or advice service.

The Public Library Development Incentive Scheme (PLDIS) funded by the Department of National Heritage and administered by the British Library Research & Development Department is also available to voluntary organisations.

Training and Enterprise Councils (TECs) are an important local source of funding, much of it coming from the Department for Employment. They will be particularly interested in projects that stimulate local employment, provide help for the unemployed. Or offer educational guidance. From 1992/3, TECs are administering an Ethnic Minority Grant which forms part of Section 11 funds but projects will almost certainly need to involve training, employment and/or enterprise. Unlike local government bids for Section 11 funding which can only cover revenue costs, TECs will be able to cover project costs.

Rural Development Commission is concerned to alleviate economic and social problems in rural England. Its Rural Social Partnership Fund supports voluntary organisations in partnership with other agencies which aim to tackle problems of rural disadvantage. This fund was set up for three years, starting in 1989, so you will need to contact them to see if it is continuing.

Local and national trusts are increasingly a useful source of funding for capital expenditure items but are less likely to provide revenue funding, except for innovative or experimental projects. Charities and trusts often have rules concerning what kind of project they can support. It is useful if you can find out what these are before applying since a little redrafting of your proposal could make it more acceptable. District Councils are supposed to keep a list of local charitable trusts and their terms of reference, but failing that the local CVS or RCC will usually be able to advise on possible sources of local funding. National trusts and their areas of interest are listed in *The directory of grant-making trusts*, an annual publication from the Charities Aid Foundation. You should find a copy in the reference section of most major public libraries.

A similar type of trust administration that has appeared in recent years is the 'community trust'. Community trusts are independent bodies who receive money from a variety of sources—trusts, industry, local government—and give grants to volun-tary projects. Applications may have to be siphoned first through the local CVS or RCC. Directory of Social Change also publishes a magazine, *Trust monitor*, which contains information on new trusts, changes in policies, facts and figures, feature articles, etc.; three issues a year, subscription £20.00.

Commercial organisations are unlikely to provide funding for the day-to-day running costs of an information service but may be a useful source of capital funding for equipment, furniture or special projects. They may also give help in kind—donations of redundant equipment, training, etc.- or offer sponsorship deals for fundraising events and publicity. Directory of Social Change also publishes a quarterly magazine, *Corporate citizen*, which gives up-to-date facts and help with understanding the corporate viewpoint; this costs £30.00 a year for voluntary organisations, £55.00 for others.

European Community, in certain circumstances makes grants to local authorities and to voluntary organisations for schemes which seek to alleviate deprivation or inequality. The European Social Fund is open to organisations that arrange training aimed at providing the skills needed for specific kinds of jobs. Applicants need to have agreement from central or local government to fund at least half (35% in Northern Ireland) of the costs of the training.

The allocation of ESF grants has been decentralized and, as far as the voluntary sector is concerned, applications are handled and placed in priority order by the National Council for Voluntary Organisations. Final decisions are taken by the Depart-ment of the Environment. The European Community also administers many small schemes for making grants. These small schemes very rarely have more than a few thousand pounds available for any one project and rarely make more than one grant for the same activity. Grants must also be used in the year they are made. They are thus not much use for core funding but may contribute to set-up costs. Areas covered by schemes include employment, families, older people, disabled people, human rights education, women and combating racism and xenophobia. There are numerous guides to obtaining grants and fundraising which cover all the sources of funding listed above and many others.

Some of these guides are general in extent, others cover particular areas of concern or geographical areas. Directory of Social Change also produces a set of 8- and 12-page Fundraising leaflets on Setting up; Planning a capital project; Drawing lip a budget; Raising money locally; Earning money; Organising an appeal; Doing research; Writing an application; Social sponsorship; Developing a strategy; Organising an event; Fundraising sources. If a statutory organisation, such as a library, wants to set up a community information service then, in addition to whatever funding can be provided from within its own budget, the following are the most likely sources of funding:

The Public Library Development Scheme (PLDIS) was set up in 1988 to encourage new enterprises designed to extend or improve public library services in England. Activities likely to promote cooperation between public libraries and other libraries or organisations in the public or private sector are of particular interest. The Scheme is funded by the Department of National Heritage and administered by the British Library Research & Development Department. It was originally funded for three years, but in September 1990 the Minister for the Arts set aside up to £250,000 per year for the three financial years 1992/3-1994/5.

The Scheme provides up to 40% of the funding for projects, the remainder to be found by the library authority or other organisation and its partners. Applications can be made by such as the following:

— English local library authorities or their co-operative agencies, such as regional library bureaux;

— any public or private organisation (including those in the voluntary sector) able to demonstrate that the proposed development will contribute to the quality and cost-effectiveness of public library services in England or in a particular region; applicants are normally expected to involve one or more public libraries in the project.

Types of project in the community information field that have been helped through this Scheme include a feasibility study and implementation of a Training Shop in Peterborough Central Library, and Camden's Free Leaflets Information Service. At the time of writing, it is not known whether PLDIS funding will be available for a further three years. Details may be obtained from

Christine Burden, Public Library Development Incentive Scheme, The British Library Research & Development Department, 2 Sheraton Street, London W1V 4BH.

The British Library, Research & Development Department has given support over the years to innovative community information services such as South Hackney School 'Right to Know' project and South Molton Community Information project. If your proposed information service intends to break new ground then you may be able to interest the British Library (BL) in a research proposal. It would, however, need to cover the research element of the work.

Only in exceptional circumstances has the BL provided financial help towards the setting-up and running costs of projects. The Department has a five-year plan for priorities in research of which the broad areas of concern are the applications and implications of information technology, information as a tradable commodity, and the effects of economic and social constraints on services. Further details of current priorities are contained in their booklet, *Priorities for research* 1989-1994, available from

The British Library Research and Development Department, 2 Sheraton Street, London WIV 4BH. Although most of the possible sources of funding listed above are for either capital items or relatively short-term running costs and do not solve the question of how to keep the service going in the long term, nevertheless they do make it possible to get services off the ground, to establish them on a sound footing and to demonstrate their worth to the community. Hopefully, this will then attract more secure and lasting financial support. Many services provided by local authorities are encouraged to pursue income generation as a means of supplementing or making up a shortfall in budgets. There does not appear to be much scope in the field of community information for income-generation activities, other than marginal activities such as the sale of mailing lists to commercial organisations (a dubious practice at best).

The one exception is in the provision of support activities, such as Camden's Free Leaflet Information Service, which is attracting support from libraries and other organisations nation-wide through a subscription system. Other organisations like the National Association of Citizens' Advice Bureaux successfully market their information service but this does not represent a major proportion of their funding.

A community information service that is intended to be simply an extension of an existing statutory service will still need to be costed and the effect on other parts of the service assessed. It is highly unlikely that there will be spare capacity—either finance, staff or accommodation—lying around waiting to be used. A sufficiently well thought out and argued scheme might attract additional funding from the authority or via other sources of finance, but the most likely scenario is that it will have to be provided out of the existing budget. This then means that some kind of re-assessment of current services must take place, in order that priority be given to the proposed service, and resources diverted to support it. It hardly needs to be said that for such a process to take place and be successful, both senior management and staff in the workplace need to be convinced of the value of the new service and to be committed to its development.

The climate for developing such services in public libraries in the mid-1990s is not of the best. Government legislation has focused attention on the 'core' services—lending books and providing reference and study facilities—and other services are expected to be self-financing. Pressure on local authority budgets as a result of rate-capping or the threat of it has meant a retraction of staff involved in outreach services, such as community information. Nevertheless, public libraries are still managing to come forward with innovative schemes, but the watchwords now are 'partnership' and 'income generation'.

Facilities

The choice of a suitable location for your information service will depend to a certain extent on what can be afforded and on the community you will be serving. If you already have suitable premises with spare capacity which can be used, this will help keep costs to a minimum but, if not, you will need to look elsewhere. It is always a good principle to try to locate an information service where it will be most accessible for its users.

Even in a 'closed' community, such as a school or organisation, there may be parts of the building that are natural congregating points, e.g. hall, refectory, social/recreational rooms, by the drinks machine. Obviously, the location of an information service which does not deal face-to-face with clients, but mainly via the telephone and post, is less crucial. Research into the use of advice centres indicates that most people use them because they are familiar and very local. They also tend to use those which are near their homes in preference to those which are near their workplaces.

So the ideal location for an information centre that is to serve the public is likely to be in the neighbourhood shopping area. This will not only make it accessible for the purposive user but should also encourage casual use, especially if it has windows that can be used to promote the service, Such locations, however, can rarely be afforded by one agency alone and you might need to consider sharing with other agencies.

Currently, with the recession at its height, there are vast numbers of shop premises lying empty which landlords Might consider letting on a short-term basis for a reduced rent. Sometimes district councils have empty property available for short-term lets. And short terms have a habit of being extended... If obtaining your own prominently sited premises, either alone or shared, is out of the question, then consider the possibility of being housed by another organisation that already has premises in a suitable location, such as a library, community centre, council offices, nearly-new shop or even a commercial concern.

Failing that, then the next best thing is to seek for premises where there is a significant traffic flow, even though it may not be with shops—for example near a popular bus stop, a school or clinic, on the way to a shopping centre, or in premises which regularly attract a large number of people, e.g. a community centre, library, health or day centre. An information service that is intended to help those with special needs, such as people with disabilities or elderly people, might be best located in a place where they already meet for other purposes—a day centre or workshop for the handicapped, for example.

The following are some other features to look out for in locating a community information service:

— ground-floor accommodation for ease of access, especially for elderly and disabled people;

— prominent location—not tucked away in a back room or having rear access;

— facilities for display, such as a large picture-window;

— informal atmosphere—some buildings can look too official or have unpleasant associations which may constitute a deterrent to users;

— drop-in facility so that potential users, especially the more timid, have a legitimate reason for going into the centre for the first time to 'suss it out' without being challenged.

Space

The space requirements for your community information service will depend very much on the type of activities it will be undertaking. A *self-help service* makes little demand on office accommodation and does not require an enquiry desk, but will need a prominent location near the major traffic flow in the building and space for noticeboards and leaflet/display racks. A *support service or* one that does not deal face-to-face with clientele may only need an office in any habitable location with space for processing materials. A purely *information-giving service* dealing face-to-face with the public may need a waiting/browsing area that is welcoming and relaxing, space for leaflet display and noticeboards, an enquiry desk prominently sited near to major traffic flow, and an office/workroom for the staff. An *advice/counselling service,* in addition to the above, will need an interview room(s) for those clients who need privacy.

Some advice services put more emphasis on informality and seek collective solutions to problems through group discussion, rather than through a one-to-one approach. Here, the centre becomes more a social facility, encouraging people to drop in for a cup of tea or coffee and a chat, out of which information needs can arise incidentally. This style of operation calls for a kitchen or at least, space where drinks can be made, and a comfortable lounge-type area. An interview room may still be necessary for those clients who prefer privacy.

Furniture and equipment

Desks, tables and chairs. The importance of the enquiry desk being located near the main traffic flow has already been stated. It should be immediately visible on entering the building/room and clearly signed. Where the location is unfavourable, this can be overcome to some extent by good directional signs. The desk should be low and form the least possible barrier between the information seeker and the staff. It will need to have a fairly large surface to accommodate such things as card files and/or computer, telephone, frequently used quick-reference books, etc. Drawers will be needed for pens, stationery, frequently used information files and cash (where the service has items for sale).

A chair will be required for the use of staff, preferably one that is adjustable if more than one person is going to use it, and with a swivel where the staff need to turn round frequently to consult shelves or a noticeboard. There should also be a comfortable chair for clients at the enquiry desk and others nearby for those waiting to use the service, with possibly a low coffee table and some magazines for browsing while they wait. An information service that handles a high volume of very quick enquiries, like a tourist information centre, might find it more convenient to have a higher bar-type counter with enquirers and staff either standing or using barstools.

Telephone. This is likely to be the most important item of equipment for the staff and the public in your information service. Some information services conduct most of their business with clients over the telephone. In such cases, where it is desirable to link a telephone enquirer immediately with another service, this can be achieved by means of a three-way or conference-line facility.

The most useful location for the telephone is on the enquiry desk, although further lines or extensions may be required in interview rooms or offices. Opinions differ as to the desirability of having telephones in interview rooms. In some instances, when seeking information or trying to sort out a problem with another organisation on behalf of a client, it can be helpful to have the client by the phone so that points can be clarified as soon as they arise. On the other hand, there will be occasions when you will want to talk frankly to another organisation without the client overhearing; in which case it is better if the telephone is located in a private office. Ideally, both options should be available but if this is not possible, then you will have to decide on the basis of which will cause the least inconvenience.

Where possible, your information service should have its own separate telephone line so that clients can make contact direct without having to go through a switchboard or waiting for lines to become available. If that is not possible, then an extension exclusively for the information service is the next best thing. It is helpful if you can obtain a telephone number that is easily remembered by users. There are several instances where people living in more remote areas have been provided with free telephone access to a central information service through the installation of a direct line from a public building, e.g. a branch library. This has been used as an alternative to providing an extension bureau or to compensate for the withdrawal of local offices.

The main space requirements would be for a soundproof booth or office. A number of information and advice services have made it easier for clients to contact them by operating a Freefone service or using an 0800 number. Some information services, who need to recover the costs of providing information, are using pay lines, whereby the customer pays not only the cost of the call but also a fee for accessing the information. In these cases, the information is usually provided by means of recorded tape(s). Details of free telephone access services and pay lines can be obtained from your local British Telecom office. You may consider that it is important for your information service to be able to offer help outside its normal opening hours. In this case you will need to install a telephone answering machine, so that at any hour of the day or night when the service is closed, enquirers can leave messages.

Some answering machines also enable you to record a message or information which is played back to callers when they ring the service. The kinds of information which might be appropriate to record in this way are contacts for emergency help, hotel vacancies, 'what's-on' events, bus or train times, etc. British Telecom produce a useful free booklet, *Telephone helplines: guidelines for good practice,* which gives practical advice on setting up and running telephone helplines. Copies are available from your local BT office.

Computer. Now that microcomputers are within the reach of most information services, they are looked on as being a necessity rather than a luxury. However, if the computer is needed solely for the organisation of information, then it may only be of value where you have a particularly large database or need to access the information through a variety of search terms. Otherwise a card index system could be cheaper, quicker to consult and more user-friendly. Generally, a computer is needed for a variety of functions, e.g. maintaining client records, keeping statistics, correspondence, accessing online databases, designing publicity, etc.

Card files. If you are not using a- computer for storing your information, it is most likely that your information file will be kept on cards, the most popular sizes being 5in × 3in (127mm × 76mm), 6in × 4in (152mm × 102mm) or 8in × 5in (203mm × 127mm). These cards will need to be housed either in drawers in a wooden or metal cabinet or in open boxes/drawers (wooden or cardboard). Open cardboard boxes designed for card filing are fairly cheap and can be found at most office equipment suppliers. If you are really desperate, shoe boxes make a good substitute.

Open wooden boxes are much more expensive but anyone with a smattering of carpentry should be able to knock up some from offcuts of wood. They don't need to be very sophisticated or load-bearing. Open boxes are easy to access and, with appropriate guiding, display the information clearly, but they also have some disadvantages: it is not convenient to stack one on top of the other; they are open to dust, drips from coffee cups, discarded chewing-gum and other unmentionable objects; and, if knocked over, the cards spill out and you have the tiresome job of re-filing them.

Again, you can get cheap drawers made of cardboard or expensive ones in wood but the most common type is the two- and four-drawer metal filing cabinet. Each drawer holds approximately 1,000 cards and, if you need greater capacity now or later, units can be stacked one on top of the other. Some drawers have a rod which holds the cards in place but this can be a nuisance if you need to take cards out frequently for updating or have information on the back of cards. For even greater storage capacity you will need to consider a free-standing metal or wooden cabinet, but these can be expensive items.

With more and more public libraries going over to microfiche or computer catalogues, there may well be an opportunity to pick up such a cabinet at a knock-down price. Enquire at your local public library—but don't mention my name!

There are on the market other more sophisticated files which usually have their own specially shaped cards. If you decide to buy one of these, you will need to take account not only of the cost of the equipment but also of the continuing cost of the specialized stationery. The systems described previously use standard sizes, so that it is possible to use scrap cards or print your own with a predetermined grid to save costs.

One card unit that does have some useful features is the Rondofile which, as the name suggests, works on a turntable system, enabling the user to consult a large number of cards from one sitting position. Cards are easily removed for amendment and are available in a variety of colours, so it is possible to introduce an elementary colour-coding of information, say by area, subject or type of organisation. A Rondofile is compact enough to be housed on the enquiry desk and thus can also be accessible to the public, if desired.

One file holds 1,000 cards and, if more capacity is required, a second unit can be stacked on top. For details and up-to-date prices of Rondofiles contact M Myers & Sons Ltd, PO Box 16, Vicarage Street, Langley Green, Oldbury, Warley, West Midlands B68 8HF. The same firm has other card filing systems, including the Rondex, a rotating desktop file that holds up to 1,000 cards, available in three versions to take any of the standard card sizes referred to above. A similar card filing system using a vertical rotary action is made by Rotadex Systems Ltd, 3/5 Fortnum Close, Kitts Green, Birmingham B33 0JL. There are 24 models in the range suitable for five different card sizes, the largest housing 9,000 cards.

Many office equipment suppliers have these systems in stock.

Filing cabinets. Filing cabinets and dividers will be needed for keeping flimsy publications such as pamphlets, leaflets, broadsheets posters, etc. as well as correspondence. Cabinets come in one-, two-: three- or four-drawer units, usually in metal, although there are some cheap cardboard ones on the market. At a pinch you could always make do with cardboard boxes and used manila envelopes!

Bookshelves, Virtually every information service will have some reference books, varying from a mere handful to many hundreds of volumes. Small numbers can be kept on the enquiry desk itself using bookends (any heavy weight or 'posh' commercial ones), a book slope, or one of those lethal coiled-spring contraptions. Slightly more could be housed on a book trolley and sited conveniently near the desk for quick reference. Larger numbers will require some form of book shelving, even if it is only cardboard or wooden cartons laid on their side or planks suspended across house bricks.

There are an infinite number of commercially made metal and wooden shelving units, either free-standing or wall mounted. Your local library should be able to help you with addresses of library furniture and equipment suppliers. Their shelving tends to be more substantial and you may find that bookshop type shelving is both adequate, attractive and cheaper. Some of the major furniture retailers, like Habitat or MFI, have cheap shelving available in a range of bright colours. Sloping shelves may be needed for displaying magazines, leaflets or information packs face outwards.

Most modern library shelving systems have facilities to incorporate sloping shelves. Murrell's and Point Eight also do sloping shelf units, either free-standing or wall mounted.

Noticeboards. Noticeboards are needed for displaying posters and information sheets for your clientele. Rarely does a community information service have sufficient noticeboard space, so be generous in your estimate where funds allow. Nothing looks worse than seeing a noticeboard with posters all higgledy-piggledy and overlaping. For cheapness, buy a large sheet of pin-board and cut to size to fill empty wall spaces, pillars, doors, etc. Boards do not need too smart a finish since most of the time they will be hidden by posters. A noticeboard standing or hanging in a window of your centre and visible to the public can be used to feature special events, information campaigns, surgeries, or out-of-hours information.

Alternatively, consider using a mobile blackboard or external wall-mounted notice-board for this purpose. External noticeboards are best covered, using vandalproof glass or perspex. There are many commercially produced free-standing noticeboards.

Leaflet racks and dispensers. Considering the vast number of leaflets available of all, shapes and sizes, the choice of ready-made equipment for displaying them is not wide and what does exist is often expensive. All the more reason for trying to make your own. The following are two cheap suggestions:

Cut stiff manila envelopes of the size required to make pockets, glue them in rows on a large piece of card and pin this onto a wall or noticeboard. An alternative material to use for pockets is adjustable book jacketing, which has an added advantage in allowing all the leaflet to be seen through the plastic front.

Screw cup hooks into a sheet of blockboard or similar material, attach to a wall, and hang leaflets from the hooks by punching a hole in the top of 'them. A copy of the cover of each leaflet could be pasted onto the board to act as an *aide memoire* when stocks have all been taken.

More up-market leaflet dispensers are available from

Point Eight Ltd, Shaw Road, Dudley, West Midlands DY2 8TP, including the best one I have seen for holding flimsy A4 leaflets or single sheets. Point Eight also do a range of perspex holders for multiple copies of a single leaflet. If money is no object, then you might be better off with a custom-designed and made leaflet dispenser.

Display boards. Display boards will be needed if you intend to put on free-standing exhibitions or displays. There are innumerable makes available in a variety of price ranges, many offering special features or accessories. It would pay you to look around first and get advice from someone in the know, such as the publicity officer of a local authority, large firm or other public body. Consider such matters as portability and stability—particularly if you are going to use the boards outside the centre or outdoors—and ease of assembly. If any display boards can be said to be universal, then it must be those of Marler Haley Exposystems Ltd, who do several different systems that are easy to erect, versatile and attractive. They also have a variety of free-standing noticeboards and a range of accessories such as shelves, lights, leaflet dispensers, etc. which go with both display boards and noticeboards. Prices vary according to range.

Strip indexes. Strip indexes may be used as an alternative to card files or as a way of presenting information for customers to use. They are limited as to the amount of information that can be contained on a strip, although a variety of widths is available. Strips are more awkward to interfile and update but they have the advantage that it is possible to photocopy quite easily the whole file or sections on demand. As personal computers (PCs) become more universally available, it is difficult to see a future for strip indexes. Kalamazoo do a variety of holders and strips but these are a little expensive.

Other furniture and equipment. It is possible to list a

great many other items of furniture and equipment that a community information service might need, depending on the nature of the service, the resources available, and the existence or otherwise of back-up secretarial help. Simply note a few items that may be considered:

— pigeonholes for storing leaflets;

— bench or flat surface for assembling packs or publications;

— type-writer;

— photocopier (be very careful about leasing a photocopier—preferably get legal advice before signing any contract);

— machine for recording number of users/enquiries ('clicker');

— fax;

— duplicator—stencil or offset.

Stationery

Pamphlet boxes may be needed for storing booklets, leaflets and other ephemeral materials for use by staff or clientele. They are available in several sizes and varying quality, from cardboard to plastic, closed or open at the top. Lawtons Ltd, 60 Vauxhall Road, Liverpool L69 3AU do a cheap A4-size cardboard pamphlet box, called the Lawco Box, which comes flat and is then folded into shape. A more up-market A4 fold-up file box in brightly coloured plastic-covered card is produced by Esselte Dymo Ltd, Spur Road, Feltham, Middlesex TW14 0TR. The same firm also has a more rigid (and more expensive) polystyrene plastic pamphlet/magazine file box in bright colours, sizes A4 and A5. Library stationery suppliers also have ranges of pamphlet boxes on offer. Addresses from your local library headquarters.

Manila folders and envelopes to file cuttings, leaflets, information sheets in vertical files. Plastic wallets are even better, if you can afford them, as they enable the contents to be immediately visible.

Cards: 5in × 3in for subject indexes or brief information, 6in × 4in, and 8in × 5in for recording more detailed information about organisations and services. Cards can be overprinted with a grid for entering information in a standard form. Use scrap cards for cheapness or 'greenness'. Cards are available from most office stationers.

Forms, headed paper, standard letters for collecting information, issuing press releases, correspondence, etc.

Notepads, printed with your logo, opening hours and services, on which to write information for enquirers. These can act as a form of publicity for the service. *Statistics sheets* for gathering information about the use made of the service.

Many organisations, from national campaigning bodies to local tenants' groups, from time to time identify a need to set up an information service to meet the requirements of the following:

— their own staff or membership;
— the general public, as a whole or belonging to a defined geographical area;
— sections of the public with particular needs, such as disabled or elderly people;
— workers and public associated with a particular purpose, e.g. a redevelopment scheme or anti-dampness campaign.

It may sound obvious to state that, before setting up an information service, you should ask yourself, first of all, some very basic questions—like those a journalist asks when writing a story: who?, what?, when?, where?, why?, and how?—but not necessarily in that order. Surprisingly, there are many instances where these questions have not been asked and services have been set up which were either not wanted, the wrong type of service to meet clients' needs, a duplication of already existing services, too ambitious for available staffing or resources, or lacking in commitment from the organisation's management or staff.

The moral is that careful thought and preparation at the outset can save a lot of wasted effort and be the sound foundation on which to build a successful service. It is always better to start modestly and grow, than to be too ambitious and have to retract or fail completely. This book tries to follow the same principle in the way its information is presented, moving from simple, cheap solutions to the more sophisticated. But first of all, let us consider those basic questions. Everybody has information needs but not everybody is equally capable of satisfying those needs. This is increasingly so in what has been termed our 'information society', with its complexity and rapidly accelerating rate of political, social and economic change.

Information is now also seen as a commodity, with a market value that may well put it beyond the reach of the 'have-nots'. More and more, it is being made available in electronic forms which may require the possession of special skills on the part of those wishing to access it. Therefore, a good reason for setting up an information service may well be to make it easier for individuals or groups of people who do not have their own adequate information networks to gain access to information that can be of benefit to them. Some places or groups that warrant particular attention are the following:

— *inner-city areas:* where multiple deprivation exists - bad housing, high unemployment, inadequate schools—or where there is a greater proportion of ethnic minorities and transient populations;

— *housing estates:* which lack basic social and other amenities—meeting places, recreational space, shops—where transport is inadequate or expensive, housing is bad, repairs deficient and vandalism rife;

— *rural areas:* where facilities—shops, post offices, doctors, clergy, local government services, transport—are fast disappearing;

— *groups with special needs—low-income* families, elderly and disabled people, ethnic minorities, young people, patients, community and social workers.

There has to be substantial evidence of need for such a service in the local community or amongst your clientele to justify provision. This leads in turn to the next question.

Community profiling

This is a systematic process developed initially by corporate planners and adopted by other agencies, including public librarians, to enable them to plan and provide services which meet the needs of a given community. A typical profile will include:

— *Statistical data* about the population: size, rate of growth, age ranges, sex, marital status, religion, ethnic groups, diseases and mortality, employment, education, housing, etc. Much of this information is obtainable from census documents, supplemented and updated by figures from local authority departments, health authorities, employment centres, police, etc.

— *Socio-economic information:* types of economic activity,

community services—statutory, voluntary or private, recreational facilities, meeting places, clubs and societies, etc.

— *Local issues:* redevelopment, unemployment, poor housing, transport problems, racial prejudice, etc.

— *Residents' viewpoints:* letters to the press, community newspapers, local radio and TV, action groups, community noticeboards, graffiti, informal discussions with those who come into contact with a wide cross-section of the community, informal contacts in pubs, shops, public meetings, etc.

The important thing to remember when compiling a community profile is not to rely on one type of information alone as this will give you a biased view. Try to get a fully rounded picture by including both statistical data and subjective assessment, official opinion and residents' reactions, majority and minority viewpoints. Obviously you must tailor your approach to the kind of community you are analysing.

Community profiles were initially designed for analysing geographical communities but the same principles will apply, although the techniques and sources of information may vary, if your community is a 'closed' one, such as a school or organisation, or a group with special needs, like elderly or disabled people. There are also some spin-offs from compiling a community profile. If you do decide to go ahead and set up an information service, the information gathered for the profile could form the basis of your local information file and might also be made available to your clientele in printed form.

The valuable contacts made with indivi-duals and groups will form the basis for your infor-mation network. The following conclusions, taken from the above issue of

Library trends, sum up concisely the right way to approach the question of who needs an information service:

1 Formal and informal methods ... are essential both for developing a clear and useful picture of 'who is out there' and for an understanding of what they need/want.

2 There is no substitute for direct, active information-seeking ... in order to avoid acting on unsubstantiated assumptions about groups of people.

3 Just as different communities will want or need different services, different approaches will have to be used ... There is no single approach which will always work, but respect and flexibility are always essential.

Remember also that some information needs may not become apparent until your community information service is up and running and it ought, therefore, to be flexible enough to adapt to them. Determining needs is not a once-and-for-all exercise but a continuous process.

What community information services already exist?

There is one more step that needs to be taken before you can get down to putting flesh on your ideas and that is to find out if there are any other agencies in your area operating identical or similar services to the one that you are planning. You may, in fact, want to take this step at an earlier stage or you might have found out the information in the course of conducting a community profile. Either way, it is an important stage that should not be omitted, since it is in nobody's interest to duplicate existing services, especially if there are gaps in provision elsewhere.

Information about existing services in a particular neighbourhood can be collected by means of a questionnaire. This will give you only the bare outlines and will need to be expanded by personal visits.

The kind of information you will need to collect about each agency consists of the following:

— location, premises and equipment, opening hours, how to contact the agency;
— staffing, information resources, training;
— the agency's activities;
— referrals, relationship with other agencies;
— the agency's users;
— feedback to policy-makers;
— publicity;
— management and funding.

This list was taken from *Who knows?: guidelines for a review of local advice and information services, and how to publicise them* which is an excellent guide to conducting such reviews and provides more details under each of the headings advice services and preparing local development plans. If it is local agencies that you want to identify and you are not a public library, then try your local library for a start.

Other sources might include the Citizens' Advice Bureau, Council for Voluntary Service, Rural Community Council, Social Services Department, civic information bureau and individuals, e.g. community workers, social workers. Having gone through the above process, you should now have a clearer picture of which community infor-mation services already exist in your community or area of interest and where there are any gaps in provision. You should also have some idea of the strengths and weaknesses of existing services and thus be in a position to make a decision about your own proposed service. At this point there are several choices open to you:

Maintain and strengthen the existing provision. It may be that your community is adequately covered by information services, in which case your efforts might best be channelled towards helping to strengthen and maintain those services. The costs of providing an information service rise continually and finding for many organisations is frequently precarious.

Material support or behind-the -scenes lobbying to help existing services will usually be more than welcome.

Extend an existing service. The solution to meeting the information needs of your community does not necessarily have to be your direct responsibility. It may not be appropriate, anyway, if your staff do not have the training, flexibility, time or independence to provide the kind of service that is required.

There may well be an existing information and advice service which is prevented from providing an adequate service or extending its work through badly located premises or lack of funds for staffing, training, information resources, etc. Your organisation could make an appreciable difference by:

— offering free use of suitable accommodation to relocate the service in a place more accessible for the public;

— offering similar accommodation for the location of extension services;

— offering the use of mobile service points, where feasible, so that remote areas of the community can be reached;

— providing help with staffing or resources, e.g. you may have staff who can offer a particular expertise on a surgery basis or you might be prepared to supply loan collections of more expensive reference materials;

— providing access points for the public in unserved areas on behalf of the information service, e.g. by having available postal enquiry forms or providing a direct-line telephone link to the service's central office.

Cooperate. Although your analysis may show that there are gaps or shortcomings in existing provision, that should not be a signal to leap in immediately and set up a new service. At a time of financial stringency, it makes sense to explore first of all the possibilities for cooperation and thus to get a more rational and coordinated use of resources. This could take the form of one or more of the following suggestions:

Sharing information. Public libraries, for example, could explore ways of putting their extensive information resources, both materials and staff, at the service of other information and advice agencies by agreeing to keep and update files of local information or by producing a directory of local information and advice services.

Joint collection, processing and dissemination of information. Often several agencies in a community will be collecting local information. This is wasted effort, as the information needs to be collected only once, and causes annoyance to those supplying the information. A joint approach is called for, either one organisation collecting the information on behalf of the others, or a consortium of organisations sharing the task.

Shared premises. There are distinct advantages in several agencies sharing premises, in addition to that of economy. It provides better access for the public who can see a number of agencies in one place without a time-consuming and often expensive run-around. Referral is made easier, which is particularly useful in multi-problem cases. There is the possibility of not only shared accommodation but also shared information resources, shared publicity, shared case-notes, etc. Sharing can make the service available for longer hours than one agency on its own could possibly attain.

Support groups. Cooperation of the kind listed in this section can be fostered by the formation of an 'umbrella' group which brings together all the community information agencies in a particular community or area of interest. Such a group could take on activities such as information sharing, joint collection of information, cooperative approach to funding, shared publicity, training and generally creating a greater awareness and understanding of each other's work.

Sometimes a number of agencies in an area, who are heavily involved in handling problems of a particular kind and do not have the resources or time to cope adequately with them, can benefit from the creation of a specialist support group to provide training, research, practical assistance (e.g. tribunal work), information materials, current awareness services, or expertise in certain areas, such as law, debt counselling, housing, planning, tax, etc. Many public libraries have been involved in setting up and running 'umbrella' groups.

Face-to-face contact with clientele

This is the passive function, whereby a community information service is located in a particular building or room and the clientele call in person to seek information for themselves or from the staff by enquiry at an information desk. It has the advantages that the most up-to-date information is available, provided the service has carried out its information-gathering efficiently; the client can be questioned to reveal exactly what information is required; and a member of staff familiar with using the files or databases is on hand to search out information, to make contact with services, or to suggest further possible courses of action. There is some evidence to suggest that many people prefer information to be transmitted verbally, especially if they have low literacy skills.

Some disadvantages to having one defined location are that, unless it is prominently sited (in the High Street or shopping centre), it may be difficult to bring the service to the attention of potential users without a continual publicity campaign; moreover, it can be expensive to operate in terms of the resources needed to staff the enquiry desk continually and to stay open outside normal office hours. Dealing with people face-to-face requires a certain amount of skill but, above all, is needed a pleasant and approachable personality, a characteristic that is not so easily learnt. The following guidelines may be helpful in dealing with clients:

— First of all, try to make the enquirer feel at ease, so that s/he is not afraid to ask questions or discuss a problem. It may seem a trivial enquiry to you but could be causing the client much anxiety.

— Do not exhibit feelings of shock, horror, amusement, disbelief or repugnance at anything the enquirer says. It is not part of your job to pass judgment on a client whose behaviour or ideas are contrary to the norms of society.

— Listen to the whole query and don't start jumping to conclusions before the enquirer has finished. Listen 'actively' by asking appropriate questions to clarify what is specifically being asked, since most people tend to phrase their questions in general terms. What the client seems to want may not necessarily be what s/he needs.

— When you think you know what is being requested, state it in simple terms so that the enquirer can confirm that you are on the right track. I once spent ages looking through modem dance manuals to answer a request for information on 'how to jive' only to find, after proudly presenting a suitable book, that the enquirer had a speech impediment and really wanted to know 'how to djive a car'!

— Try to identify with the enquirer's problem, at the same time remaining impartial and emotionally uninvolved. Such a counsel of perfection is probably unattainable but is only a warning that sometimes people ask the impossible or want confirmation or support for a course of action when they are in the wrong. Even where a service sets out to be impartial, it cannot support clients irrespective of whether they are right or wrong. It may be necessary at times to give information or advice that is contrary to what the client expects to hear.

— Before any information is given it should, wherever possible, be double-checked to ensure that it is correct and, if reasonably brief, written down to give to the client.

— Where there are alternative courses of action, explain these to the client in simple terms and leave her/him to make the choice unless you are specifically offering an advice service.

— Suggest where else the client may go to find an answer, even making a telephone call, if necessary, to fix an appointment or make an introduction. If the enquiry needs further investigation and is not urgent, take down the details and offer to phone or write with the answer as soon as possible. Suggest that the enquirer calls back after a certain interval if they have not had a reply.

By telephone

The physical location of a community information service whose work is mainly or entirely conducted on the telephone is less important. Staff can be occupied with other work in between calls and do not have to be tied to an enquiry desk; thus it may be possible to offer longer hours. With the additional use of an answerphone, a service could offer a 24-hour, sevendays-a-week service.

A conference-phone facility enables three-way link-ups to be made and clients can be put in direct contact with a service that can help them. If in order to answer enquiries you need to move away from the telephone or for periods of time it has to be left unstaffed, then you may need to consider the convenience of a cordless phone.

However, telephones are still by no means universally available in Britain and public call-boxes are frequently inconvenient because of location, continual use or lack of privacy. Some people are deterred from using telephones because they experience difficulties in expressing themselves via this medium or the cost of making calls is a financial burden. Some services have overcome the latter difficulty by offering a Freephone or 0800 number, or by a policy of ringing back the caller as soon as contact is made.

Telephones are best suited for answering enquiries that are brief, clearly stated and uncomplicated. Time does not allow for lengthy interviewing of the client over the phone, nor is it possible to pick up those non-verbal signals which often help in assessing the true need of the client. Likewise, the client cannot see you—so make your voice welcoming. Here are some tips on answering the telephone, based on an English Tourist Board booklet supplied to Tourist Information Centres, called How can *I help you?*:

— Make sure you always have a supply of pens and paper near the telephone and that the most used sources of information are readily to hand.

— Answer the telephone promptly. You may think that letting it ring and ring is a smart way of getting over the message that you are busy, but it only annoys the caller, who imagines that you are either drinking tea or having an interesting discussion about last night's television programme or football match.

— Never use 'Hello!'—it is too casual and, at this stage, the caller may be uncertain whether they have got through to the right service or not. State clearly the name of your service, your name, and offer to help, e.g. 'Exville Information Service. This is Joan Smith. Can I help you? If you don't want to give your name straight away, it can be left to the closing remarks, such as 'If you need to ring back, my name is Joan Smith. Thank you for calling.' If the caller gives their name, always use it.

— Do not smoke, eat, or drink when speaking on the phone, and definitely not all at the same time, as it impedes your speech.

— Jot down the details of the query as it is given and confirm with the caller the essence of their enquiry before answering.

— If you have to ask the caller to wait or need to leave the telephone to look up information, explain what is happening, how long you might be and, when returning, thank the caller for waiting.

— If it is obvious from the start or after an initial search that the query may take some time to answer, offer to ring the caller back—*not* forgetting to take down their telephone number and name (if you haven't got it already). If the enquirer is ringing from a public call-box, either ask them to phone back later (try to specify a time or length of time) or take down name and address and post the reply.

— When answering an enquiry by telephone, ask the caller to read back any crucial information such as amounts of money, telephone numbers, etc. as a check that they have been taken down correctly

— At the end of the enquiry, thank the person for calling. Be positive even if the reply is negative. It's better to say 'Sorry, we haven't been able to help you on this occasion but thank you for calling and please get in touch again if you have any other queries' than 'Sorry, can't help you'—click.

A very useful adjunct to the telephone is a fax machine which will enable you to transmit and receive documents to and from other information services.

By post

Requests for information by post do not as a rule figure prominently in the work of a community information service, but they are just as important. There is a temptation to assume that postal enquiries are less urgent than the client who is breathing down your neck or hanging on the end of a telephone, and so can be dealt with whenever there is a spare moment—in other words, never! However, every enquiry is important to the person making it and should be dealt with expeditiously.

A fairly common type of postal enquiry from individuals, organisations and commercial concerns is for lists of clubs and societies on a particular topic or in a particular area. It is obviously an advantage if you have a filing system or a computer database which enables you to print out a section on request. An alternative for frequently requested information is to have it pre-printed as a list, broadsheet or leaflet. Where a postal request is likely to take a little time in being answered, send off a pre-printed acknowledgement slip on receipt of the enquiry, saying something like: 'Thank you for your enquiry, which is receiving our attention. We will send you a reply as soon as possible.'

By display

People have an innate tendency to browse, picking up information in a casual fashion. An information service can take advantage of this by providing well-sited, attractive and interesting displays for putting over information to clients and passers-by. There are four main aspects of display: noticeboards; thematic displays; window displays; and outside display.

Noticeboards. A great deal of information is available in poster or broadsheet format. Some of it is free, some will come unsolicited and there are a few posters for which you have to pay. There are basically four types of poster:

— the event poster gives details of something that is to take place at a particular time;

— the *service* poster gives details of a service that is available—its opening hours, location, who is eligible, how to contact, etc.—and is not, as a rule, restricted to a finite date;

— the *information* poster presents hard information in an encapsulated form—benefit rates, changes in legislation, health education, eligibility for grants, etc.;

— the *persuasive* poster seeks to sell a product, change opinions, or enlist sympathies.

The displaying of posters is an activity that can frequently arouse great passion, particularly those posters concerned with moral, political or religious issues on which strong opposing views are held. This applies not only to campaigning posters but also to ones presenting straightforward information, such as an event or hours of opening of a service, e.g. family planning clinic. You need also to be sensitive to the location of a poster.

A poster showing how to fit a condom may be appropriate for display in a youth information centre but not on a board just outside the children's library. Ideally, a community information service or its parent organisation should draw up guidelines on what is or is not allowed to be displayed.

Try to avoid the overly simplistic approach of displaying either everything or nothing at all. An open door' policy may, in theory, sound fine but in practice it can throw up just as many problems, such as your right to refuse to display a poster which may not be in the public interest but does not necessarily contravene the law. It has been usual to rule out commercial advertising posters, although some services now accept these but make a charge in order to raise money for the service.

There is more to displaying posters or other notices than simply sticking in a few pins. The following are a few points you might find useful:

— You can never (or rarely) have enough noticeboard space, so in planning your service— think BIG!

– If you have several boards, categorize them: coming events, sources of help, places to visit, official notices, etc.

— Don't overcrowd your noticeboards—posters should never be overlapping and obscuring each other. If you have only a limited space, change the posters regularly to give each one a chance.

— Arrange posters to look attractive—contrast posters of different shapes or colours to add interest. Move long-term posters around from time to time to give the impression of change.

— Check noticeboards regularly to ensure that out-of-date posters are not left on display and long-term posters have not become faded or tatty.

Thematic displays. Displays devoted to a particular topic or theme, if well produced, can be a useful way of drawing attention to information that is available. The theme may be:-

— concern a problem area identified from an analysis of enquiries;

— relate to a current change in legislation or benefit rates;

— be aimed at improving public awareness of an issue of current concern;

— draw attention to benefits, grants, services or rights of which your clientele may not be aware;

— canvass support for a cause; or educate your clientele on personal matters, e.g. health, finance, etc.

There is some skill required in preparing materials and mounting an effective and attractive -display. Identify someone in your organisation who has a flair for this kind of work and is willing to help. There are a number of organisations and government departments which have displays that can be borrowed free of charge or with carriage paid one way.

Window display. If your information centre is blessed with large windows looking onto a thoroughfare, then they can be used to good effect in giving out information not only to users of your service but also to casual passers-by. Displays such as those described in the section above, placed in the window, enable the information to reach beyond your own clientele and may even attract use of the service. An external window can also be used for displaying essential information when your service is closed, such as addresses and telephone numbers of emergency services, hotel or bed-and-breakfast accommodation. A number of commercial organisations have produced microcomputer-driven information points which usually stand in a window and feature local information and advertising.

The computer either scrolls pages automatically or is controlled by means of touch terminals mounted on the outside of the window. Windows or glass entrance doors may be also be used to display small ads and job vacancies. Small ads may seem trivial but they do fill an important information need in most communities and also have an added bonus of attracting people to look in your window and, perhaps, thereby become more aware of the service and of what it can offer.

Small ads can also be a useful source of income for your service but, in setting up such a service, be sensitive to other small ads services in the immediate vicinity. A job vacancies board is a much appreciated service, particularly at times of high unemployment and where your service is located some distance from the nearest Jobcentre. Either contact local firms, businesses, shops, etc. and ask if they would be prepared to display their job vacancies in your window—you might even make a charge and earn a bit of income for the service - or contact your local Jobcentre who may be prepared to let you have job vacancy cards on a regular basis. If you can afford to do so, offer to contact the firm or Jobcentre on behalf of any client who is interested in a particular job advertised, to see if it is still vacant.

Outside display. As well as displaying information in your own centre, consider the possibilities of display in other buildings. It may be possible to circulate such displays around a number of centres and thus reach a much wider audience. Some commercial businesses, like banks and building societies, who rarely have anything interesting to show in their windows, encourage organisations to use these for displays. With displays located on other people's premises, you will have to accept their right to reject all or part of your display if it is objectionable to them or not produced to a high enough standard.

Find out first if the organisation or business has a policy on what can or cannot be displayed and whether they have their own display equipment which you can use. For outside displays, other than simply posters pinned to a wall, you will need spare display boards that can be released for a length of time and the means of transporting them. The display should be checked regularly to maintain stocks of any give-away leaflets, etc., to ensure the currency of the information, and to keep it in good repair.

Another possible outlet for information is community noticeboards, which are usually located in prominent positions such as market squares, shopping malls, etc. They are most likely to be owned by the local council but it is not unknown for councils to assign the running of them to a local information centre. The sort of information best suited for this type of board is directional (map of village, town or neighbourhood and street index), showing places of interest and sources of help or coming events.

Selective dissemination of information (SDI)

This is a rather forbidding term to describe a process for transmitting information which many information services adopt quite naturally without ever having heard of the phrase. It simply means taking note of the subject interests of particular individuals or groups who use your service and supplying them with new information on their areas of interest as it becomes available. 'Taking note' can be a fairly organized and formal system involving the sending out of a questionnaire initially to discover users' interests and maintaining a card or computer file (usually arranged by subject) of those interests. However, more often than not, it is an informal system stored in the information worker's head (I know Joe Bloggs is interested in this, I'll send him a copy').

Good information workers can even anticipate the interests of their clientele. SDI is most often used by services whose clientele are a closed group—a voluntary organisation, for example—rather than ones who serve the general public. Where generalist services operate SDI, it will usually be for other information and advice workers, community workers, professionals or groups. An SDI service can include regular scanning of new publications, journals, newspapers, press releases, annual reports, product literature and other ephemeral material or it may be rather unsystematic and random.

Either way, it is a useful service, particularly for those individuals, organisations and groups who need a supply of new information in their area of interest but do not have the time, resources or expertise to search it out. It is an excellent way to win friends for your information service who in turn may be able to help you on other occasions.

Deposit files and collections

One solution to the problem of having one fixed location from which to give out information is to duplicate your information file or database and make it available to other centres. This would make it more accessible to a wider clientele but has the disadvantages that

— you need to have a mechanism for keeping these files or databases up to date, especially if you have to rely on someone else to do the updating, and

— staff, where they exist, need to be trained in using the file or database so that they can help clients. Files using loose-leaf binders or strip indexes are easier to duplicate than card files.

Computer databases can easily be copied onto floppy disk(s) but depend on the recipient having compatible equipment. Those information services whose databases are stored on a mainframe computer may be able to offer other centres online access. Some community information services have made available collections of books and other material for deposit in centres which have particular needs, such as youth clubs. This is quite a costly service to provide in terms of both resources and staff time in preparing the collections and keeping them up to date. With this type of service, it is desirable to have a monitoring mechanism so that the value of the collections can be appraised. A good example of an information service that is duplicated and made widely available is that operated by NACAB.

The material consists of specially prepared loose-leaf information sheets; leaflets and booklets.; reference books; a comprehensive index; and other supplementary material, such as sources of leaflets and information about useful reference books. The system is updated by means of monthly packs containing amendments to the information sheets and leaflets; new information sheets and leaflets; a booklist of new publications; *update—a* magazine which provides a comprehensive summary of changes in the law, etc.; and new editions of reference books.

As the system is so comprehensive, it provides the factual resource for a wide range of advice and counselling services. However, it does require a substantial amount of staff time to update the files each month and occupies several feet of shelving or a whole four-drawer filing cabinet. For many organisations the costs may also be prohibitive: £644 (voluntary organisations), £900 statutory and commercial bodies) to set up the system, while the annual updating subscription from April 1993 is 040 (voluntary) and £566 (statutory and commercial).

For those organisations who do not have this kind of money or do not need such detailed information, NACAB also produces a Basic Pack, contained in two loose-leaf binders, costing £29.50 (voluntary), £ 78.50 (statutory and commercial) to set up, with the annual updating subscription costing £37.00 (voluntary) and £61.50 (statutory and commercial). Further details can be obtained from NACAB, 115-123 Pentonville Road, London NI 9LZ. If your problem is lack of space or staff time to update the hard-copy version or you need an information system that is portable, NACAB also caters for these needs with a microfiche version of the hard-copy pack. Microfiche are 6in × 4in transparent cards which contain up to 60 pages of information.

Publications

Well-produced and attractive publications enhance the image of an information service and help to attract custom. The commitment of information to print inevitably attracts corrections, additions, etc. which enable your service to maintain an even more accurate and up-to-date database. Producing publications of reasonable quality can be costly in terms of both time and money, depending on the system used for storing your information base and access to in-house printing facilities. If your database is stored on computer then there are a number of options, as follows:

If you have a word-processing or desktop publishing package on the same computer or access to these within your organisation, it may be possible to transfer the whole or sections of the database file into these packages and manipulate them to produce the required format and layout for publication; at which point there are again several choices:

— print out the publication on demand or in small quantities (assuming your computer has a printer)—not practical for lengthy documents;

— print off one copy on your computer printer and photocopy best for short documents with a limited run where quality is not critical;

— produce printed master copy for printing in-house or by a commercial printer using offset litho—master copy needs to be produced on good quality laser or bubblejet printer; (Tip: You can improve the appearance of text produced on a dot matrix printer by reducing it slightly on a photocopier or, better still, asking the printer to do it photographically—don't forget to allow for this by making your document format slightly larger.)

— copy the document to a floppy disk and take it to a printer who has equipment and software compatible with yours.

If you don't have access to word processing or desktop publishing, you may still be able to copy your database or sections of it to a floppy disk which can be read by a commercial printer with compatible equipment. The production costs will be higher as the printer will need to format, design or lay out the publication according to your specifications. When you are planning the computerisation of your information system, it is worth ensuring that all your software packages are compatible not only on your computer but also with systems that are to be found in most printing firms nowadays. It may be worth investing.

A little more to get an integrated package that offers a suite of facilities—database, word processing, spreadsheet, graphics and communications service—that allows you to swap documents or bits of documents from one facility to another with ease. If you have a manual database then a lot more work is necessary to transcribe the data into a form suitable for printing. Once you are at that stage, and if you do not have in-house printing facilities, it will pay you to shop around for printers. Get at least three estimates - you may be surprised at the variations in both price and the size of the publication (if this has not already been determined).

Alternatively, explore the possibilities of:

— joint publication with other organisations;

— obtaining a grant from an appropriate body who may have an interest in your publication;

— sponsorship; and

— advertising, or a combination of these.

Once information is printed, it is static and, therefore, liable to date in a short space of time. When producing a publication always consider your ability to sustain not only one issue but also any future new editions which may be necessary, to distribute copies, either as a one-off or regularly, or to handle sales. All these can be very time-consuming. It is an acceptable strategy, of course, to publish one issue in the hopes that its value will be recognized and future issues will attract funding. The frequency with which you need to update the publication should determine the format you choose—whether it should be loose-leaf or not, a leaflet or a booklet.

Publications may be aimed at basically two kinds of user: those whose work or status consists wholly or in part in informing others and those whom we might term your general clientele. They may be the public, a section of the public, or members of a particular organisation or group. The major differences between the two in respect of publications will lie in the degree of detail and the way the information is presented.

How do you know what to publish?

— The kind of enquiries your community information receives will be one indicator. Frequent requests for the same type of information, e.g. addresses of playgroups, could be answered more quickly if a printed list or leaflet is available to give away.

— Identification of a gap in the coverage of a topic as a result of analysing enquiries or seeking information.

— Recent development or change which has not yet spawned any interpretative literature.

— Local issues.

— Discussions with other information and advice workers.

— Identification of specific groups who have defined information needs, e.g. elderly or disabled people, parents with children under five, school leavers, or the unemployed, which might be met with a suitable publication.

Types of publication

A list can be just a single side of paper or several sheets stapled together. The arrangement is usually straight alphabetical or alphabetical under subject or place headings, depending on the topic. Lists are given out in response to an enquiry, so do not require a great deal of creative design in their production.

The use of an attractive pre-printed headed paper with the logo of your service, if you have one, its address, telephone and fax numbers, can make a humble list a little more attractive and helps to publicize the service. Small numbers of lists can be run off on a photocopier or, where you have a computerized database, printed out on demand; for longer runs use a stencil duplicator or an offset litho printer. If you do not have print facilities yourself, most towns of any size nowadays usually have at least one instant-print shop where good-quality copies can be obtained at a fairly reasonable price and quickly.

Leaflets

A leaflet in one respect is a kind of extrovert list; it goes out of its way to attract attention—and thus encourage people to pick it up -through design and format. This is the *information* type of leaflet, the contents, of, which may be much the same as a list. The two other main, types are the *educational* leaflet, the objective of which is to increase understanding or awareness of a particular subject, and the *campaigning* leaflet, which sets out either to convert someone from one point of view to another, to gain sympathy and support for a cause, or to change a certain state of affairs for the better. Thousands of leaflets are produced each year by all kinds of organisations.

The quality of these leaflets varies from the extremely glossy and eye-catching to the cheap and nasty. If you are going to enter this arena; then it is important to give as much attention as possible to the design of your leaflets as to their contents, since they will have to compete for attention with commercially designed products. However, you do not have to be an artist or designer to be able to produce an attractive leaflet. Look -around at examples of commercially produced leaflets for inspiration. Advertising can also be a source of abundant 'free' or non-attributable art to illustrate and add impact to your own leaflets. Other sources of material might include old engravings (particularly of the Victorian era), drawings of the great masters (Leonardo da Vinci, Durer, Michelangelo, etc.) and instant art books. If you have access to a computer, the possibility is opened up to you of investing in a graphics package which enables you to draw and design your own artwork or to buy in copyright-free art files that can be manipulated for your own purposes.

Lettering in a wide variety of styles which can be rubbed onto artwork is available in large and small sheets from most stationers, or your organisation may well have invested in a lettering machine. Use cartoons, diagrams, graphs and photographs to liven up the text. Keep wording simple and short. Standard sizes of leaflets are A5 (149mm × 210mm) and 1/3A4, but experiment with unusual sizes based on standard sheets for added impact. Have enough copies printed to give a wide circulation and distribute them through as many outlets as possible, particularly those which attract large numbers of people. If the leaflet is aimed at a particular group in the community, identify specific ways of reaching them.

Posters

The aim of a poster is to present a small amount of information with the maximum amount of impact so that 'he who runs may read'. Use posters to advertise events or your service, to draw attention to a few sources of information and advice, or to point out eligibility for a service or benefit. Much of the advice given above about the design of leaflets applies equally to designing posters.

The design of a poster should emphasize and complement the information that you want to convey. Remember that some of the most successful posters contain no words at all. Let the image do the talking. Don't make the poster too—big as this may create problems for those whom you might wish to display it, since most organisations do not have unlimited display space. A3 (297mm × 420mm) is the most popular and useful size; A4 (210mm × 297mm) is a little small to make a great deal of impact but may be more acceptable if you want organisations to display the poster for a long time. Ideally, you should produce posters in a variety of sizes to suit varying locations.

A one-off poster can be prepared by hand if you have someone artistically inclined, but for any quantity you will need to have access to printing facilities or a good photocopier capable of enlarging and reducing. Use coloured copier paper for effect if you are printing only in black. Colour photocopiers are becoming more widely available but copies are considerably more expensive and may only work out cheaper than printing for very short runs. Another method of reproduction for posters is silk screen, which is a kind of stencil process. Some community arts centres make silk-screen facilities available to groups and will show you how to go about it.

Directories

A directory is one of the most useful publications that a community information service can produce. It may cover the whole of a community, be confined to the interests of a particular client group, or contain information about a certain type of organisation, e.g. social welfare agencies, local government services, etc. A directory plays an important role in community development by informing people about the services that exist and thus encouraging them to take a more active part in community life. It helps newcomers fit into the community and is a tool for those people to whom others turn for help and advice. A directory will usually be based on an information service's database but reproduced in a format that is easy to understand and use. There are a number of decisions to make before you embark on producing a directory, regarding such as the following:

How many copies will be required? This will depend on whether you decide to distribute to everyone, in which case you need to obtain an estimate of your target group. If it is not feasible to give it such a wide distribution, then you must decide on how many copies it is realistically possible to produce within your budget. You will need to work out as accurately as possible what size the directory will be so that estimates can be obtained from printers. Allow for advertising space if you are using this method to finance the directory.

Newspapers work on a formula of two thirds advertising to one-third editorial (information) but they have greater overheads to, contend with. Half-and-half or even less may be an acceptable proportion, depending on your advertising rates and whether the advertising is intended to cover the whole cost.

How is it to be funded? From your own budget? By special allocation from a parent body? Joint funding with other agencies? Grants from outside bodies? Sponsorship? Advertising? Sales? Or a combination of several of these? Local newspapers often take a strong interest in producing directories of their communities. These are generally paid for by advertising and are distributed free of charge either as a pull-out supplement or as an integral part of a particular issue of the newspaper. It may be worth pursuing this alternative at the outset as it could save your information service much time and expense, and ensure that the information is made widely available.

What format? This will depend to a certain extent on the number of copies to be produced and the target group. A directory aimed at the whole of a community and containing a lot of information will need to be produced as a book, rather like a telephone directory. An alternative is to publish it as a supplement to a newspaper, but this carries the danger that it will be discarded with the newspaper and not kept for reference. Consider any special needs of your target group, e.g.. elderly people will require larger type, people with disabilities will require a format that can be handled easily.

How is it to be distributed? Delivered free to all households? Supplement in local newspaper? Insert in a community newspaper? On request or sold at certain specified centres? Through individuals who have contact with the public or target group, e.g. social workers, health visitors, teachers, etc.?

Content and arrangement It is not possible here to go into detail about the scope and arrangement of directories because these will vary depending on the nature of the directory, but the following guidelines may be of help:

Scope. This should be clearly defined before you start. Decide the geographical area to be covered and the topics included. The majority of space will be taken up with entries for organisations, clubs, societies, agencies, services, etc. but some directories may include a certain amount of 'hard' information, even if this is simply a profile of the area. There is a thin line between what constitutes a directory and what a handbook.

Detail of entries. This will depend on the directory's target group. If you are producing it for use by other information agencies or community workers, then you may need to provide the full range of information collected for your database, as those using the directory will need as much information as possible in order to assess the usefulness of an organisation to their clients. For general use, it is best not to give too much information as this may result in confusion and render the directory too cumbersome for efficient use.

The minimum amount of information for each entry should give the name of the organisation, persons to contact, address and/or telephone number, and a brief description of the aims of the organisation where this is not self-evident from the name. The examples listed here show a full and a short directory entry.

Arrangement. Directories can be arranged in a number of ways fairly common method is alphabetically by name of organisation under broad subject groups which in turn may be further subdivided. Where the directory covers a number of distinct and separate towns or neighbourhoods, you may want the primary arrangement to be geographical. Other possibilities include one alphabetical arrangement by name of organisation, with a subject index if required or an A-Z by subject.

A contents page at the beginning may be necessary to locate sections quickly. Also include at the beginning any information that may be required, urgently, such as emergency services. Directories are used mainly to locate specific items of information quickly, so if the arrangement is not clear and well signposted, you may need to provide an alphabetical index. Certainly, in a directory aimed at other information services, there will be a need to index by the subject interests of agencies, groups, etc. as well as by their names. If there is more than one entry per page, then each entry should be given a running number to which the index should refer, rather than a page number.

Current awareness bulletins

Pleas for up-to-date information are often made by workers in many spheres of activity who do not have the time themselves to search the literature. Community workers, social workers, information and advice workers, doctors and health visitors are just a few of the groups which might benefit from a regular flow of information. Current awareness bulletins are one of the best ways of supplying that information in an easily digestible awareness bulletin is a duplicated listing of items of information which would be of use to a certain group or groups of workers.

Where a publication or periodical is available locally, it is helpful to state this at the end of each item using for brevity, if necessary, some sort of code to indicate location, with a key provided at the beginning or end of the bulletin. Each item should be given a distinctive number so that requests for further information, photocopies or loan of material can be identified clearly and simply. The usual method is to use a combination of the year and a running number, e.g. 83/1, 83/2, etc.

The most common way of arranging the entries in a current awareness bulletin is to group them under subject headings with a contents page at the beginning. Under each subject group arrange entries alphabetically. Before deciding to compile your own current awareness bulletin, find out what is already produced both locally and nationally, to avoid carrying out work that is already being done elsewhere. The bulletin shown here was produced jointly by an Advice Workers' Group and the public library, with finance from the local CVS. If necessary, to cover costs or postage, the bulletin can be made available on payment of a subscription. You might be able to save on postage by using another organisation's distribution network, e.g. CVS, library, local government.

Handbooks often contain directory-type information but mainly the text comprises descriptive information, e.g. about services, rights of individuals or groups, advice on personal matters, courses of action, etc. Handbooks are usually aimed at groups of people who have particular needs—elderly people, people with disabilities, parents of children under five, young people—or they may cover a defined geographical area. You may have to get help with writing the text from people who have knowledge of the subject. The arrangement of a handbook will depend to a certain extent on its subject but a simple method is to use broad headings arranged alphabetically.

A contents page and index are essential for locating specific items of information quickly. Use illustrations to break up the text and add interest. Handbooks can be expensive to produce and you will probably need to get help with finance. Packs are an increasingly popular form of making information available, especially to people who perhaps do not have a habit of reading books. They are also useful for community information services that have limited staff resources and where the service offered is mainly of the self-help type.

Packs vary from a simple plastic bag to specially embossed or printed folders. Their chief attraction is that they enable a number of flimsy items on a related theme such as leaflets, information sheets, small booklets, flowcharts, sample forms and letters, booklists and address lists, etc., to be brought together in such a way that the whole is greater than the sum of the parts. Sometimes it is necessary to link items with a specially prepared text. Packs are easily duplicated for distribution to outlying centres and, if well produced, can entice people to browse through them who otherwise would not use a more conventional book form.

Some, disadvantages to packs are that they need to be displayed face outwards for maximum impact; they need to be regularly checked and updated (less easy the more they are dispersed); and without careful and attractive presentation they can so easily appear to be just a rag-bag of assorted ephemera.

The following guidelines may be helpful in preparing packs:

— *Choose the topic*—this might well be (i) a subject of frequent enquiry, e.g. buying and selling a house, adoption, writing a CV; (ii) a subject on which there is very little information in book form or that which exists is not readily understandable to the layperson, e.g. pensions, VAT registration; or (iii) a subject that meets the needs of a particular group e.g. one-parent families, those with debt problems.

— *Identify* suitable material and obtain in required quantities.

— *Write or compile* any linking material, lists of addresses and further sources of information. Get help from people who have special knowledge of the subject, if necessary.

– *Number* items and list them on a contents sheet.

— *Design* a title sheet which can be inserted into or stuck on the pack.

Manila wallets for packs can be obtained from most stationer, usually in A4 or foolscap sizes. You may also be able to find a stationer who stocks ready-made transparent plastic folders but, if not, Celsur Plastics Ltd stock these and will make them to your specifications, if necessary. If your funding will stretch to it, then you might like to go in for custom-designed plastic or manila folders.

The media

The media will often readily accept offers of free material from outside organisations, provided it is presented to them in the right way and would be of interest to their readers, listeners or viewers. The great advantage in using the media is that your information will reach a much wider audience than it ever would by any other means of dissemination, even if said means is not a very permanent one. Of course, the decision as to how that information is presented to the public will be out of your control.

However, we have found that in the case of regular articles, columns or scripts, provided you have clear guidelines on what is required by the particular media in terms of length, style and content and keep to them, the material will not be altered very much.

Information Base

The information base of your service is most likely to include the following types of information:

Soft information—details of clubs, societies, organizations and services; individuals; events, etc. Usually this information will not be available in a published form, or at least not in sufficient detail, and it will be necessary to make a conscious effort to collect it. This information may comprise the major part of the resources file.

Hard information—factual information on a specific subject e.g. benefit rates for single-parent families, how to get legal aid, how to change your name. This information will be available in a variety of Banns, some ephemeral such as leaflets, pamphlets, booklets, broadsheets, posters, periodical articles, etc. Such items are usually kept in a vertical file, in storage boxes or similar receptacles and accessed via some form of index or classification scheme. Other hard information may be in the form of books, multi-volumed reference works, law books, or even audiovisual forms. If there are many items of this type, they will need to be classified and shelved.

Supplementary information is information already produced in a particular format—directories, handbooks, diaries, annual reports, constitutions, newsletters—of organizations appearing in your information file.

'Soft' information

It is highly unlikely and undesirable that an information service should need to 'go it alone' in the collection of information. Such is the volume, complexity and variety of sources of information in present-day society that, unless your service has very narrow terms of reference, it will be virtually impossible for it to collect and keep up to date all the information that is required. Therefore, it is important that you first of all identify the information providers, support services and 'gate-keepers' in your community and establish effective contacts with them.

These links may already have been forged in the process of conducting a community profile. They now need to be fostered and strengthened, so that there can be a mutual exchange of information. These contacts will also be able to provide you with useful feedback from the community as to the success or otherwise of your service. The network of contacts can be maintained on a fairly casual basis as the need arises, or you might want to formalize the arrangement.

Some ways of doing this include irregular 'get togethers', informal luncheon clubs, regular meetings with agendas and minutes, or the circulation of a newsletter or bulletin. Other activities that could develop out of such meetings are joint collection of information, shared publicity, compilation and publication of directories, information handbooks and leaflets, training, and general discussion of common problems. Collecting information is a time-consuming process and there is no one method of going about it. You will probably have to use a combination of several techniques to build up a satisfactory information base.

One thing definitely to be avoided is duplicating work that has already been done. So first of all identify the following:

Existing information files. Contact all the other community information services, council departments and organizations who are likely to maintain information files and ask if they would be willing to share this information. Try to offer something in return, either an exchange of information or some other help you can provide.

Local directories. There are several types of directory that may be available in your area and which are useful sources of soft information:

— local government authorities often produce directories or town guides of their area which contain a certain amount of local information or they may produce a guide to council services;

— telephone directories, especially *Yellow pages* which have an alphabetical subject arrangement;

— area directories, such as those produced by Thompson's Newspapers, which are similar to *Yellow pages* but also contain a section of community information—your local newspaper may produce a directory of local services, sometimes in conjunction with local information groups;

— citizen's guides may also be produced by the local

newspaper as a supplement to an existing newspaper;

— CVSs or RCCs sometimes produce directories of voluntary organizations in their area or you may find these listed in your local CVS/RCC annual report;

— directories covering a special subject, such as accommodation, halls for hire, etc.;

— directories aimed at a particular interest group or groups e.g. people with disabilities or senior citizens.

National directories are useful not only for the wider network of services but also for identifying local offices of a national organization. Other methods to use in building up your information base and maintaining its currency include:

Looking and listening. A lot of information can be gathered by simply walking around your community, looking at noticeboards, picking up leaflets, or attending open meetings, fairs, fetes and other community events. This method of collecting information is unpredictable and requires more than a 9-to-5, five-day week.

Contact with individuals. People are a major source of information in any community and there are always those to whom others naturally go for information. Try to identify such people and enlist their help, possibly by offering something in return—bartering is a time-honoured system! Direct contact with individuals in other information services and organizations is often a better way of eliciting information than impersonal methods and also paves the way for further cooperation. Pay regular visits to such centres.

Scanning newspapers, magazines, newsletters, etc. can turn up details of new organizations; changes of personnel, premises or hours of opening; new services introduced; and may highlight problem areas where information may be needed.

Other documents, including council minutes and agendas, planning regulations, annual reports (ask to be put on mailing lists for these), leaflets and manifestos.

Media publicity. Local press, radio and cable television stations may be prepared without charge to put out a call for organizations to contact your service. If not, then consider inserting an advert or, where there is, a local directory produced, have a tear-out slip included for organizations to fill in and return to you. As a result of these various methods, an amount of raw material will have been obtained which may be of use to your information service.

How accurate, up to date and complete the data is will depend very much on the reliability of the source. In most cases, unless you have every confidence in the source, the information will have to be checked before it is entered in a more permanent form in your resource file. So, at this stage, simply record it onto say a scrap 5in × 3in card and put it into a temporary file. The information you have obtained will be of several different kinds but the most common will probably be that relating to organizations, clubs and societies. This is the most difficult type of information to collect since it is ever changing and therefore unrelenting effort will be required to achieve even reasonable completeness or accuracy—100% will be impossible.

However, with a good system for collecting and updating the information, you should be able to build up and maintain an acceptable file. A lot of staff time will be needed to carry out this work, so first of all investigate whether there are other local information services that need this type of information and would be willing to help in its collection. It may be possible to collect the information through an umbrella group, where the work can be farmed out so that it is not too great a burden on any one organization.

Alternatively, a joint approach can be made on behalf of a number of organizations. Ideally, the most effective way to collect information of this kind is to pay a personal visit to each organization or service, but rarely will that be possible without exten-sive staff resources or a very small community. The chea-pest and quickest way to collect this information is by telephoning. Prepare a standard list of questions to ask so that entries in your information file follow the same format. Telephoning is only practicable if you have a reasonably small number of organizations to contact, say up to one hundred. If visits and telephoning are ruled out, then the information can be collected initially by postal questionnaire, with a request for up-to-date information sent at least once a year and also when it is known from other sources that changes have taken place.

A covering letter should be sent with the questionnaire or update request, explaining why the information is needed and asking for cooperation. If the information is to be passed on to other organizations or commercial bodies, either free or for payment, this should be drawn to the attention of the recipient of the questionnaire, so that they have an opportunity to decline to give the information or insist that it is not so disseminated. If the information is to be stored in a computer, then you will need to meet the requirements of the Data Protection Act. If it can be afforded, include with your questionnaire some means of returning it free of charge, as this will significantly improve the response rate. Separate forms may be required to collect different kinds of information.

The following is a suggested list of headings which you might need to include on forms for collecting information from two of the most common types of organization.

Clubs and societies

— *Name:* the name by which the club is best known, plus the full name if different. Indicate relationship to larger body, i.e. branch, regiment, lodge, etc.

— *Secretary's name, address and telephone number* or those of a similar person if the organization has no secretary.

— *Place, day and time of meetings.*

— *Purpose of organization* if not self-evident from the name.

— *Eligibility:* any restrictions by age, sex, ethnic group, occupation, status (single, divorced, widowed) etc.

— *Subscription:* any charge to become a member or to attend meetings.

— *Annual general meeting:* the date of an organization's AGM can be a useful indication of when to send out update forms as this is when officers or policies are likely to change.

— *Other officers:* names, addresses, telephone numbers of treasurer, president, chairman, publicity officer, membership secretary, etc.

— *History of the organization* including special events or persons associated with it.

— *Publications:* newsletter, diary, commemorative brochures, annual report, etc.

— *Date* the information was obtained and/or last updated or checked.

Agencies and organizations providing a service

— *Name:* popular name and full name, e.g. CHAT (Come Here and Talk), SHAC (Shelter Housing Action Centre), plus relationship to parent body where necessary.

— *Address:* street address and postal address, Post Office, box number if used.

— *Telephone and fax number,* including—service number, administration number, after-hours or hotline numbers.

— *Contact person:* personal name, title and address, if different from above.

— *Hours of opening:* days and times; note if seasonal, e.g. holiday period, term time.

— *Services provided:* advice, counselling, practical help, etc.; types of enquiry the service would like to have referred to them.

— *Eligibility:* age, income, sex, residency, status.

— *Application procedures:* walk-in, appointment or waiting list; what papers or documents need to be brought.

— *Cost:* free, fees, means-tested, donations; any facilities for payments to be spread over a period; help available from local or central government, charities, etc.

— *Geographical area served:* neighbourhood, city, county, region, *ad hoc* area; no geographical restrictions.

— *Branch offices:* extension bureaux, mobiles, surgeries,

etc.; include hours of opening, routes and times of stops.

— *Director,* administrator or executive director of the service; name and telephone or extension.

— *Volunteers:* does the service use volunteers and for what purposes? Method of recruitment.

— *Publications:* directories, handbooks, leaflets, annual report, etc.

— *Funding:* local government grant-aided, donations, etc.

— *Special facilities:* foreign languages spoken, access and facilities for people with disabilities, photocopying or fax service, escort, advocacy, etc.

— *Transportation:* how to get to the service, e.g. bus route numbers, underground line and station, etc.

— *Date* information was obtained and/or last updated or checked.

These two lists represent most of the facts that a community information service might need to know about an organization or service. In practice, depending on the scope of your service, it may not be necessary to include all the fields in the questionnaire. It is a good idea to get the person filling in the questionnaire to sign it, thereby giving the information service some protection against claims of giving out wrong information—a not uncommon occurrence, especially when the information is committed to print. There are other types of 'soft' information that your service might need to collect, for example halls for hire, places of local worship, accommodation, 'What's-on' events, local industry. The procedure is much the same:

— Decide what information you need to know.

— Devise a standard format or list of questions to ask.

— Identify possible sources of information.

— Decide which method or methods to use to collect the information: telephone, personal visit, postal questionnaire, press advert, etc.

How to store 'soft' information

There are various methods that can be used for storing information: A *list* is easy and quick to consult, can be photocopied for clients to take away and can be faxed, but has very little flexibility for inserting and updating information. A *strip index* provides flexibility, can easily be photocopied, and is available in various forms: large binders holding many pages, smaller folders containing just a few pages, address books, wall-hung panels, rotunda units, etc.

Strips are available in several colours, which allows for a simple categorization, and various widths. Even so, they are limited as to the amount of information that can be contained on them. It is also not quite as easy to insert new strips as the manufacturers claim. *Cards* are still one of the most commonly used systems for storing information. They are infinitely flexible, easy to insert and update, can be sorted into any preferred order, and require very little technical know-how.

The most popular sizes are 5in × 3in, used mainly for indexes or temporary information waiting to be checked, 6in × 4in, and 8in × 5in, which are large enough to contain sufficient information about most organizations or services and to be preprinted with a standard grid for recording the information. There are more superior types of card file available, such as the Rondofile or Rotadex systems which use custom-designed stationery and therefore tend to be more expensive. With systems that use standard cards, you can—if you are hard-up or want to save trees—use the reverse of scrap cards.

Card files have a number of disadvantages: they are not so easy to carry around, they are not easily reproducible if someone wants a copy of a particular section, multiple access (e.g. by name, subject, area, service, etc.) requires duplication of cards, and the updating process can be tedious. You may still find around *edge-punched cards* which offer a primitive type of multi-access to the information on the card through the strategic use of knitting needles or rods. Personally, I would save up and get a computer.

Loose-leaf binders with one sheet for each entry, sometimes called 'sheaf' binders, have a similar flexibility to cards. They are slightly slower to add to and amend but are more portable. They are suited best for alphabetical arrangements as they are difficult to guide.

Microcomputers now have the capacity to handle immense information files that can be accessed by any number of predetermined variables or even free-text searching by keyword, depending on the software used. With a printer attached, all the information or sections of it can be printed out on demand or to provide a master for printing by conventional methods.

Personal computers now begin at prices that bring them within the range of most community information services. However, there is danger in automatically seeing the computer as the best solution for maintaining your information file, as this may not always be the case. A lot depends on the size of your file and its complexity, what you want to do with the file, and to what other uses you want to put the computer. The importance of the computer in, information and advice work is such that it merits a chapter to itself, and you will find these and other aspects dealt with in more detail in Chapter Eight.

Filing system

Whichever method is chosen for physically storing the information, except for that by microcomputer, it will be necessary to decide the best way of arranging entries so that the information can be retrieved swiftly and accurately. In order to ensure that the total resources of your information service are used to the full when answering an enquiry, it will help if the system used to organize the information file can be integrated with that for the vertical file and the bookstock. This point needs to be borne in mind now, although it will be dealt with more fully later.

The bulk of the information file is likely to comprise 'soft' information which you have collected about organizations, clubs, societies and services and, to a lesser extent, about individuals who are a valuable source of information or advice, plus items of 'hard' information not available or conveniently available in printed form.

There are several ways in which you might want to retrieve this information—by the names of the organizations, by subject (i.e. area of interest), by clientele, by the type of service (e.g. counselling), or by place. In practice, the 'clientele' and 'type of service' approaches are usually catered for through the subject file rather than as separate files.

Organizations file

The master file for the whole system will usually be an alphabetically arranged sequence of entries by name of organization. It is generally recommended that the full, official name of the organization is used, with references from other forms of the name. In practice, it does not really matter as long as there are references from the alternatives to whichever form is chosen.

There is a good argument for putting the main entry for an organization under the form of name by which most people refer to it, even if this differs from or is an abbreviation of the official name. This is especially so where the file is to be used by the public. In addition to details of organizations, each entry in the master file may also contain certain 'housekeeping' details relating to the maintenance of all the information files, plus references to appropriate headings in the subject file, where relevant information can be found, and a classification number.

Subject file

Most enquiries received by a community information service are likely to be about the need for a service or activity or for help with solving a problem, rather than for information on a specific named organization. So the information you have collected about organizations, services and individuals will also need to be accessible by the services and activities they provide.

There are two ways this can be achieved, by either using a subject index or having a subject file of organizations. In both, you will need to choose or adopt a set of subject headings which will adequately describe the information on file or elsewhere in the system and the interests of your clientele. If you are compiling your own list of subject headings, choose terms that are in common use by your clientele, especially if they will be consulting the files directly, rather than the 'official' term, e.g. OUT OF WORK or ON THE DOLE instead of REDUNDANT. Always refer from alternatives not used to the chosen term. A *subject index is* rather like the index to a book. It is an alphabetically arranged file of subject heading cards on which reference is made to where information on that subject can be found.

The cards themselves do not contain information. The subject index can contain references to organizations, individuals and other supplementary material such as pamphlets, periodical articles, audiovisual material, books, etc.

A *subject file* consists of an alphabetically arranged set of subject heading cards behind which are filed copies of the organization cards appropriate to that heading and possibly cards containing items of 'hard' information. An alternative is to arrange cards according to a classification system either devised by yourself or adopted from another service, such as the NACAB classification scheme.

Some arrangements will have to be made for organizations which do not conform to the pattern, either because the place-name does not feature at the beginning or because it is not contained in the name of the organization at all. In these cases, an additional card can be made out with either an inverted heading (e.g. EXVILLE, ROTARY CLUB OF) or the place-name can be prefixed.

Filing alphabetically

There are two recognized methods, known as 'word by word' and 'letter by letter'. In word by word, entries are initially sorted by the first word in the heading, then headings that begin with the same word are sorted by the second word and so on. Another way to describe this method, which may be more helpful, is to treat spaces between words in a heading as an imaginary letter coming before 'a' in the alphabet, then sort letter by letter. In letter by letter, you simply ignore any spaces in the heading and sort one letter at a time from left to right. Here is how a small group of headings would look sorted by the two methods:

Word by word	*Letter by letter*
DO SOMETHING! BOYS CLUB	'DOG AND BONE' DARTS TEAM
'DOG AND BONE' DARTS TEAM	DOGSBURY RESIDENTS' ASSOCIATION
DOG SNIFFERS ANONYMOUS	DOGS HOMES
DOGS HOMES	DOG SNIFFERS ANONYMOUS
DOGSBURY RESIDENTS' ASSOCIATION	DO SOMETHING! BOYS CLUB

There are several other niceties to do with filing alphabetically but we only need mention here that hyphens are treated as spaces in word-by-word sorting and numerals are spelt out as said, so that 1900 (the year) is considered for sorting as NINETEEN HUNDRED and 1,900 as ONE THOUSAND, NINE HUNDRED.

File 'housekeeping'

In addition to the information needed to answer enquiries, there are other items of information to do with the maintenance of the file which may usefully be included on each entry, such as the following:

— the date the information was obtained, last updated or last checked, which will indicate not only the degree of reliability to be placed on it but also when to update;

— the date a questionnaire or update letter was sent - a check for chasing up non-returned forms;

— additional contacts or other information which does not fit into the main part of the entry;

— subject headings used in the subject file;

— place headings used in the place file, if not obvious from the name of the organization;

— feedback—comments from users of the service;

— 'tracings', i.e. a list of other cards that refer to they can be traced and amended or withdrawn when necessary.

The amount of this 'housekeeping' information you need to include will depend on how sophisticated you need your file to be. The bigger the information service and the larger the file, then the more likely it is that you will need to introduce a systematic procedure for processing information.

In such a case it is usual for the housekeeping information to go on the reverse of each entry, using a standard grid like the one illustrated here. It is arguable that if your information file requires this degree of sophistication, you ought seriously to consider keeping it on computer. For a small community information service, it may be quite adequate just to note the date when the information was collected, checked or updated.

Interim updating

All the entries for organizations should be checked at least once a year to ensure they are still correct. In between times, however, new information will be brought to your attention by various means, including word of mouth, newspaper reports, organization newsletters, company reports and by direct contact with the organization itself. If the source of information is reliable, it can be substituted immediately for the out-of-date information in the database but, if not, it should be noted and a further check made to verify its accuracy.

A simple way to add new information to an entry in a card file is to write it onto self-adhesive labels or slips (obtainable at most stationers) which can be stuck over the original information. Even though an entry has been updated in between times, it should still be checked formally once a year.

Annual updating

Once a year is probably a reasonable time-span for updating your database but a shorter interval may be necessary if the information content changes frequently. You will need to decide how the annual update is to be carried out. Some organizations like to update the entire file at the same time, so that they can say the file was as accurate as possible at a particular date. However, this does create a tremendous amount of extra work for a period of several weeks and you may feel it necessary to get extra paid, work-experience or volunteer help.

Another disadvantage of this method is that it captures a picture of organizations at a set moment in time. Some organizations may be just about to make changes, and your records for these would be out of date for almost a year. Alternatively, you may decide to update on a continuous basis by using either the date the record was added to the database or the organization's annual general meeting (AGM) date as a trigger. This is easy to do if your database is kept on a computer, since a date field can be used to produce a subset of records and, by linking the database with a word processing package, a personalized standard letter can be printed out for sending to each organization. It is less easy with a card or any other kind of file.

You can get little coloured metal tags to clip on to the top edge of cards, a different colour for each month, or you could use an appropriate symbol on the heading of the card, such as a coloured dot, a letter or number. Tags can make the file look a bit messy and are easily knocked off if it is in constant use; symbols require the whole file to be checked through. My preference is to update records shortly before or after each organization's AGM, since most organizations, if they are going to change their officers or constitution, generally do it once a year at the AGM.

An alternative to writing to each organization is to phone, but this is time-consuming and costly, and only feasible if the number of organizations to contact is fairly small. Avoid sending out updates at times when people are likely to be away, such as during the summer. There are certain times when it is more appropriate to update other kinds of information, e.g. social security benefit rates (which usually change in April and September), adult education classes or school, college and university courses which change termly. When an updated entry is returned it should be checked to see if the subject or place headings still apply.

Minor changes can be recorded on the master card and any other cards in subject or place files; major changes may require a new set of cards to be produced. For those with computerized databases the process is simpler as just the one record has to be updated. Don't forget to change the date the information was last checked or updated.

'Hard' information

Most information services will need a certain amount of 'hard' information to answer enquiries. Short, unrecorded or inadequately recorded items of 'hard' information, as we have already seen, can be incorporated into the database. However, the majority of hard information will usually be found in one or more of the vast range of print forms, starting from locally produced free broadsheets to extremely expensive multi-volumed loose-leaf reference works. Within the scope of this book, it is not possible to go into detail about the sources of this material, since they will vary considerably according to the type and subject range of the service you are operating.

Community information dates rapidly so any printed sources should be treated with care. However, you might find useful a chapter on the sources of community information that I contributed to *Printed reference material and related sources of information*, 3rd edn, Library Association Publishing, 1990, which concentrated on organizations and on those items which are regularly updated. The following framework for collecting community information was originally devised by Grainne Morby, who at the time was working for the Community Information Project, with some additions of my own:

Distinguish between subject areas

In other words, identify the main topics into which the subject scope of your information service naturally divides. Throughout this framework I will take as an example an information service for which the main area of interest is housing. It is sometimes useful to apply a consistent criterion when dividing up a subject, although obviously this would not be so easy for an information service whose scope covers as broad an area as, say, 'community information'. However, taking housing as our example, you could decide to divide it by type of accommodation, e.g. owner-occupied, private-rented, council-rented, New Town, Housing Association, institutional accommodation, tied accommodation, mobile homes, etc.

In most cases you would probably need an additional category for subjects that cut across all or more than one category. In the case of housing, this might be 'squatting' or 'homelessness'. Since the material you want to collect will usually be written to meet a particular need or needs, it is advisable to collect information around those needs rather than for fitting into a theoretical framework.

The kind of broad client groups that might be identified in the field of housing are landlords, tenants, owner-occupiers, squatters, transients, elderly people, people with dis-abilities, the homeless. Then, one could identify client groups who share a common problem or need associated with their particular type of accommodation, such as eviction, dampness, house repair, renovation, harass-ment, mortgages, rent arrears, planning permission, redevelopment, etc.

Once these subject areas and client needs have been identified, it should give you clearer guidelines when you come to select material from the various sources identified in the next part of the framework.

Print sources
Official

(a) National

— Pre-legislation: political party manifestos and policy documents, speeches by Ministers, the Queen's Speech at opening of Parliament, White Papers, Green Papers.

— Legislation: Bills, Hansard reports of debates in both Houses of Parliament, Acts, Statutory Instruments.

— Guidance to local statutory bodies: circulars and letters from Ministers, guidance notes, reports of Inspectors.

— Reference books: collections of legislation, e.g. *Statutes in force, Legal aid handbook.*

— Periodicals from government departments and agencies, e.g. *Department for Employment gazette.*

— Guidance to the public: leaflets, posters, videos and other A/V material.

— Ombudsmen.

(b) Regional

— Health authorities, British Rail.

— Privatized utilities: gas, water, electricity, telephone.

— Consumer watchdog bodies: Post Office Users' National Council (POUNC), Office of Gas Supply (OFGAS), Office of Electricity Regulation (OFFER), Office of Telecommunications (OfTel), Office of Water Services (OFWAT).

(c) Local

— Local authority policies and decisions: agendas, minutes, standing orders, by-laws and regulations.

— Guidance to the public: handbooks, leaflets, etc. from local authorities, area and district health authorities, Community Health Councils, local offices of government agencies.

2 *Non-official*

(a) National

— Reference books and handbooks from commercial publishers.

— Voluntary organizations.

— Pressure groups, self-help groups.

— 'Umbrella' organizations, e.g. National Council for Voluntary Organizations, Federation of Independent Advice Centres.

— Professional bodies, e.g. The Law Society.

— Trade associations, e.g. National Association of Retail Furnishers.

— Educational bodies, e.g. National Extension College, Open University.

— Trade unions.

— The media.

— Practitioners in the field who publish.

(b) Local

— Claimants' unions.

— Law centres, other specialist advice centres.

— Neighbourhood and generalist advice centres, resource centres.

— Local 'umbrella' groups.

— Pressure groups, campaigning groups, action centres. Voluntary organizations.

— Local media: newspapers, community newspapers, radio, cable television.

(c) New technology

— Videotext systems: Prestel, teletext, private viewdata.

— Online computer databases, e.g. Volnet.

— CD-ROM, videodiscs, etc.

Howard Matthews, in his book *Community information* has drawn up a set of criteria for selecting community information materials. It is aimed particularly at library community information services but may be generally helpful for anyone setting up such a service.

1. Selection should be done by those who know the community best.
2. Material should relate to specific, local, identified needs.
3. All material should be current.
4. All material should be written at a level appropriate to its intended use.

5. Material should be concerned with the practicalities of problem solving.
6. All new material should either fill a gap, offer a new viewpoint, or promise something better.
7. Material should take into account the level of use the client will make of it.

Obtaining publications and other material

Once the material you require has been identified, you will need to obtain it. Some material will be priced, in which case you will need to order it, and some will be free.

Priced publications

The procedure for obtaining priced publications, particularly in the field of community information, is not as simple as you might suppose. Since a lot of the material may well be fairly cheap and from small or community publishers, booksellers and library suppliers are reluctant to obtain it as the profit margin is likely to be too low for the amount of effort involved.

The alternative is to order direct but this also has its difficulties as many small publishers now insist on money with order, and this can cause problems for some organizations through the need to raise a cheque or limitations on the amount that can be spent from petty cash. A few national voluntary organizations, e.g. Age Concern England, operate a standing-order system for their publications—this is one solution, although you may need to accept blanket coverage of the organization's output. In the larger cities, you may find a community or alternative bookseller who is prepared to supply this material to order.

A directory of alternative bookshops is published annually by the magazine *Radical bookseller.* Whatever the method of ordering, it is important to keep a record of what has been placed on order and from whom to avoid duplication of titles and as a check on supply. For each title make out an order or slip—this can be either a scrap 5in × 3in card or one specially printed with a standard grid. The following indicates the kinds of information that need to be recorded:

— title of publication—more important than author for this kind of material, since authorship is often unclear;
— author—might be an individual or an organization;
— price, date of publication and, if a periodical, frequency;
— supplier—this may be a bookseller, library supplier or the address of the producing body;
— date of order;
— source of information about the item;
— location, if you are ordering for more than one centre.

You may find it helpful to use the order cards later as the basis of a catalogue of the publications in your information centre; in which case, leave space at the top of the card for either a subject heading, classification number or filing code. After an order has been placed with a supplier, the order cards are filed, preferably by title, in one alphabetical sequence known as the 'order file'. When a publication is received, the order card is removed from the file and accompanies the publication to the next stage if it is to be used later as the catalogue card. If not, you may find it useful to file the order card in a 'publications received' file, until such time as the publication is permanently recorded in the system, after which the card can be thrown away.

Periodicals

Publications which arrive at regular intervals—weekly, fortnightly, monthly, quarterly—will not require an order card but you will need to keep a record of each title taken. This should include the following items of information:

— title of periodical;
— frequency;
— supplier;
— when subscription is due for payment;
— a grid to record receipt of each issue;
— instructions for disposal of back copies.

For those using computers, there are software packages available for periodicals management but these are aimed at organizations who take an extensive range of periodicals and such packages are not cheap. If you have a database management package on your computer, you would do better to devise your own periodicals database.

Organizing hard information

We have already seen that hard information can be found in a great variety of forms. For the benefit of organizing it, the following categories can be identified:

Material in book form for use by clientele or information workers will be best arranged on shelves in the broad subject groups identified when acquiring the material or according to a classification scheme.

Ephemeral material for use by information workers is best stored in a vertical file using the same subject headings as those in the subject sequence of the information file, though probably with more subdivisions, or using a classification scheme. Alternatively, the material could be kept in file boxes on shelves using broad subject headings.

Ephemeral material for use by clientele on the premises is best kept in file boxes, ring or display binders and ideally interfiled with books. Vertical files are not recommended for public use as they tend to be a deterrent. Another way of dealing with ephemeral materials is to gather them together in packs on particular topics and, for maximum impact, to display them face outwards on sloping shelves.

Ephemeral material for the public to take away can be displayed in special leaflet dispensers, on a sloping surface or on tables. Ideally, they should be displayed in broad subject groups or by originating organization, e.g. Benefits Agency, Department for Employment, but this is rarely possible because even within organizations leaflets are produced in varying sizes.

Supplementary information

Many organizations produce printed material in the course of their work or activities. The most common types of material are directories or address lists of members (individuals or constituent groups), newsletters, events sheets or cards, annual reports, constitutions, posters, leaflets, funding appeals, campaigning literature, advertising brochures, balance sheets and commemorative booklets (anniversaries, etc.).

All this material is potentially useful as back-up information to the database but there is no sure way of obtaining it. When sending out the original questionnaire to organizations, you can ask to be put on their mailing list for this type of material, if one is maintained. Some organizations that operate on a shoestring may make a small charge for their mailing list facility. Even when you are put on a mailing list, regular receipt of material may depend very much on the enthusiasm or efficiency of the secretary of an organization. Often the best solution to obtaining material is to maintain regular contact with organizations and to pester them continually.

When material arrives, it should be dated, so that you know roughly how old it is, and carefully filed for future use. The simplest method is to have an envelope or folder for each organization. Write on the outside of the envelope the name of the organization as used in your database and arrange envelopes alpha-betically in boxes or a vertical file. You should also add to this file any cuttings from newspapers or magazines concerning those organizations.

The file should be checked regularly, at least once a year, to remove out-of-date material. When writing to organizations for updated information for your database, ask them for any new literature. Before throwing away the withdrawn material, check to see if it would be of use to some other organization or section of your service which collects material on local history.

Classification

It is not my intention to go into any great detail about the classification of community information materials. For most small information services, it will be quite adequate to arrange material by broad subject groups subdivided according to the form in which the clientele's needs and problems are presented. For ease of labelling vertical files, book spines and boxes, a simple notation can be used based on the initial letter or letters of subjects. For example, Cambridgeshire Libraries' community information service covers 21 categories:

Ben	Benefits	Gov	Government
Bus	Business	Hea	Health
Car	Careers	Hou	Housing
Com	Community	Law	Legal rights
Con	Consumer	Mon	Money
CR	Community relations	SC	Senior citizens
Dis	Disability	Tra	Transport

Edu	Education	Ump	Unemployment
Emp	Employment	Wom	Women
Env	Environment	You	Youth
Fam	Family		

Some libraries also include as separate categories: Death, Equal opportunities, Fuel (or Energy), Gay rights, Leisure, and Trade union rights. These categories can then be broken down into smaller subcategories as necessary. Taking the earlier example of Housing, a possible range of subcategories with a mnemonic notation might be:

A	Agricultural accommodation	Re	Rented accommodation
H	Homelessness	ReC	Council housing
I	Institutional accommodation	ReH	Housing Association housing
M	Mobile homes	ReP	Private rented
O	Owner-occupied	S	Squatting

Numerals could be introduced for more detailed subdivisions, e.g. O1—Buying and selling a house; O2—Home insurance; O3—Planning applications; O4—Development; etc. An effective method that can be used where you have only a small number of broad categories (no more than ten and preferably less) is colour coding. Allocate a colour to each subject and attach an appropriate coloured sticker or tape to the spine of each book or file box.

Colour coding can be used in conjunction with notation to provide more detailed subdivision of a subject. When a community information service grows to a size where broad categories are not adequate to contain all the material and allow efficient retrieval, then it may be necessary to consider using a classification scheme. Two choices are open to you, either using or adapting a ready-made scheme or constructing your own. There are a number of general classification schemes used in libraries, of which the most well known is the Dewey Decimal Classification.

These schemes have been constructed to organize the whole of knowledge and subjects are usually arranged on philosophical or logical principles. Consequently, they may not be sufficiently detailed or treat subjects in the way your clientele express their information needs. Most schemes have a degree of flexibility and it might be possible to adapt them.

4

Network Communications

A computer network is intended to connect together a wide range of information technology equipment, which varies in the design and operation of the equipment itself, in the information types it handles, and in the internal processing which it undertakes. In order to be able to communicate successfully, these various systems must have a common 'language' for the exchange of information, while retaining their local independence. As well as an agreed form for communication the network units must also agree on the *process* of communicating—the rules which govern the procedures for the exchange of information and the co-ordination of action between participants.

In daily communication we use a language to express our ideas and intentions, and the voice as a means of transmitting this information to other people. To ensure that the communication is successful, we must converse in an agreed language which the hearer is able to understand, and we must be able to respond to messages asking for clarification, repetition, and so on. In any conversation, there are well-understood rules which govern the process of communication—taking turns, allowing others a chance to speak, indicating that one has finished speaking, waiting until another has finished before speaking oneself, and so on. These signals are often given implicitly, through signs such as gestures or tone of voice. The rules for communication must be well defined and standardized; there is little room for 'working out' what a participant in the exchange really meant to say. This process underlies the development of sophisticated and 'user-friendly' applications which depend on network communication, even though this may not be immediately apparent. A goal of information networking is to allow users to work in this medium as naturally as possible, finding the least obtrusive fit with the natural work environment.

A dialogue which is mediated by computer communication places certain structural constraints on the process due to these underlying factors; the task of design is to find ways of incorporating the equivalent of the contextual factors which inform human communication while working within these constraints. A basic model of the communication process identifies the entities involved, and their respective roles. There are three main elements:

— a sender, which originates the message, and is responsible for representing the content of the message in an agreed format;

— a channel, which carries the message from sender to recipient through some physical medium;

— a recipient, which receives the message, and is responsible for interpreting the format in order to extract the information content.

The communication is not simply one way, and the roles will at times be reversed: the recipient may wish to send a reply to the original message. In network communications explicit signals and format rules are vital to the success of the communications process. For a computing machine to manage this role effectively, rules governing these issues must be highly detailed and agreed in advance, and encapsulated in software programs.

Data and communications software must be able to deal with management of the exchange process, not only by sending and receiving messages for transmission but also by encoding and decoding between the internal format used by the computer and the format used for external communication. It is also necessary to monitor the quality of the exchange and to co-ordinate activity between participants at each end of the process for longer data exchanges. This is problematic because the channel which links the participants will have characteristics of its own which may affect the communication process.

The sender and recipient exchange the encoded message as a physical signal transmitted in some way through a common channel. The environment of this channel can potentially interfere with and distort the signals in the process, resulting in the loss of some information content and delivery of a corrupted message. This kind of interference is known as noise—the general effect of corruption and garbling of the signal which occurs after it has been transmitted, and before it is received. For example, noise may result in the appearance of unreadable characters on a computer screen in the midst of a normal text message, as the receiving system attempts to interpret corrupted signalling codes.

Although the use of more reliable technology for the transmission medium has reduced the problem of noise in recent years, the rules which govern the process of communication must still be capable of detecting and recovering from the effects of noise by returning a message to its original form. This requires the communications software to have some means of matching the two versions of the message—that sent and that received—and entails the addition of control information to the actual data content by one means or another. Thus the exchange will consist of more than the simple data content of the message. Techniques for dealing with the effects of noise are concerned to preserve the quality of the message by ensuring that the integrity of the signs used to represent the information content have not been compromised.

The communication process must also therefore be concerned with co-ordinating the system of codes which is used to express the semantic qualities of the data exchange—what might be loosely called the 'meaning' of the message; with the physical representation of the chosen coding system as transmittable signals; and with any control information which binds different elements of the message together. There are various different coding systems for the task of mapping information generated by user applications into the binary codes used by the computer. For text, the ASCII (American Standard Character Set for Information Interchange) is widely used both within a computer and for data interchange purposes; however, completely different character sets are used in some circumstances, for instance the EBCDIC character set which dominates the IBM mainframe world. There are several different representation formats for graphics, which may be either bit patterns or geometric coordinates, and for other forms such as video signals and multimedia information.

Information to be exchanged there must be agreement between the end systems on the method by which the message is represented for transmission, even though this may not affect the actual exchange of data symbols through the channel. Since there is little standardization in the internal processes of computer equipment itself, the actual physical signals which the end systems generate must also be standardized for inter-operability, and may need translation between different physical forms in order to make use of different communication channels.

Synchronous Communication

The additional control information which is appended to the user data content carries information used in processing the message, and must also conform to some agreed system. A simple text message, for example, may contain an, overhead of information which is used to indicate boundaries between characters or chunks of text; this will appear as binary digits apparently identical to the data content unless there is some common method of 'reading' the stream of symbols.

A multimedia message which contains both sound and video elements requires control information to synchronize timing of the audio output with the screen display, which must be interpreted correctly. There is a need to synchronize the flow of information between the two end systems, so that signals which will conflict with each other are not generated simultaneously, and so that the receiver is ready and capable of processing the incoming signals at the rate which they are sent—controlling the 'turn taking'. Communication can take place in one of two alternative patterns, and in each of these synchronization is achieved in different ways.

Asynchronous communication might be characterized as 'on demand' use of the communications channel. All network users have equal access to the channel, and use it to send messages at random intervals, characterized by short bursts of activity with quiet periods of varying length in between. The receiver waits passively once the connection is made, and is activated by the receipt of some message.

A typical example of this type of activity would result from a user seated at a terminal screen, alternating interaction with a remote computer with periods of planning and thinking. Synchronous communication depends on a fixed cycle, in which each user, and both sender and receiver, have access to the channel at defined time intervals for a fixed period.

A typical use for this approach would be for large data file transfers in situations where the transfer is being managed completely by the computer systems as a background process, with no human intervention, or for the synchronization of composite sound and video signals in videoconferencing systems. This synchronicity characteristic delineates the time/response dimension of the process, defining the appropriate activities in the end systems to control the process; there is also a characteristic of the communication channel which will affect the process.

Communication through a transmission channel can occur in one of three different modes determining the allowed direction of, and activity in, the transmission. Each of these requires a different level of sophistication in control of the communication process:

— in simplex mode, the communication is in one direction only;

— in half-duplex mode, the communication can be bidirectional, but at alternate times only;

— in full-duplex mode, the communication is bidirectional, and both end systems may transmit simultaneously.

The term *channel* is normally used to denote the more abstract concept of a logical channel rather than the actual physical media. One physical link may potentially offer several logical communication channels, which can be thought of as separate entities. Since a network is a medium which is shared by many users, management of the communication process is a more complex affair than is suggested by the simplified one-to-one model. As well as agreeing on the terms by which the exchange will be conducted, the communication program must be able to supervise and regulate the dynamic elements of the process, making necessary adjustments as the exchange develops and operating conditions fluctuate. The communications program must be able to:

— establish and maintain a connection across the communications channel between the sender and recipient, agree the terms on which the exchange is to be conducted, and terminate the connection-once the transaction is completed;

— regulate the flow of information between the two participants to prevent overloading of data by the recipient, if it is unable to process it quickly enough, and a consequent possible loss of information;

— control the quality of information received by checking for the presence of errors and taking corrective action as necessary, perhaps by requesting a re-transmission of corrupted information.

The term bandwidth is an indication of the information capacity of an individual element in the process: the higher the bandwidth of the channel, for example, the higher is its information carrying capacity. The overall communication process (including the end systems) can only utilize the information-carrying capacity of the element with the least available bandwidth in any particular situation; either the transmitter, the receiver, or the channel will have a more limited bandwidth and will define the overall information exchange rate. In many situations, the bandwidth of the communication channel will be the limiting factor. The capacity of a channel is normally expressed as the number of distinct symbols per second which can be passed along it. This maximum *data transfer rate* is usually given as a figure measured in bits per second, since the number of bits which make up a useful 'unit' of information will differ according to the information type—between characters of text and scanned images in bit-map form, for instance.

In this way, a channel which is described as having a particular data transfer rate can be matched to different information transfer processes through a common comparable measure. In some circumstances, particularly in modem communications, the term *baud rate* is popularly used as an equivalent to this measure of bits per second; although this is not a strictly accurate use of the term, it can normally be taken to mean the same thing.

Transmission channels can also be characterized by the method of signalling which is used. In *baseband* signalling the capacity of the channel is monopolised by a single message for the duration of the transmission, typically by varying the voltage along an electrical cable in a pre-determined pattern. *Broadband* signalling enables a physical medium to be shared by more than one transmission by varying the frequency of the signals to ensure separation of one from the other—as a radio can distinguish different frequency transmissions. Broadband offers a higher bandwidth, and is therefore more associated with information networking applications which require higher capacities, such as multimedia.

A goal of advanced network technology is to support a flexible, use of bandwidth among multiple users according to fluctuating demand, changing the allocation dynamically according to the transmission needs of the moment. A communication channel is a logical concept that can be implemented on a variety of physical media, each of which has its own particular characteristics, such as bandwidth. The choice of which to adopt depends on the purposes of the network and the kind of applications it must support, the predicted traffic and data rates together with required response times, and a cost/benefit calculation on the relative importance between these factors. The most widely used physical transmission media are mentioned here.

1. The *twisted pair* is the simplest form of transmission cable, two simple electrical cables carrying small voltage signals. This is a very cheap method of connecting individual computer devices to a network, and is easy to install, but is not suitable for carrying traffic from many devices due to the limited bandwidth which it possesses, nor for applications which require more than a 1 Megabit per second (Mbps) data rate.

2. *Co-axial cable* uses a more substantial copper cable to offer a higher bandwidth suitable for multiple access from a limited number of nodes on a local network; and for the transmission of information forms which require a higher throughput of data, such as video signals, at data rates of up to 10 Mbps. This higher capacity is bought, at the expense of a higher material cost and a more complex installation process.

3. *Optical fibre cable* provides a means of transcending the physical limits of electrical cable, by conveying signals on a fluctuating light beam enclosed within a very fine glass fibre. Since light waves have a much higher potential bandwidth than electrical waves, data rates up to and beyond 100 Mbps are possible, as well as providing a lower susceptibility to noisy or sensitive environments.

A single glass fibre, smaller in dimension than a human hair, is provided for each signal, and an installed optical cable may consist of several hundred fibres bundled together, providing a high throughout for existing services and spare capacity for future growth. While optical fibre provides a means of building very high bandwidth networks which can support sophisticated multimedia services, it is expensive and more difficult to install, requiring special interface equipment between cable and computer.

4. Microwave transmission offers a non-terrestrial alternative to a physical point-to-point link. Data is conveyed on radio waves through free space, and is normally used in conjunction with geostationary satellites. The data is transmitted from a ground station, called an uplink, to an orbiting satellite which is in direct line-of-sight, and the signal is bounced back to a receiving station (the downlink) at some different geographical ground location. These re-transmissions can be broadcast over a wide area for receiving by many destinations simultaneously, or be highly focused onto a single site.

   Satellite relay is commonly used to leap across long distances, such as in establishing connections between the United Kingdom and North America or the Far East, or where the laying of a physical cable would be costly or impossible across difficult geographic terrain. Microwave transmission may also be used on a ground-to-ground basis, between stations situated on high ground within line of sight of each other.

5. Network communications have also been achieved by the use of infra-red and broadcast radio signals; there is a growing interest in the use of such 'wireless' communications although few actual

installations as yet. Some use is made of radio data broadcasting at a national level.

Protocol

Essentially, a protocol is one attempt to address the basic problems of data communications which are relevant to networking within a particular arena. Since there is no universally applicable solution to these problems which will be effective in all situations, a range of protocols have arisen which have proved effective in specialized areas within the current feasible limits of technology.

Since the development of communication protocols has been carried out within the context of perceived practical problems, there is a tendency for the available offerings to be predicated on the use of particular types and make of equipment. Computer manufacturers have devised their own proprietary protocol suites intended to interconnect only their own Computer makes; and more generally applicable protocols have emerged for broader categories of computer, such as for local networks of micro-computers.

Although a protocol is a logical specification rather than a particular implementation in software, the protocol is likely to make assumptions about available levels of functionality and processing capabilities. As both computing technology and information applications have led to more complicated and sophisticated systems, so the communications process between systems has also developed a parallel level of complexity.

The complexity of modern networking has led to the use of a layered approach to protocol specification. A *layered protocol* aims to analyse the overall communications process into well-defined and semi-autonomous functional modules, each of which provides a specialized service in the overall scheme and works in conjunction with the other modules.

Network communications can then be split into constituent activities, and these may be implemented on different parts of the system in different ways, not necessarily all together on the same piece of equipment. Any particular layer may potentially contain alternative specifications for reaching the same goals, each of which is more appropriate for a particular environment or system arrangement. As long as the module provides the appropriate service to its co-operating modules in the process, the way in which it achieves this need not concern the other elements involved. The growing need for the capability of interconnecting computer systems and networks whatever their local characteristics has led to several initiatives aiming to develop a degree of standardization between the major alternatives, and to encourage the conformity of new products to these standards.

These initiatives aim to develop a framework within which the most widely accepted and established 'industry standard' protocols can fit as alternative options. At the present time networking protocols fall into two main groups:

— those emanating from or supported by national and international standards making bodies, which are more 'open' in nature with published specifications;

— those emerging as proprietary standards from major computer manufacturers, which are 'closed' by virtue of their confidential specification and non-participative development.

A set of protocols will deal with aspects which are more closely related to the physical aspects of data and network communications and those which are more related to the information transfer aspects of user activity. At the lower layers, the data communications aspects can be seen as failing into three main areas: the physical connection, basic data management, and routing through the network. The *physical level* is concerned with producing, receiving and monitoring the physical signals which are actually transmitted between systems, and with the standardization of methods for representing data in this form.

A well-known example of this is the RS-232C standard, which defines the electrical interface on equipment as a multi-pin connection and assigns a particular function to each pin. The *data link level* is concerned with error control and recovery, and with flow control. In order to achieve this, most protocols encapsulate the user data in frames by dividing the stream of data into units of a pre-defined size and adding control information for use by the receiving system. Since the network connection will be conveying data frames from other network users, the frames also contain header information ensuring delivery to the correct destination.

Special frames may also be used to send only control information, for example to establish and terminate links with a remote computer. The frames produced by this layer are passed down to the physical layer for transmission. Error control is important at this level, since noise on the channel may result in the loss or corruption of frames; one purpose of splitting the whole message up into data frames is to retain control of the transmission as it develops, and take any remedial action necessary. Error control takes a number of simpler or more sophisticated forms, some of which require feedback from the receiver, for example:

— echo checking reflects characters received back to the sender for display on the user's screen, so that any corruption can be noticed and re-transmitted;

— acknowledgement schemes require the receiver to send an acknowledgement token back to the sender for each frame, before the next is transmitted;

— check digits can be added to the data frame by the sender, based on a computation carried out on the user data itself, and which the receiver can also use to check comparability.

Flow control is concerned to ensure that the data is not sent faster than it can be received; this function can make use of some of these devices, for instance acknowledgement schemes, or add features of its own to the exchange process. The network level is concerned with the management and control of routing through the network.

The extent to which this is relevant will depend on the type of network in use and the mode in which it is operating. There are two broad modes within which a network can operate, providing two types of service:

— *connectionless mode,* in which the data is dispatched by the sender with the appropriate destination address, but no direct connection is made between them;

— *connection-oriented mode,* in which the two end systems behave as though directly connected by a physical medium and work in co-operation with each other.

The network layer will typically organize the user data into packets, splitting up a long message into several units in this way, and adding source and destination information to each packet to control its path through the network. The user data is then made transparent to the network itself, which is only concerned with the 'external' address information.

Different packets which constitute parts of the same message are then treated as independent units, and may travel through the network at different speeds and by different routes. The receiving system takes delivery of the packets and reconstitutes the message in its original format using the control information added by the sender. An X.25 network is an example of this arrangement. The network layer passes the packets down to the data link layer for the addition of error and flow control information, once it has completed its own responsibilities. In this way, user data is passed between layers in both sender and receiver, with only one actual physical network connection between them. In wider area networks, these three layers are also contained within the intermediate stages internal to the network, as well as in the end systems. The specific protocols which implement these broad functions within an individual context will depend on the particular elements of the system which is in use, and the equipment available to it.

A range of protocols are implemented either as software in communications packages, or as hardware built into data communications equipment. Some have achieved a greater popularity and therefore a *de facto* standardization over time. In order for the communication process to be successful, both systems which intend to exchange data must be capable of running the same protocol, and therefore require communications packages or hardware which are compatible with each other; larger systems may offer a range of communication alternatives which can sense the method used by a caller and select the appropriate option.

The types of device which have a role to play in the entire networking process can be placed into two categories:

1. Data terminating equipment (DTE) describes the devices which originate, or provide the final destination for, a transmitted message; either that operated by an end-user, or a computer system working autonomously. Typical examples of DTE

devices would be a desktop microcomputer, a mainframe computer system, a visual display unit terminal, a printer, or a facsimile machine.

2. Data communicating equipment (DCE) describes the devices which are used to support onwards communication of a message received from some DTE device type—acting as 'steps in the chain' rather than as end-controllers of the process. This may be a device attached to the end-user's system, or some intermediate step within the network itself.

The data communicating equipment acts as a common interface for unlike data terminating equipment, evening out the differences through the common use of a standard protocol. In this way, dissimilar types of information technology equipment can be used for information networking without requiring an end user to be aware of the physical characteristics of the receiving system; the more widely used and open the standard protocol which is used, the wider range of equipment which can interface in this way.

The kind of equipment which falls into this category fulfils specialized roles in the communications process: some of these are integral to the internal functioning of the network element itself while others are associated with user end systems. Some of the more commonly found types are described here, as indicative of the range. The multiplexor is a device for concentrating a number of terminal devices onto a higher bandwidth line, to make the most effective use of this capacity and to remove the need for installing many duplicate lines (one for each device) in parallel with each other. This arrangement would typically be used to connect several terminals situated near each other to a central computer which is located at some distance. The multiplexor is responsible for apportioning the line on an equitable basis between all the terminals connected. There are two main methods of multiplexing:

— time-division multiplexing, in which each terminal is allotted the full capacity of the channel for a fixed period of time, in a rotating sequence;

— frequency division multiplexing, in which the full channel capacity is divided between users by allowing simultaneous transmissions on different frequencies.

The most appropriate form to use depends on the applications which are using the system; commonly asynchronous enquiry-type applications, where activity is in unpredictable short bursts, use a time-division form of multiplexing. A multiplexor must be installed at the receiving end, to separate out the different terminal signals for processing. A modem is another communicating device which allows one kind of DTE equipment, typically a personal computer, to establish a temporary connection with another remote computer system by using the normal telephone line.

Since the telephone system was originally designed solely for voice traffic, which is analogue in nature, some conversion process must be used to translate digital computer data into a form suitable for analogue transmission. Digital signals are in a binary form, having two states—on and off—which can be represented as changes in voltage signals on a cable. Since the normal telephone line is designed for transmission of sound waves, these binary signals must be transformed into an audible tone by the modem. This process is known as modulation; a modem (modulator—demodulator) must be placed at both ends of the telephone link, acting as the interface between the end systems and the line, encoding and decoding the digital data signals.

A series of standards recommendations have been produced by the CCITT (Comite Consultatif Internationale de Telegraphie et Telephonic), a Geneva-based international organization concerned with issues in telecommunications development, for the use of modems. The cost of modem technology falls steadily, faster transmission speeds are achieved at a higher expense due not only to the price of equipment but also to the additional communications processing which is necessary at higher speeds.

Higher transmission speeds are achieved by a panoply of special techniques which require more sophisticated error checking capabilities to counter the increased influence of noise. While the CCITT recommendations are standard within Europe, the existence of a separate set of standards in North America, developed by the Bell Communications Corporation complicates the international situation.

The most common of these are the Bell 203 (1200 bps) and Bell 212 (2400 bps) standards; although working at the same speeds they do not have an exact correspondence to V-series standards and are not compatible. A final example of data communicating equipment is the use of an independent computer processor to handle the communications loading of a large computer system. This would typically be used where a mainframe computer is accessed by a large number of remote callers; for example, a system which makes an online bibliographic database available to users on a global basis through the use of modems over a telecommunications network. A smaller computer—such as a minicomputer—is dedicated to the task of dealing with the network communications, so that the mainframe does not become overloaded by this task, and is free to concentrate on database activity.

5

Technological Change

Communication systems have unified, to such an extent that telephone transfers and television pictures no longer circulate on separate channels. Computers and television sets are one and the same thing, telephones are linked to the Internet and mobile phones are connected to laptop computers. These changes also have far-reaching sociological implications, not only in terms of the ways we use the new technologies but also in the ways we have recourse to their services, and for what purpose.

The fact that computers can now be interconnected has marked a new step in innovation with the emergence of worldwide communication networks. At the forefront of these is the Internet, a living encyclopedia which makes no distinction between telephone, satellite or television to route the information it contains. Optimum performance of the network will not be achieved, however, until very high performance circuits have become commonplace. That movement is now under way, through the growing integration and interconnection of new information technology with telecommunications resources. It can be seen in information highways, the synthesis of technological convergence resulting in widespread interactive multimedia offers. This break with the past, one of the major undertakings for the next century, symbolizes a society in which network distributed information and intelligence will be the major forms of wealth. Most governments are persuaded that such is the case, and are already preparing vast schemes with information highways as their priority to enable their societies to take part in a new economy, to enhance the productivity of already existing industries and to create new ones.

With this in mind, economic actors in all sectors of the information and leisure industries - including suppliers of telecommunications hardware and infrastructures - are already taking up their positions. Groups are being set up for this purpose, launching intersectional alliances which have generally led to high market concentration and internationalization. These upheavals, both technological and economic are radically modifying the ways in which we use communication, both at work and in the home.

New possibilities for training, education, employment and leisure activities hitherto reserved for an elite can now be afforded by all. People communicating now have powers of transmitting and receiving information undreamed of even ten years ago. That fundamental breakthrough, which backs up the concept dear to Bill Gate of 'introduction at your fingertips', both enhances individual action and at the same time questions the very nature of the state, national frontiers and cultural roots.

Combined with geopolitical change, to raises a number of questions about legislation, the gaps existing between nations and within them, the risk of rendering local cultures uniform, and the role of public services when forced to compete with domestic and supranational private programmes. The accelerating progress in new information and communication technology is essentially based on three fundamental changes: the digitization of images, sounds and data; digital data compression; and the growing power of electronic components. These innovations have made possible the gradual replacement of analog equipment by digital systems that are clearing the way for greater interactivity between end-users and terminals.

Digital revolution

Digital technology marks a true revolution which goes far beyond purely technical upheavals. On the one hand, it will lead to the integration of information transmission networks and reception hardware, and, on the other, it will simultaneously enhance a new relationship with the media and the way in which we consume the information they convey. Basically, this revolution stems from the spectacular progress made in micro-electronics, leading to the digitization of images, sound and data. In conventional so-called analog systems, sounds and images were converted into electrical signals so that they could be transmitted on physical support systems such as wires and optic fibres, or in electromagnetic wave form via terrestrial broadcasting networks or by satellite.

With digitization, the same signals are coded into strings of numbers represented in binary form as packets of os and is, which then constitute a data processing file. The problem with these basic files, however, is that they are extremely demanding in terms of transmission capacity.

Digital compression has solved the difficulty, by reducing the flow of information to decrease the time and therefore the cost of transmission, without modifying the quality and content of the information itself. In radio broadcasting, digital techniques and particularly that of data compression will make it possible to transport, on a single transmission channel (be it via cable, terrestrial broadcasting or satellite), several services (television, radio, data transmission, telecommunication), or several television and radio programmes, with several sound tracks in each one of them, as well as a single programme based on asymmetrical loop multiplexing (Near Video on Demand [NVOD]). Moreover, digital compression makes more efficient use of the channels available and thus reduces or shares out the cost of transmission. After pervading telephones and computers, digital technology has now tackled the last link in the chain of image and sound broadcasting: use by the public at large.

The consequences for television viewers and users of images will be greater than those affecting users of computer or telecommunications technology, since television is a consumer market with a much higher penetration rate than the other sectors of the communication industry.

Electronic components

The development of digitization and its applications is based on the extraordinary breakthroughs in electronic components. Ever since their invention in 1969 by Ted Hoff and other engineers at the American company Intel, their computing power has increased at an exponential rate. Gordon Moore, one of the three founders of Intel, as early as 1965 deduced a law which has dictated their evolution ever since: 'Microprocessor power doubles every eighteen to twenty-four months.' Thirty years later, the Moore law can still be seen to hold true.

The power of semiconductors doubles almost every two years, with a corresponding drop in their price/performance ratio. Each new processor launched on to the market contains approximately twice as many transistors as its predecessor, with market launches following on every eighteen months. Between the 2,300 transistors of the first microprocessor and the 5.5 million in a Pentium Pro, the number of transistors has already multiplied by more than 2,400.

However, there is no let-up in the power-race between the industrial groups as a whole. With 8.8 million transistors, the new K6 Advanced Micro Devices (AMD) computer broke all the records in 1997, including that of Intel, which had reached the figure of 7.5 million transistors with its Pentium 11. If the curve is extrapolated, a microprocessor in the year 2000 should comprise between 50 and 100 million transistors and be capable of executing two billion instructions per second, or 400,000 times more than ENIAC, the very first computer constructed fifty years ago. This strategy of reaching ever higher goes hand in hand with the new miniaturization and storage capacities of the hard disks used in microcomputers.

Progress in this field has also been spectacular. In 1956, one of the very first hard disks, the RAMAC 305 (Random Access Method of Accounting and Control) could store 5 million characters (each character being represented in computer language by one byte, a group of eight bits), or some 2,500 pages of-text. It contained fifty disk platters, each 60 cm in diameter.

In 1997, the latest hard disk from IBM, the Travelstar VP, has a storage capacity of 1.5 billion bytes (Gb) of data, weighs no more than 99 grams, is the size of an audio cassette and is only 9.5 rum thick. It can store 3.2 Gb, or 1.6 million pages of text. The miniaturization of components and memories and the enhancement of their technical prowess are ongoing processes, making them smaller, faster, more powerful and less expensive.

Meteoric changes such as these provide the new information and transmission support media with new powers of communication. The general process of digitization has resulted in the emergence of a new feature: the convergence of telecommunications, computer and audiovisual technologies, which were previously separated by techniques, legislation and modes of distribution. The new concept has given rise to different definitions and interpretations according to each operator, institution or researcher concerned. Harmonized, common development of convergence is difficult to find, because each state is strongly influenced by its own history and the different levels of development of its telecommunications and audiovisual sectors.

However, the structural transformation of the public sector and new legislation look forward to the development of such convergence. Several angles of approach are possible. Some authors see convergence as comprising three different features or levels: the technical convergence mentioned above, economic convergence and convergence in legislation. Others add the convergence of social customs and expectations. The Organisation for Economic Co-operation and Development (OECD) distinguishes three other types of convergence: technical, functional and corporate.

Technical convergence refers to the use by the communication industry of signal digitization. It is evaluated according to the progress in the digitization process in the three communication sectors. Computer technology is by definition completely digitized. Digitization in telecommunications is an ongoing process which is already highly advanced in terms of both transmission and packet-switching.

Finally, the audiovisual industry is making giant leaps in the digital world. Technical convergence, then, refers to the adoption of the general process of digitization. Functional convergence refers to the diversification and increasingly hybrid nature of the services offered by communication media which hitherto have been distinct. This means radio broadcasting services will be able to transmit signals other than information or entertainment programmes; in addition to the conventional services of dialogue and data transmission, the telephone industry will also be able to transmit entertainment; cable-based distributors on their side will be able to provide telephone services.

Functional convergence may thus be summed up as free competition between the radio broadcasting, telecommunications and computer technology sectors, and the disappearance of the traditional boundaries between these three industries. Corporate convergence refers to the new capacities of the communication companies to diversify their sources of finance. In this way, companies telecasting audiovisual program will be able to make viewers pay for them direct, and will no longer have to limit themselves to indirect revenue such as advertising or state subsidies.

The same principle applies to telecommunications companies, which will now be able to seek other sources of finance than direct fee-paying alone. The distinction in technical terms, therefore, between the various sectors of the communication industry is less self-evident, owing to the fact that information is processed in digital form and that the transmission infrastructure itself is multi-purpose. Functional convergence and that of the companies involved is thus melting the barriers between the different sectors of activity.

While opinions are unanimous with respect to the reality of convergence, particularly in terms of its technological nature, debate is still heated about the lead times that will be needed to provide each home with programmes that are interactive, easy and fast to use. Some believe it will happen tomorrow, others talk of its realization ten or twenty years hence. Convergence is, in fact, an ongoing process.

6

Freedom of Information

The first consecration occurred in 1789 with the French Declaration of the Rights of Man and of the Citizen, whose Article XI asserts that 'the free communication of ideas and opinions is one of the most precious rights of man', and that in consequence every citizen I can freely speak, write and print subject to responsibility for the abuse of this freedom in the cases determined by law'.

Two years later, in 1791, the American Bill of Rights proclaimed a number of amendments to the constitution of the United States, including that landmark legal provision, the First Amendment, which stipulated that 'Congress shall make no law . . . abridging the freedom of speech, or of the press'. This was a fundamental revolution, for it meant that truth had ceased to belong to any one constituted power, and pertained 'solely to the constituent parties, being immanent to individual reason' and no longer to the transcendent authority of the state.

During the Second World War, the international community became alive to the way in which people's attitudes and awareness were affected by total control of the, media. It was for this reason that, in 1941, President Roosevelt placed 'freedom of speech and expression everywhere in the world' in the front rank of the 'Four

Freedoms.' In the years immediately following the war, defending freedom of information naturally became one of the objectives of all efforts to rebuild the international system.

The following year, the United Nations recognized the importance of freedoms relating to information. In 1946, the UN recalled in its resolution 59 that 'freedom of information is a fundamental human right and is the touchstone of all the freedoms to which the United Nations is consecrated' On 10 December 1948, freedom of information was enshrined in the Universal Declaration of Human Rights, whose Article 19 is the most categorical expression thereof. 'Everyone has the right to freedom of opinion and expression; this right includes freedom . . . to seek, receive and impart information and ideas through any media and regardless of frontiers. The Munich Declaration adopted in 1971 by representatives of journalists unions, adopts an identical point of view: 'The right to information, to freedom of expression and criticism, is one of the fundamental rights of man.'

UNESCO's own Constitution, adopted on 10 November 1945, assigns to the Organization in its Article 11, paragraph 2(a), the goal of 'advancing the mutual knowledge and under-standing of peoples', it particular by means of international agreements designed 'to promote the free flow of ideas by word and image' These principles were to be strengthened with the International Covenant on Civil and Political Rights, adopted by the United Nations General Assembly on 16 December 1966, whose Article 19 provides that: 'Everyone shall have the right to freedom of expression; this right shall include freedom to seek, receive and impart information and ideas of all kinds, regardless of frontiers, either orally in writing or in print, in the form of art, or through any other media of his choice.' More than ninety states have already ratified this Covenant, thereby pledging to apply its principles. Other victories for press freedom bound up with the development of the media have given rise to further international and regional declarations. All give pride of place to freedom of information as a precondition of democracy, truth as a basic duty, and respect for the human person as limit.

Among the many international legal instruments that establish freedom of information as a basic principle, mention may be made of Article 10 of the European Convention for the Protection of Human Rights and Fundamental Freedoms, adopted on 4 November 1950, Article 13 of the American Convention on Human Rights, adopted on 22 November 1969, and Article 9 of the African Charter on Human and Peoples' Rights, adopted on 12 July 1981. This principle was to be a driving force in the domestic legislation of the different countries.

Selection of professional charters on press freedom

The Munich Declaration

The Declaration of Rights and Obligations of Journalists was adopted on 24 and 25 November 1971 in Munich by representatives of the journalists' unions of the Six countries of the then European Community. It has since been adopted by the International Federation of Journalists (IFJ) and by most journalists' unions in Europe.

The declaration, which is quintessentially a code of professional ethics, states in its Preamble: 'The right to information, to freedom of expression and criticism is one of the fundamental rights of man. All rights and duties of a journalist originate from this right of the public to be informed on events and opinions. The journalists' responsibility towards the public exceeds any other responsibility particularly towards employers and public authorities.'

The Declaration of Chapultepec

The Declaration of Chapultepec was adopted by some hundred professional journalists in Mexico City~ at a conference organized by the Inter-American Press Association (IAPA) in March 1994. It has been signed and endorsed by the President of the United States, by a dozen Latin American Heads of State, by the Secretary-General of the United Nations and by the Director-General of UNESCO.

It is in line with the Santiago (Chile) Declaration on the development of the media and democracy in Latin American and the Caribbean. In addition to recognizing the fundamental role played by freedom of expression and press freedom in all democratic societies, the declaration condemns all forms of violence and coercion against journalists. It stipulates in particular that, in a truly free society public opinion alone has the right to reward or to condemn the work of journalists. All acts of violence directed against journalists must be 'investigated promptly' and 'punished harshly'.

The Charter for a Free Press

The ten principles of the Charter for a Free Press were adopted in London in 1987 by journalists representing thirty-four countries and the main organizations working in the field of press freedom. The charter urges governments to:

— put an end to both direct and indirect censorship;
— prevent all discriminatory practices in regard to the independent media, particularly in regard to access to information, means of distribution and taxation;
— permit the free flow of news and the unimpeded movement of journalists and their equipment across borders;
— not restrict the practice of journalism through any licensing system;

— ensure that journalists enjoy the protection of the law and are recognized as civilians in war zones.

The charter was signed by the World Press Freedom Committee (WPFC), the International Federation of Newspaper Publishers (FIEJ), the International Press Institute (IPI), the Inter-American Press Association (IAPA), the North American National Broadcasters Association (NANBA) and the International Federation of the Periodical Press (FIPP).

UNESCO and communication

However, in the period immediately following the Second World War, the free flow of information would very rapidly become a Cold War issue and constitute one of the major bones of contention between states. It was interpreted in terms of two fundamentally conflicting doctrines.

That of the Western democracies was based on Article 19 of the Universal Declaration of Human Rights. It advocated the dismantling of all barriers in the way of seeking, receiving and imparting information and ideas both within states and beyond their borders. For its part, the attitude of the Soviet Union and the peoples' democracies originated in Communist theory, which defined the media, as educational tools operating under state control for the purpose of expediting the construction of socialism. The media had a social function, and journalists, defined as intellectual agitators and propagandists, had a mission to -inform and to mould opinion.

To the principle of a free and unimpeded flow of information, the Soviet Union and its allies opposed that of a controlled exchange of information, conducted on the basis of intergovernmental agreements, with due respect for sovereignty and the principle of noninterference in the domestic affairs of states. For their part, the developing countries declared themselves to be the victims of serious inequalities in the matter of information flows between North and South, and considered the manner in which the media of the North reflected the reality of their national situations to be exaggerated, distorted and even totally false. In consequence, they called for a redressing of the balance of information flows, and hence implicitly for control over information emanating from the countries of the North.

The Communist countries' demand for controlled information exchange between East and West and the developing countries' calls for a redressing of the information flow balance between North and South were both compatible and complementary. These two groups of countries formed a united front within the international organizations concerned, first and foremost the United Nations and UNESCO, for the purpose of advocating, at the end of the 1970s, the establishment of a 'New World Information and Communication Order' (NWICO), regarded as being the counterpart of the 'New World Economic Order'. The discussions which took place on the subject within UNESCO were extremely stormy. Tension reached a climax in the mid-1980s when the United States (1984) and the United Kingdom (1985) withdrew from the Organization. For their part, a number of international organizations representing professional media circles put all their weight into the balance in order to isolate UNESCO and to make the international community understand that the New World Information and Communication Order constituted an intolerable assault upon press freedom and the free flow of information.

The political changes which occurred in the USSR at the end of the 1980s, and in particular the introduction by Mikhail Gorbachev of glasnost, had the result of radically transforming the overall situation in regard to NWICO.

With the emergence of democracy, a number of Eastern and Central European countries began to adopt the liberal conception of information whereby freedom of expression and media independence and pluralism are an essential precondition of any properly functioning democratic society. The major upheavals which occurred in Eastern and Central Europe drove a number of developing countries as well to embark upon the path of democratic reform. Freedom of expression, and with it press freedom and pluralism, thus gained a certain amount of ground.

The new information and communication technologies, in particular satellite television which ,enters via the roof, without having to go through the censor's office' - and the Internet, have shrunk the planet to a global village, and made information available to a growing number of people on every continent. True, information flows remain largely to the advantage of the North; but an increasing number of developing countries such as Brazil, Egypt, India and Mexico are becoming in turn producers, broadcasters and operators on a regional and even a worldwide scale.

Moreover, it is worth pointing out that the smaller countries of the North are themselves becoming ever more dependent upon the output of the major international, and particularly North American, corporations, in regard both to information (large international news agencies supplying texts, pictures and data) and to entertainment and fiction films. The twofold dichotomy between North and South and East and West is gradually being superseded by a new subdivision between the large, populous countries, which have a sufficiently strong domestic market to cover the costs of their national productions, and the smaller countries of the North and South alike, which are far more numerous but which, because they do riot possess the necessary critical mass, are doomed to import foreign programmes in order to counterbalance the quantitative inadequacy of their domestic output.

The public and private television companies of the industrialized and developing countries are indeed in danger of shortly finding themselves excluded from international deals in regard to the live broadcasting of the most popular sports events, such as the Olympic Games or the World Football Championship, since the charges for broadcasting rights are becoming, in relation to their domestic advertising market, quite prohibitive. What, then, can be said of the poorest countries of the South, in particular those of the African continent, which provide so many of today's world champions! These countries are already almost wholly dependent on the international market.

In the case of some, the situation is so critical that the systematic pirating of satellite pictures and videotapes has become the sole means of survival. Thus the disparities highlighted by the commission chaired by Sean MacBride, which served to justify the call for a new world order, the NWICO, still remain a burning issue. On the other hand, the map of these disparities has changed in relation to the situation prevailing in the 1970s and 1980s. Most Latin American and Asian countries are undoubtedly in a better position than they were twenty years ago, both in regard to media access and in terms of endogenous production.

It must not be overlooked that large sectors of their populations, notably the poorest sections, have benefited but little from this favourable trend. In the industrialized countries, while access to the media poses no special problems aside from financial constraints, the growing dependence of the small countries on the major international suppliers of texts, images and data has become an extremely worrying factor. As regards the least developed countries, their situation has worsened still further in that many have become still more impoverished, and have been left on the fringe of technological progress.

Seizing the opportunity afforded by the ending of the Cold War to move beyond the sterile discussions on the NWICO, and concerned to support the process of democratization being pursued in several regions of the world, the General Conference of UNESCO adopted, at its twenty-fifth session in November 1989 - at the very moment when the Berlin Wall was crumbling - a 'new communication strategy' aimed at meeting the needs of the burgeoning democracies and the developing countries alike. Its goals were threefold:

— Encouraging the free flow of information, at international as well as national level.
— Promoting the wider and better balanced dissemination of information, without any obstacle to freedom of expression.
— Developing all the appropriate means of strengthening communication capacities in the developing countries in order to increase their participation in the communication process.

In respect of the first prong of this 'new communication strategy', UNESCO reasserted the fundamental principle of 'free flow of information' enshrined in its constitution. In particular, it pledged to promote both freedom of expression, the cornerstone of the human rights edifice, and press freedom, itself a key component of all democratic societies. To this end, it provides assistance to intergovernmental and nongovernmental organizations whose mission it is to defend these fundamental freedoms, while at the same time preserving and developing its own means of action. In order to give concrete expression to its commitment to the democratic process in countries living through a period of transition, UNESCO, in conjunction with the United Nations Department of Public Information, has since 1991 organized a series of five Regional Seminars on Promoting Independent and Pluralistic Media.

These workshops, which brought together in all several hundred media professionals, gave rise to the adoption of firmly worded and unambiguous 'declarations' which defined the preconditions for setting up and operating a free, independent and pluralist press. An unusual occurrence in the annals of the United Nations system, these various declarations, framed and drafted by the participants, themselves all media professionals, were later formally adopted in their entirety by the states represented at UNESCO's General Conference.

In addition, the United Nations General Assembly decided, in December 1993, on UNESCO's proposal to proclaim 3 May, the anniversary of the Declaration of Windhoek, 'World Press Freedom Day'. Finally, as its most recent initiative, UNESCO established, in 1996, the UNESCO/Guillermo Cano World Press Freedom Prize, which was awarded for the first time on 3 May 1997.

In the light of the foregoing, one cannot fail to observe the developments that have occurred in the states since the end of the Cold War. Unfortunately, in so far as respect for fundamental freedoms is concerned, there is frequently a major difference between official positions, adopted 'cold' in intergovernmental forums, and the reality of the situation at grass-roots level. The fact nevertheless remains that states taken as a whole have never committed themselves so far on such sensitive issues as press freedom and the independence and pluralism of the media.

The second objective of UNESCO's 'new communication strategy' takes up one of the ultimate goals of NWICO, with this single - but major -difference: that it is no longer possible to curb or to prevent the free flow of information on the pretext that its dissemination is unbalanced. Such an argument had in fact frequently been put forward by authoritarian and totalitarian regimes, in the 1970s and 1980s, in order to justify censorship of the international news agencies, to ban the distribution of foreign newspapers on national territory and to jam electronic media broadcasts transmitted from abroad.

The new strategy does not seek to weaken the strong, but rather to strengthen the weak in order to redress the balance, in so far as is possible, in the exchange of information flows. Hence the third objective of UNESCO's 'new information strategy', namely, to develop communication capacities in the developing countries. When the General Conference of UNESCO adopted its 'new communication strategy' in November 1989, the representatives of the developing countries, somewhat at a loss after finding themselves dropped by their traditional partners among the Communist states of Eastern and Central Europe, had greatly hoped that the industrialized countries of the North, having obtained satisfaction on the free flow of information issue, would do their utmost substantially to increase their financial support for the development of communication, and in particular for the International Programme for the Development of Communication (IPDC).

This hope was strengthened in February 1992 when IPDC decided to change its rules of procedure in order to be in a position to help the media, in pursuance of a recommendation formulated some months earlier on the occasion of the Windhoek seminar. As a result, projects submitted by the private sector are henceforth admissible.

In the light of the experience of recent years, it must be acknowledged that hope has been disappointed because contributions to the IPDC Special Account have failed to increase. It is true that, since the economic crisis which hit them in the first half of the 1990s, most of the industrialized countries have severely cut back their aid budgets to developing countries.

It is also true that the needs born of the transition process in the new democracies of Eastern and Central Europe have siphoned off substantial sums, frequently to the detriment of the countries of the South. However, that does not explain everything, for assistance for communication development has lagged behind both in the East European democracies currently in transition and in the developing countries of the South. This situation is all the more surprising in that, throughout the Cold War, Western countries, and first and foremost the United States, had invested billions of dollars in order to ensure their supremacy in the strategic field of communication.

Those investments were far from fruitless, since it was the power of words and images that toppled the Berlin Wall. While it is understandable that, like the 'weapons of deterrence', the 'weapons of persuasion' should have suffered substantial budget cuts, it is difficult to imagine that only a few crumbs remain to consolidate the achievements of democracy in the communication field, since it is well known that the media were and are still in Europe, as in the other regions of the world, the driving force behind the transition to democracy. The scant interest shown by the industrialized countries in the development of communication and information becomes even more surprising when one considers the fact that the communication sector represents up to 10 per cent of GNP in some countries of the North.

It may therefore legitimately be wondered what

reasons have led the national development agencies to devote less than 1 per cent of their financial resources to date to projects relating to communication development.

The media between freedom and censorship

Satellite broadcasting, electronic printing, the explosion of the Internet and of e-mail, and the mobile telephone have resulted in a huge expansion of the potential for worldwide information flows and exchange. They have also facilitated the rapid and even instantaneous transmission of images from one region to another, transcending national borders even though some states still endeavour to raise all kinds of barriers by operating border controls, jamming radio broadcasts and banning the possession of satellite dish aerials. All these defences are today increasingly eroded by the new progress being made by the media, the intensification of output and the higher levels of technical performance.

The new communication technologies, or the new ways of optimizing the old, have become an essential dimension in all thinking about the issue. For they are capable of producing positive effects and helping to speed up the democratization process, just as they may constitute a curb upon, and a threat to, freedom of expression and democracy.

The media, allies of freedom and democracy

The media have played a key role in several countries in bringing about the democratic progress recorded throughout the world during the 1980s. Their ability to transmit, continuously and in real time, current national and international news has had the effect of both driving events along and speeding them up. Examples are legion. In the Philippines, the clandestine use of video (and also of photocopying) at the time of the assassination of the opposition leader Benigno Aquino, as well as the high-profile presence of foreign media during the 1986 elections, contributed in large measure to the fall of Ferdin and Marcos. Radio Veritas was occupied by the citizenry during the 'people's power' movement in order to rally the Population against Marcos's army. In South Africa, in Haiti and in Palestine, the pictures of apartheid, repression and of the intifada prompted reactions solidarity and support throughout the world. They enabled the international community to condemn the abuses, to defend human rights and to encourage democracy. The impact of the media can also be of paramount importance when they describe and present to peoples deprived of freedom another way of life other political systems, other democratic values.

The example of the former communist regimes provides an excellent illustration. In the ex-German Democratic Republic, citizens could receive the radio stations and television channels of the Federal Republic of Germany. They were kept regularly informed about certain political and other events that their government preferred to cover up. That was how, in 1989, they learned of the great demonstration in Leipzig, the opening of the Hungarian borders and the first cracks that were appearing in the Berlin Wall.

After the fall of the Berlin Wall, the peoples of the neighbouring countries, who were following the events on foreign radio and television stations, decided in their turn to take to the streets. Here too, pictures invaded every sphere and played a crucial role in bearing witness to the process of liberation. They neutralized official pronouncements and undermined the authorities' position. During the same period, in Czechoslovakia, the students had installed television screens throughout the streets of Prague in order to show police brutality against the demonstrators, and to broadcast the speeches of the playwright and future President of the Republic, Vaclav

Havel. In Poland, the majority of journalists found themselves on the front line with all other citizens calling for democracy. Dailies such as Gazeta wyborcza exerted considerable pressure on behalf of the democratization process. In Romania, television played a key role in rallying the population and helping to spread support for the liberation movement, which was filmed, monitored and broadcast live throughout the world thanks to the famous Studio 4 of the Free Romanian Television company. In striking contrast to the macabre faking of the mass grave in Timisoara, this movement established itself as a formidable force in the fight for democracy.

Determined to bear witness on behalf of that revolution, citizens set up as amateur reporters to impose their video recordings by way of popular testimony in the first meetings organized by the revolution's leaders. Reaction to the events was extremely powerful, thanks to a press and television that, having thrown off their shackles, acted as catalysts in generating a genuine new awareness. In the Federal Republic of Yugoslavia, the popular demonstrations against the authorities' refusal to accept the results of the municipal elections won by the opposition were widely and favourably reported on the Internet.

Several sites made it possible to monitor in real time the evolution of the protest movement. Sites such as 'Protest 96', named after the student movement, made their voices heard through-out the world by posting reports on demonstrations, and by publishing their 'Declaration of Decency', a manifesto on behalf of respect for constitutional rights. Thsse sites also showed photographs of demonstrations, and of graffiti observed on the walls of Belgrade. The Internet was thus instrumental in enabling the popular movement to keep up a dialogue with the outside world by receiving thousands of e-mail messages of support from all over the world." These non-stop demonstrations, monitored continuously by the international community, drove the public authorities to confirm the opposition's victory in the capital and in several provincial cities.

In a similar context, the live broadcasting of the first trial in the history of the UN International War Crimes Tribunal has enabled international public opinion to discover the full extent of the atrocities committed in Bosnia and Herzegovina. In other regions of the world, such as North Africa and the Near East, certain media have played and still play a key role in fostering the progress of democracy. In the Maghreb, satellite dish aerials, installed on a wide scale in the region, continue permanently to defy the public television channels operating under state control. Their unstoppable spread is breaking up monopolies and triggering off a veritable cultural and political revolution.

In Algeria, the October 1988 uprising sparked a genuine democratic awakening that was immediately reflected in the emergence of a profusion of newspapers of every persuasion, and of go-getting journalists whose credo was and remains freedom of speech. In Africa, use of the video recorder has greatly increased access to information sources and to a whole range of messages. This, technology has contributed to a relative democratization of African society, which neither radio nor television had managed to achieve, for it has provided access to a greater number and variety of programmes than are offered by the traditional networks, whose coverage is limited and which generally operate under state control. Such programmes have in most cases been used to supplement or even to replace the information made available by the official media.

Thus the events of the century's closing decades have

provided, ample proof of the close ties that exist between the media and democracy. The two are intimately linked, and develop in tandem. They demonstrate that there is no more reliable criterion for judging the quality of a democracy than press freedom and the pluralism and independence of the media.

The media

In most democracies, the press is perceived as both an outward sign and a guarantee of democracy. Regarded empirically as the fourth estate, it ensures that democracy functions properly, condemns abuses and clarifies the options available. Pursuing these aims journalists enjoy certain professional rights that are supposed to guarantee their editorial independence *vis-à-vis* both the public authorities and their employer.

In practice, however, many media professional regularly denounce the restrictions which undermine their independence - clear proof that the struggle for press independence is never over in democratic countries, even if it has lost much of its intensity. First and foremost, journalists are concerned by the curbs placed by many governments upon the free flow of information. Access to public information sources, which is a precondition for ensuring that citizens are kept properly informed, is often limited if not deliberately restricted. In most cases, states stir impose strict regulations. For example, press coverage of military conflicts is subject to rigorous control i certain countries.

There is a growing trend to limb the war correspondent's autonomy, freedom of movement and access to the front. This development has been particularly striking since the Viet Nam War in the United States, where access to information has c several occasions been channelled by the Pentagon. In most cases, the culture of secrecy continues to hold sway, usually cloaked in a series of regulations, statutes and conventions that limit both the volume and the nature of the information which may be disclosed to the public. In reality, as the international monitoring organization Article 19 contends, 'governments invoke a wide variety of reasons . . . for justifying secrecy... Many reasons lack justification in the sense that they are not recognized as permissible restrictions under international law, and in fact may have illegitimate aims, such as the suppression of criticism and unorthodox ideas .

The French media historian and former Secretary of State for Communication, Jean-Noël Jeanneney, has pointed out that in a modern democracy 'we must beware of all secrets, and flush out everything that is hidden in the shadows: ultimately, all curiosity is legitimate'. Thus the obligation imposed in certain cases upon journalists to reveal confidential information which they alone possess, the common tendency to confuse secrets that could jeopardize the interests of states with those that would simply harm political administrations, and the repeated attempts to thwart journalists' investigative missions are all, generally speaking, detrimental to the citizen's right to information and, hence, to the public interest as a whole.

Furthermore, media professionals consider that they are not safe from threats and intimidation. Infringements of, and obstructions to, freedom of information increasingly take the form of a whole range of obstacles placed in the way of journalists: these include house searches, indictments, the forced suspension of publication, violence and even murder. The use and the interpretation made of libel actions, of requests to exercise the right of reply, of public order disturbances, provisional or emergency measures, and actions for damages are usually governed by the circumstances of the moment.

The enforcement of these restrictions, which are moreover considered to be outmoded by the profession, generates a climate of insecurity and suspicion that weighs heavily upon freedom of information. Certain court rulings are experienced by journalists as intolerable infringements of their professional rights and, consequently, of the public's right to be kept informed. In the field of electronic media, the threats exercised by the courts also remain extremely powerful.

In the print media field, trials relating to the disclosure of documents deemed to be secret or confidential are becoming increasingly common, and are usually aimed at smaller newspapers, whose limited financial resources reduce their ability to defend themselves or to pay the fines and damages awarded against them. Media professionals consider that these judgements represent a direct threat to freedom of information and investigative journalism, understood as the concern to go beyond official sources in the search for information.

They face journalists with an unacceptable dilemma, since they are liable to be convicted of libel if they publish confidential information without providing proof of the facts revealed, and convicted for possession of stolen property if they hold and publish the evidence confirming their allegations. However, the Munich Declaration emphasizes the right to information by affirming that journalists may claim free access to all information sources and the right freely to investigate all events that affect public life. It adds that the secrecy of public or private affairs cannot in such cases be adduced as justification for denying journalists these rights save in exceptional circumstances and on clearly stated grounds.

This trend towards freeing access to information sources from legal impediments has been enshrined, in most states of the United States of America, in the so-called shield laws', which shield journalists against being forced to give testimony. It has also been regularly reaffirmed by regional and international courts of justice. Several recent cases have, for example, provided an opportunity to reassert the right of journalists to protect their sources.

The one that attracted most attention was the ruling by the European Court of Human Rights on 27 March 1996 which condemned the United Kingdom for failure to respect journalists' rights in this respect. In countries in transition, acceptance of the principle of a press that is free, independent and openly critical of all the authorities is a relatively recent phenomenon.

Theoretically, most of these countries support the principles set forth in Article 19 of the Universal Declaration of Human Rights and reiterate them in their new constitutions. Nevertheless, such support, often solemnly proclaimed, has not solved all the problems affecting freedom of expression and the free flow of information. In many countries, particularly arbitrary forms of obstruction of and restrictions upon the freedom of information still remain. Such obstacles stem by and large from the prevailing system of media ownership and management. The majority of broadcasting networks are still state monopolies subject to strict controls. In countries with authoritarian or totalitarian regimes, the prevailing ideology leaves but little room for pluralism.

The main dailies and weeklies are controlled, subsidized and administered by the state. Likewise, the co-existence of several newspapers or television channels does not necessarily constitute evidence of pluralism, in particular when their proprietors are close to the establishment. In such contexts, the public, the target audience of these media, is self-evidently not in a position to forge an enlightened and unbiased opinion of its own. Censorship may take a variety of forms, depending on whether it is practised officially or unofficially. The ban upon satellite dishes in force in many countries, and the controls exercised on access to electronic media and the Internet, deprive citizens of alternative information sources.

Moreover, various administrative measures may prove just as effective as overt censorship. These range from restrictions upon, for example, the use of newsprint and other professional materials and hardware, to more direct forms of interference: control over the printing at newspapers, monopoly on the importation of paper, right of scrutiny of newspaper circulation figures, control over the award of advertising contracts, exorbitant taxation of certain publications, etc.

In order to explain the strengthening of their control over the print and broadcast media, and even to justify the censoring of news-reporting that does not serve their interests, the authorities generally put forward the same reasons: imperatives bound up with issues of national security and public order. Thus many countries grappling with terrorism and outbreaks of irrational violence have adopted public order measures that have inevitably eroded press freedom severely. In Spain, the Bill on the secrecy of defence matters presented by the Spanish Government in June 1996, which was interpreted by media professionals as an attempt to restrict freedom of expression, was finally abandoned.

The activities of the ETA continue to be publicized by Spanish news agencies and reported by the media. For its part, the United Kingdom adopted on 16 September 1994, as one of its measures to deal with the Irish question, a Bill known as the 'Ulster Rule Bill' which imposed very strict controls upon news coverage of IRA activities by the

BBC.

For example, the BBC was not allowed to grant air time to IRA representatives. In order to circumvent this ban, the Corporation hired Irish actors to deliver the terrorists' statements. The same restriction was imposed upon the independent British television stations, which were required to sign specific agreements regarding the coverage of terrorist activities. In Algeria, the Government published a decree in June 1994 relating to the reporting of security issues. That decree established a 'communication unit' to be responsible for issuing official communiqués exclusively through the Algerian news agency APS.

Article 3 of the decree stipulates that in reporting on terrorist and subversive activities, all categories of media are required to disseminate only official communiqués'. Lastly, Article 4 provides that 'the dissemination of any information relating to security matters that is not covered in the framework of an official communiqué or a public press release shall be forbidden' In Egypt, the law on 'crimes of publishing' authorizes journalists to be held without trial for an indefinite period in accordance with the law instituting a state of emergency. The new law also makes provision for lengthy terms of imprisonment, should the court decide that a crime is involved, in the case of journalists found guilty of 'tendentious writings'.

Freedom of information may be limited by other entities than governments (terrorist and extremist groups, the Mafia, paramilitary groups, and drug cartels). In some countries, extremist groups resort to force in order to prevent families from picking up foreign television channels that spread values alien to their own. Others launch fat was against intellectuals, artists and journalists. Others still go to the extreme of murdering journalists and other media professionals. In this regard it should be pointed out that, in almost every case, inquiries into crimes committed against journalists have come to nothing, and neither those who carried them out nor those who ordered and paid for the killings have ever appeared before the courts. Concerned by this 'culture of impunity', professional organizations such as the Inter-American Press Association have set up their own committees of inquiry.

International Freedom of Expression Exchange Network (IFEX)

This initiative was launched by several professional and non-governmental organizations concerned to pool information more effectively and to enhance the impact of their interventions, which set up an electronic alert and co-ordination network to react whenever freedom of information is threatened. Operational since September 1992, the network is run by the Canadian Committee to Protect Journalists, in Toronto, with the support of UNESCO and its International Programme for the Development of Communication (IPDC).

The IFEX Network today has twenty-seven members, including the major organizations. The network, which is a vitally important point of contact for all journalists and professional media organizations, comprised in May 1997 more than 300 subscribers in eighty countries, 160 of them located in the developing countries. This was achieved thanks in particular to the International Programme for the Development of Communication, whose aid has enabled the professional organisations of those countries to form a majority within the network.

In five years, the network has made it possible not only to improve the gathering, production and disorientation of news and information on topics relating to press freedom on an international scale but also to strengthen the development of South-South exchanges, and, finally, to set up a veritable system of alert and solidarity among all the protagonists: 1,600 alerts are issued each year, as well as a weekly press release in three languages. Joint campaigns are also conducted. A data bank has been created on the Internet which makes available the information gathered by IFEX on a World Wide Web server (http:Hwww.ifex.org).

The media in the service of hatred

In conflict-tom countries, gaining control of the media and their use for partisan purposes constitutes a major objective of the parties in conflict. This practice may lead to a downhill spiral with ever more dangerous consequences. In the former Yugoslavia and in Rwanda, for example, newspapers, radio stations and television channels, press-ganged into the service of the various factions, have begun to launch public calls to violence, ethnic cleansing and even to genocide. The self-styled journalists working for these media no longer see their mission as being to report on events in times of crisis but as a veritable combat on the side of one or other of the parties in conflict. By resorting to the procedures of totalitarian propaganda, based on techniques of crowd manipulation, conditioning and disinformation, such media, co-opted or hijacke, to serve as the tools of xenophobic and hate-filler, politicians, have become vehicles or carriers of way.

The authorities no longer confine themselves the, censoring publications that might damage their image, but seek to orchestrate the entire system of the media in order to turn it into a political tool. It is well-known strategy of totalitarian regimes. In the former Yugoslavia, the media have been turned into veritable war machines putting out ~ mixture of crude lies and war-mongering propaganda For nearly five years, they have sown the seeds of hatred between the Serb, Bosnian, Croat and Muslim communities.

The consequences have been tragic since they have fostered the emergence of various forms of chauvinistic and xenophobic nationalism Be it in Serbia, in Croatia or in Bosnia and Herze govina, most of the media have been used as instruments of war and intercommunity violence. Brought very early on under the control of the parties in power, they have embraced the most extremist causes. Their persistent rhetoric inciting to hatred and ostracism has been regularly condemned by the international community.

In Rwanda, media such as the broadcasting stations Radio-Télévision Libre Mille Collines (RTLM) and Radio Rwanda, and the periodical Kangura, have contributed actively to campaigns inciting to racial hatred and genocide targeted against the Tutsis. Although RTLM, which was set up in April 1993, claims for itself the status of a 'free', commercial station, it was in fact financed entirely by members of the family of President Juvénal Habyarimana, who was assassinated on 6 April 1994. Installed directly opposite the presidential palace, the station became the propaganda centre of the Habyarimana clan, well known for its hostility to the Arusha peace accords of August 1993 between the government and the opposition party, the Front Patriotique Rwandais (FPR).

The station succeeded in winning a wide audience thanks to live shows and musical broadcasts distinguished by a degree of professional expertise. The station's presenters gloated daily over the massacres, and the non-stop flow of their commentaries, personal messages and jokes was tinged with racial hatred directed against the Tutsi minority. This process of 'ethnicization' clearly won support throughout the region of the Great Lakes. In Burundi ' Radio Rutomorangingo, a pirate radio station set up by Hutu extremists, as well as both Tutsi and Hutu extremist newspapers, have enlisted in the service of ethnic hatred.

Resistance and international support

Faced with this dangerous drift by the media towards hatred-inspired campaigns of disinformation, some journalists are nevertheless striving, frequently at the cost of their personal safety, to do their job conscientiously, reporting events in an honest and unbiased manner. In Rwanda, André Sibomana, editor of the country's oldest independent newspaper, Kinyamateka, founded in 1933, narrowly escaped the massacres on several occasions. Having been a victim of harassment, threats and censorship, this newspaper resumed publication in December 1994, thanks to aid provided by the international community.

In the former Yugoslavia, while many journalists have thrown in their lot with the nationalists by espousing their doctrines, others have opted for a professional approach and strive first and foremost -despite the threats and obvious risks to report the facts and to tell the truth as impartially as possible. While the former have consciously consented to take part in campaigns aimed at manipulating public opinion, for example by stirring up feelings of hatred and vengefulness, the latter have by contrast done their utmost to give a balanced and unbiased picture of the situation.

Today, the problem of the media's independence in these countries has still not been resolved, despite the efforts of the international community, and in particular of UNESCO, to create the conditions in which pluralist and independent media can develop and take an effective part in the process of reconstruction and democratization.

UNESCO in a period of conflict

During the war years, independent journalists in the former Yugoslavia came under heavy political pressure. At a time when the independent media were fighting for survival, access to unbiased information was also becoming increasingly difficult for the public. In December 1992, in accordance with its constitutional mandate 'to promote the free flow of ideas by word and image', UNESCO launched a pilot programme to assist independent media in conflict areas, special emphasis being given to the former Yugoslavia.

After the signing of the Dayton Peace Accords in December 1995, UNESCO renewed its support to independent media so as to pave the way for democratization and the peace process, thanks in particular to the aid supplied by several donors, and in close collaboration with other United Nations agencies and professional media organizations.

UNESCO's strategy in the former Yugoslavia was and remains threefold:

— To provide the technical and material assistance needed in order to keep the existing independent media alive and to start up new media for the promotion of pluralism in the press.

— To encourage information exchange between nonpartisan media in the region and with the rest of the world.

— To foster the establishment of the conditions required to ensure press freedom.

In four years, the Organization has supplied several tonnes of newsprint to independent newspapers, delivered equipment to non-partisan electronic media and news agencies and trained journalists in most of the republics and territories of former Yugoslavia. In 1996, UNESCO was designated 'lead agency for assistance to independent media for the reconstruction period in former Yugoslavia' by the UN Inter-Agency Appeal. As such, the Organization has lent backing in Bosnia and

Herzegovina, the Federal Republic of Yugoslavia and the Republic of Croatia to eleven TV stations, ten radios, seven newspapers, three press agencies and three production companies.

The journalist: torch-bearer of democracy

Aside from the extreme cases described above, there exist throughout the world dozens of conflict situations in which the media perform a more traditional but no less essential role as 'witnesses' Their supposed mission being to report everything that occurs in these regions and to reveal violations of the fundamental principles of humanity, the media are in a position to keep international public opinion informed and to alert it to the most horrendous situations. The journalist then becomes, as it were, a torch-bearer of democracy by reporting on what he or she has seen and learned in order to supply the citizen's basic need for information.

A report on violations of the fundamental principles of humanity, whether enshrined in the Geneva Conventions or in the human right., conventions, can in itself serve to alert public opinior and thereby constitute a major exposure of the crime,, committed. In certain cases, such a report may serve to set in motion mechanisms or procedures for putting an end to those crimes. However, in situations of armed conflict, the journalist's job is a difficult and dangerous one opposition groups and civil and military authorities alike generally find it in their interest to conceal certain compromising realities.

Some do not their hesitate to take appropriate steps in order to curb the activities of reporters. Harassment, threats and even murder are unfortunately becoming increasingly common in dealings with journalists who get in the way too much. In this 'no-man's-land' of freedom, the reporter's sole means of protection is frequently his own experience and common sense.

At present, the status of journalists on professional missions in areas of armed conflict is defined in the first Protocol Additional to the Geneva Conventions of 12 August 1949, in Article 79 relating to 'Measures of protection for journalists.' This article provides that 'journalists engaged in dangerous professional missions in areas of armed conflict shall be considered as civilians' As such, they enjoy general protection against dangers arising from military operations, and shall not be the object of attack, acts or threats of violence. In an effort to go beyond the legal protection afforded by international law, the efficacy of which remains wholly contingent upon the willingness or otherwise of the warring parties to comply therewith, various non-governmental organizations have taken initiatives aimed at assisting journalists on dangerous missions. For example, the International Committee of the Red Cross (ICRC), whose delegates are present in virtually all the planet's conflict areas, set up in 1985 a hotline which operates round the clock.

7

New Information and Communication Technology

The 1886 Berne Convention was the first multilateral agreement instituting the international protection of literary and artistic works. The digital revolution combined with the setting up of open, interconnected, interactive networks has fostered a number of radical changes, the most important of which have resulted in the dematerialisation of products, growing concentration in cultural sectors and the globalisation of communication networks. The overall trend, associated with the free circulation of products around the world, raises a number of questions of a statutory, cultural and political nature.

Over and above the issues raised by the progress in technological convergence and industrial conflicts, there remain a number of problems: those concerning the place of copyright and neighbouring rights in the future information society, those with respect to national cultures and their diversity in the general trend towards globalization, and finally those of the new information and communication technology in economic, social and cultural development. All these areas are both significant and strategic in the quest for enhanced democracy in the information society - the only factor that might induce the participation of all political, cultural and linguistic viewpoints around the world.

Copyright and intellectual property

The scale of the technological upheavals that go hand in hand with the dematerialization of products has confused the judicial concepts on which intellectual property rights were based, and has sparked wide-ranging debate about the ways in which copyright should be applied and complied with in a digital environment. Copyright and neighbouring rights form one of the very first areas of international co-operation.

International structures for the protection of copyright were set up from the end of the nineteenth century onwards. Since then, the convention has been revised several times, most recently in 1971. It guarantees creators a high level of protection of their rights (moral rights, economic rights relating to the reproduction, representation or public performance, broadcasting, adaptation and translation of their work). The Universal Copyright Convention, adopted under the aegis of UNESCO in 1952 in Geneva and revised in Paris in 1971, obliges signatory states to ensure effective and adequate protection of copyright, leaving them free to adapt that protection to the requirements of their socio-economic reality.

It was this convention that introduced the @ symbol followed by the name of the copyright holder and the year of first publication, to replace the registration formalities required by certain legislations. Finally, the Rome Convention, signed in 1961, provided a flexible, inter national legal framework for the protection of performers, producers of phonograms and broadcasting organizations. All these texts were drafted well before the digital revolution, and cannot directly take into account the developments that have occurred in this area since 1961. Digital technology also provides a major opportunity for intellectual and creative works in that they can be disseminated an infinite number of times. That self-same power of dissemination, however, can also lead to the violation of copyright, notably through piracy and other forms of computer crime.

Around the world can be seen an increasing number of flourishing unauthorized businesses manufacturing and marketing illegal 'smart card' decoders for the reception of telecasts without the payment of any licence fee. Piracy and the other forms of counterfeiting are a major problem whose economic consequences cost tens of billions of dollars every year. All these risks are a cause for concern among creators and have led states to examine the usefulness of creating a special legal system for the new digital environment.

At the international level and as part of the work carried out by the World Intellectual Property Organization (WIPO), most participants consider it unnecessary to draft new special legislation. Two basic viewpoints have emerged on the subject, however. The first consists in applying distribution rights together with reproduction rights to works transmitted via digital means. This is, for the most part, the position defended by the United States, which proposes to consider transmission as a form of distribution, whether it involves 'on-line' transmission or the dissemination of the reproduction of a work recorded on a material medium. The American position requires that international transmission be considered as a form of import.

The second viewpoint regards the act of digital transmission as an act of public communication. This is the position of Argentina, Australia, Canada, Japan, the member states of the European Union, and Uruguay, a point of view backed by several nongovernmental organizations. Public communication rights would be combined with reproduction rights when the end-user makes a copy of the work transmitted.

The WIPO treaties on copyright and neighbouring rights adopted on 20 December 1996 in Geneva contain no provision with respect to reproduction rights in the digital environment for lack of agreement on this sensitive point. On the other hand, Article 8 of the Copyright Treaty implies that the digital transmission of works via networks is an act of public communication governed by the exclusive rights of right-holders.

The adoption of this article, however, was linked to an interpretative statement to the effect that 'it is understood that the mere provision of physical facilities for enabling or making a communication does not in itself amount to communi-cation within the meaning of this Treaty or the Berne Convention. The declaration further indicates that the provisions of the treaty with regard to limitations and exceptions do not prevent a signatory from applying of the Berne Convention.

The statement seems to suggest that the provision of the physical facilities for enabling or making a digital communication is not a sufficient stage in the digital communication of works to warrant protection under copyright laws. It leaves a number of questions unanswered with respect to the liability of providers of wide-area networking servers in the process of digital transmission.

Balancing interests and agreement

At regional and national levels, the issue has become particularly acute with the publication of the US White Paper of September 1995. Drafted by the Working Group on Intellectual Property Rights of the White House

Information Infrastructure Task Force set up by President Clinton in 1993, the document contains detailed proposals for adaptation of the US Copyright Act to cyberspace. Their concern has also been echoed in Canada with the report of the Information Highway Advisory Council, which was published the same year.

The importance of protecting intellectual property also led the European Community in 1988 to present a Green Paper containing an economic and judicial analysis of the various problems raised by the new information technology in legal terms. Multilateral discussions held during the drafting of the paper resulted in the adoption in 1995 of the Green Paper on Copyright and Related Rights in the Information Society. It lists a catalogue of fifty-five problems concerning future copyright.

The paper followed the Bangemann Report of June 1994, which considered the protection of intellectual property to be a crucial element in the development of a European multimedia market. The European Commission has announced another Green Paper specially devoted to the legal protection of encrypted signals, and has raised the possibility of intervention by the Union to make technical protection systems mandatory when the former have been sufficiently developed and accepted by industry. Finally, also worthy of note is the CITED project (Copyright in Transmitted Electronic Documents) developed under the ESPRIT programme.

UNESCO's contribution

For its part, UNESCO, which initiated the Universal Copyright Convention (1952), was an active participant in the Diplomatic Conference organized by WIPO in December 1996 with a view to adopting a new protocol to be appended to the Berne Convention. The presence of UNESCO at the conference, as well as at those organized by the European Commission on Copyright and Related

Rights on the Threshold of the Twenty-first Century (June 1995) and at the Intellectual Property Conference of the Americas (July 1996), was intended primarily as a means of achieving a consensus on an arrangement reconciling the respective rights of authors, producers, copyright holders and the general public, as well as those of exporters and importers of protected works. UNESCO also launched a wide-ranging consultation with specialists in the field of communication, publishing and development. In that connection, worthy of note was the organization in co-operation with the Spanish Government of an International UNESCO Symposium on Copyright and Communication in the Information Society.

Discussions at the symposium focused on three major subjects:

— The outlines of a national policy to set up the basic infrastructures for the digital transmission and broadcasting of information (the role of the state and of private operators), and the norms that should govern the operation of those infrastructures, as well as the principles for regional and international co-operation in the area.

— The guidelines to follow in order to adapt national legislations so as to ensure that they protect the legitimate rights of authors and other right-holders in the digital and multimedia environment and enhance harmonization of those rights at the international and regional levels.

— Strategies for national policies aimed at fostering the creation and development of cultural economic sectors, the digital broadcasting of works and performances, and distance teaming, with a view to international and regional cooperation in this area. The discussions also enabled Member States of the Organization, especially those from developing countries, to acquire up-to-the-minute legal and technological data in the field of intellectual property rights.

The symposium was followed by a series of regional meetings of Committees of Experts on copyright in the information society (basic infrastructures, the Protection of rights and their social and cultural impact). The first of these, for Latin America, the Caribbean and Canada, was held in Bogotá in September 1996. The second, for Asia, the Pacific and the Arab States, was organized in New Delhi in November 1996. The Committee of Experts of Europe is scheduled to meet in Monaco in March 1997 and that of Africa in 1998.

On the whole, the various meetings have agreed on the need to simplify legal rules at the international level, in order to maintain a three-way balance of

(a) the rights of authors in relation to those of the traditional cultural economic sectors and of information highway service providers,
(b) the rights of right-holders in relation to the public interest (both of which are contained in the Declaration of Human Rights), and
(c) the interests of countries exporting 'copyright' in relation to those of importer countries, notably the developing nations.

The above balance is closely connected to the issue of the access to information and to new communication technology and contrasts the views of three groups of thinkers: those that relate network access to a fundamental fight on the same grounds as other rights; those that consider access must be modulated in relation to the varying contexts and types of information in question (information which is access-free, in the public domain or restricted); and finally, those that would make all network access part of a commercial service. The problem is complex and multidimensional. The absence of legal protection is not supportive of creativity worldwide, and it is equally obvious that over-protection is not conducive to access to the networks by research workers and academics of developing countries.

The correct balance therefore remains to be found between the right of creators to benefit from the use of their work and the needs of users to access those works and use them freely. One further suggestion, developed by a number of non-governmental organizations in particular, militates in favour of a political alternative, based on non-market mechanisms ensuring right-free access for underprivileged countries to digital productions connected with social and economic development. Other ideas, based for example on consumer initiative or on codes of ethics developed ad hoc by information professionals, may suit the complexity of the problem and ultimately be more effective. This only underlines, however, the vital role of dialogue and co-operation among the various parties concerned, which, alone, may enable the right balance to be found between the interests of some, the duties of others and the solidarity of all.

Major imbalances

The development of the information society raises the issue of the inequalities which are a feature of both the industrialized and the developing countries, and which at the same time come between the rich and poor within the same society. The developing nations are confronted with the challenges of the new technology, the production and distribution of which take place outside their frontiers. A large majority of these countries feel excluded from that progress and some continue to denounce the aggravation of the obvious imbalances in the flow of information exchange between the North and the South. The debate began as long ago as the 1980s within UNESCO and in other international circles, about the idea of the New World Information and Communication Order (NWICO).

How to approach copyright and intellectual property rights: the Canadian example

The Final Report of the Information Highway Advisory Council, published in September 1995, examines copyright legislation and practices in the context of a digital environment. Salient excerpts ore presented below.

Principles

In the context of accelerated digitization of information, the federal government should adopt principles for copyright based on the following:

— maintaining a balance between the rights of creators to benefit from the use of their works and the needs of users (including the education and (earning community) to access and use those works on reasonable terms;
— encouraging industry, creators and user communities to develop and implement an administrative and regulatory framework that is easily understood and implemented by all interested parties and not seen as a barrier to access or use of the content on the information highway;
— recognizing creativity as required for the information-based economy and the multiple roles of individuals of the information highway (creators, disseminators and users of information);
— encouraging the creation of works that are critical to a national and cultural identity and economic development,

Browsing

The new technologies present unprecedented challenges

for the protection of works. If the information highways are to be viable and sustainable, creators must be guaranteed continued protection of their works. At the same time, users must be assured of fair and reasonable access to those works. In its final report, the Copyright Subcommittee concluded that 'the act of browsing a work could mean either accessing a work, even if it is temporary or ephemeral in nature, or the making of a copy.

Fair dealing

In the context of copyright, accessing and reproducing works in a digital environment is increasingly complex. It is important that users comprehend better the extent and nature of copyright liability.

Moral rights

Moral rights include, among other things, the right to paternity and the right of integrity of the work. The right of integrity is attached to the honour and reputation of authors who, in order to seek remedy, must show that their reputation has suffered from the modification of their work. The alteration or mutilation of originals of certain artistic works also infringes the author's right of integrity.

Crown copyright

In the council's view, ensuring universal and easy access to public information on the information highways does not require the abolition of Crown copyright, but instead a more liberal approach to making works of the Crown available to the public should be adopted.

Distribution right/ownership

The right to communicate to the public by telecommunications currently contained in the Copyright Act clearly applies to the electronic transmission of works to the public. There is therefore no need to introduce any new rights, such as an electronic distribution right.

Administration

Upon review of the range of mechanisms that could be developed to track and enforce copyright on the information highways, the council concluded that the above combination of technological, policy and legislative solutions was appropriate. The industry itself, with the assistance of the federal government, is best suited to developing the technological solutions.

Public education

Both users and creators and the industry in general need to better inform themselves about the rights of creators and the responsibilities of users on the information highway. The federal government can lead by example by exercising copyright in a responsible manner, by participating in copyright enforcement programmes and by ensuring that government works are broadly and routinely distributed. The talks have at least brought to the attention of international opinion the extent of the disparities and distortions that exist in the area of communication and new technology, imbalances suggesting that the vision of a global village which so many have held for so long will basically be attained by the richest or most recently industrialized countries in which the data banks, software systems and programs are gathered and stored. The gap is particularly wide in Africa, which has only 1 per cent of the telephone lines available in the world, but 12 per cent of its population.

In 1994, there were more telephone lines in the city of Tokyo alone than in the whole of Africa, when the population of the continent is thirty times greater than that of the Japanese capital. Inside Africa there are also remarkable differences in development. Over the last decade, the number of telephone lines per 100 inhabitants - known as teledensity - has doubled in the Maghreb. In South Africa, the number has increased by more than 200 per cent and is now close to 10. Teledensity in sub-Saharan Africa has stagnated, emphasizing the disparity between the affluent and the underprivileged countries. The same observation holds true of information and communication.

The inequalities are just as pronounced in terms of audiovisual equipment as for the production and content of their programmes. The same applies to the consumption of the written press. Average connection fee and monthly subscription fee for residential telephone service by region, 1995 (in US dollars) television programmes, and to the flow of programmes from producer to consumer countries. This imbalance has been still further highlighted with the emergence of digital technology and the broadcasting of programming streams. Market globalization favours communications between developed or newly industrialized countries or within such countries, or links between major cities and rural zones.

In the economic sphere, the imbalances reflect both the highly unequal economic development of "nations, the diversity of their political systems and the specific character of each society. They can be explained as much by the past as by certain current effects of globalization. These somewhat pessimistic observations must, however, be tempered by the emergence of a number of Asian and Latin American countries that have worked wonders where telecommunications and audiovisual technology are concerned.

Some even form the driving force behind economic growth rates that contradict the climate of recession in the rest of the world. Others have begun policies for technology transfer and adaptation b offering attractive subcontracting capabilities and thereby offshoring communication multinationals.

Cultural and linguistic obstacles

The imbalances between nations and within them,

together with the acceleration in the globalization of the contents of programmes, also arouse concern about the dangers of cultural and linguistic standardization.

Developing countries are at risk from standardization of local cultures through a form of planetary brainwashing caused by the white noise of poor programme content. These dangers may have grave consequences, such as the marginalization and possible disappearance of fragile community cultures, the weakening of cultural foundations, the temptation to withdraw into an identity coinciding with religious beliefs, and the threat of violent inter-ethnic conflict. While the existence of these dangers raises questions of ethics and political sovereignty, they have also been used by some states and their single parties as a convenient alibi to justify their stranglehold on the media and the use of the media.

The member states of the European Community also appear to be jealous of their cultural identity and make it a fundamental factor in their national sovereignty. They are striving to protect their audiovisual production by a policy of broadcasting quotas adopted within the framework of the directives of the 'Television without Frontiers' programme. The economic issues implicit in quotas became a subject of confrontation with the United States during the GATT trade talks in 1993. There are two contradictory viewpoints on the subject.

The United States is pushing for the free circulation of programmes, while Europe and Canada intend to protect their cultures and their film industries by arranging programming rules. The Americans wish to encourage a form of total market internationalization and the globalization of trade, whereas Europe and Canada consider the audiovisual field to be a service whose cultural purpose justifies its treatment as a special case in relation to the overall GATT agreements. Hence the importance for the European Union to have an audiovisual and cinema policy designed to preserve cultural identities, to strengthen economic development and to create jobs in the audiovisual sector.

However, according to the European specialists, the results of the GATT trade talks (in December 1993) hardly changed anything, either in terms of the current market situation, which favours American programmes, or with respect to the risks of furthering their market domination with the arrival of digital clusters of TV programming streams. As digital technology rapidly develops, however, the scope of deregulation is widening in Europe to include the private telecommunications sector. The latter is to become a competitive market from 1998 onwards, and should facilitate the circulation of images.

In addition, the future prospects outlined in the European Commission's Green Paper on the audiovisual policy of the European Union are already those of a demand focus on profitability in an open, dynamic global market' based on a largely free trade attitude. On top of this, the renegotiations of the 'Television without Frontiers' directive reached a compromise with some difficulty as a result of strong reluctance on the part of countries such as Germany, the United Kingdom and Italy, all of which demanded the straightforward abolition of the quota policy. Together, these new trends have led the European Union to think about implementing a different policy basically aimed at strengthening the broadcasting industry.

The other major issue is the risk of linguistic standardization. An example frequently quoted is the fact that the vast majority of programmes circulating on the Internet are in English and that the main navigation software systems are not capable of reading characters other than those of the Latin alphabet. These fears apparently are being allayed by the market trend towards linguistic diversification throughout the system. With the stupendous growth of the Internet, English-speaking countries owned only 70 per cent of sites in January 1997 as against 90 per cent a few months before.

Today three language groups are extending their reach throughout the network: Germanic (German, Dutch and the Scandinavian languages) with 11 per cent; Romance (French, Italian, Portuguese and Spanish) with 9 per cent, and Japanese with 5 per cent. The world's other languages are used on only 5 per cent of the sites. This is a poor showing if the Internet is to be multilingual and sensitive to the whole family of cultures. Yet the latest technological progress in automatic translation makes data processing possible in a number of languages.

Moreover, for exponential growth of network navigating and surfing tools, the setting of common standards adapted to the various non-roman scripts, and public and private investments in on-line services, could transform the network fundamentally in the medium term by giving every user access to a huge amount of data in foreign languages using non-roman scripts.

The future of the public service

Media globalization together with the arrival of competition from international and national private television channels raises the issue of the status, role and future of the public service in the new audiovisual fields around the world. For many years, public television channels enjoyed a period of stability based on a monopoly. There are three main reasons for their domination. The first of these is technical, and concerns the use and distribution of frequency spectra considered to be a collectively owned, rare resource.

In this area, the state played the role of a microwave 'regulator', to prevent frequencies from being used in a disorganized and anarchic manner. This function is generally performed today by an authority independent of the government, its role being to enforce conditions of fair competition. The second reason concerns the public service role which is conferred on all the broadcasting services.

The power of radio and of television seems truly vast from the political, social or cultural viewpoints, since it provides the general public with access to cultural information programmes that they would not be able to receive elsewhere or otherwise. The third and final reason is linked to the traditional distrust of public authorities with respect to the market's capacity to perform the public service assignments imposed on the broadcasting industry.

The crisis in public service broadcasting

The arrival in the 1980s of private operators and distributors on the market had as its consequence the end of the supremacy of public television channels, a setback which then depleted their audience ratings and advertising market share. Technological innovations in the satellite area also led to the development of new markets, accompanied by an increase in private capital and publicity investments in television. Since then, the growth in private channels has taken place to the detriment of advertising revenue for public television, undermining the traditional balance between the public and private sectors.

These various reversals have occurred in an environment of increasing internationalization and worldwide televisual exchange. All around the world, clusters of private, general-interest or specialized digital television channels are springing up in audiovisual market-places which are becoming increasingly turbulent. Against this backdrop, the public channels have had to face stagnating or diminishing public subsidies, forcing them to reduce their expenses or seek other sources of revenue such as the introduction of TV commercials. Reduced government involvement in public service channels in several countries, notably those in Europe, has accelerated the rate of change in the audiovisual marketplace and thrown the public television sector into disarray.

The public service challenge

The future of public service broadcasting depends on a clearer distinction between public service and public sector, which are two very different concepts altogether. Privately owned television operators exist that provide educational or cultural programmes, traditionally classified as being the role of the public service. In the United States, for example, the major networks such as CBS, ABC or NBC also provide programmes of an educational and cultural nature, as does the federal CBC Radio Canada network. These programmes are all part of a complementary, diversified offer. The assignments and obligations of the public service are not necessarily incompatible with the ownership of corporate capital, and the difference between private and public as diametrically opposed sectors is no longer pertinent.

The concept of public service seems nevertheless to be gaining ground in Europe, and is even moving towards that of universal service, notably where the texts of the European Union are concerned. Universal service is relatively far removed from the Canadian or French concept of public service, and lies somewhere between the Latin and Anglo-Saxon definitions. Generally speaking, a universal service is seen as a compensatory factor within a market- controlled regulation system. The future of the public service also depends on a clearer distinction between public service and commercial television, which obeys market laws first and foremost.

The public service should be free of economic and financial considerations dictated by audience ratings and market share, to carry out its role as a social link. In a world open to the internationalization of data flow and image exchange, a public service should provide basic landmarks of a historical, cultural and political nature for a nation.

8

Computers in Schools

The electronic heart is part of a teaching tool George is putting together for eighth-grade biology classes. A few feet away sits Pam Miller, 14, a ninth-grader with long, brown hair draped far down her back. She is operating a computer program—or software—that simulates the workings of a nuclear reactor. Today she is fine-tuning the section that governs the control rods, those regulators of the reactor's nuclear fires. Tapping away at the keyboard, Pam explains: "You have to maximize the power output without destroying the reactor." Suddenly, flashing numbers burst upon the screen. "There," says Pam, her face lighting up. "Reactor overheated. Power output low. Reactor core damaged. Melt-down!"

A disaster that she has brought on intentionally, just to show how it could happen. Other disciples, seated at terminals scattered around the room, are no less absorbed. Meilin Wong, 15, chic in blue velour blouse, jeans and Bass moccasins, is trying to figure out what went wrong with her business data management program. She is an old hand at such troubleshooting, having spent much of last semester "debugging" a program that, when printed-out, stretches over 30 ft. Jim McGuire, 13, is creating a video game called Spaceship, which will let electronic star warriors zap a boxy-looking orbital intruder. A more mundane program is emerging from 15-year -old Dave McCann's terminal: a verb test for seventh- and eighth-grade Spanish classes. Off in a corner two youngsters are putting the impish face of Mad magazine's cartoon hero, Alfred E. Neuman, onto the computer screen. Says Muller, as he presides proudly over these after-hours computer converts: "No one told them they have to be here.

They're not usually doing assignments. They're experimenting. They're letting their imaginations run free." *t*-Muller's disciples are not all math whizzes. Or straight-A students. Or particularly precocious. They are reasonably normal youngsters who have grown up with computers. For them, in ways that few people over 30 can understand, manipulating these complex machines is as natural as riding a bike, playing baseball or even solving Rubik's cube. Like thousands of others across the country, they are part of a revolutionary vanguard: the computer generation.

Not only is this generation propelling traditional education down promising avenues, it is tugging at the entire social fabric, foreshadowing changes at least as startling and momentous as those ushered in by a new generation of automobile users more than a half-century ago. In the classroom, where youngsters are being introduced to the machines as early as kindergarten, they astound—and often outpace—their teachers with their computer skills. After school they gather at the mushrooming number of computer stores (more than 1500 at last count) or join the computer clubs that are becoming a regular part of the youthful landscape.

Huddling around any available machine, they argue over their programs, thresh out computer problems and swap software as intensely as kids once haggled over baseball cards. In the summer, they may even go off to computer camps, another growth industry, and if they are Boy Scouts, they may try for a computer merit badge.

During mischievous moments, they may tinker with one another's programs, writing in steps that will flash an unexpected insult or obscenity across a buddy's video screen. Some try to pick the encoded electronic locks on copyrighted software, taking glee in outwitting their elders, or spin fanciful plots to break into computer networks.

A few turn their skills to profit by showing baffled businessmen how to get idle, new computers to run, or by establishing Delaware-based corporations to market their own software creations. To the bafflement of their parents, they talk in a jargon of their own ("Hey, Charlie, you should have POKED instead of PEEKED"). As with so many other changes in contemporary life, the spark for this revolution is technological: a bit of silicon sophistication variously known as the personal, home or microcomputer. No larger than an attache case, apart from its video screen, this mighty mite packs the computing power of machines that two decades ago occupied a full room.

Yet the micros, as they are affectionately called, are a relative bargain to buy and are becoming steadily cheaper. Many models cost under $1000, bringing them within reach of schools, parents or the children themselves. Last week, in the sharpest price break yet, Timex announced it will begin selling a small home computer for a suggested retail price of $99.95. But size and price cannot explain why computers have taken such a strong hold on so many youngsters. Certainly their interest has been stirred by a related rage, video games, whose computer-generated flashes, zaps, and pings have not only all the appeal pinball machines had for their elders but go a significant step further: they pique young minds to learn more about all that electronic prestidigitation. But many experts, and most of the young operatives, agree that the overwhelming attraction of the machines is the lure of control, the pleasure of being able to think out and then make something happen, a satisfaction all too often denied children. Recognized by students and teachers alike as his school's best computer programmer, Lewis works afternoons as an instructor for a computer consulting firm, introducing younger children to the machines.

Last year his employers sent him to Chicago, where he displayed his special teaching gifts before a meeting of educators. As Lewis told *Time* correspondent Peter Stoler, "we love these machines. I've got all this power at my fingertips. Without computers, we don't know what do be. With them, I'm somebody." Perhaps because of the faintly macho side of computers, the bug seems to strike many more boys than girls in the pre-adolescent years. Says Steve Siegelbaum, Lewis's teacher: "Maybe it's because boys are pushed more toward math and logic than girls are. Maybe it's because boys are just more aggressive."

Paradoxically, the computer passion is often stirred in youngsters who seem least likely to be interested in high tech. Jay Harstad, 12, of Minnetonka, Minn., litters his house with poems and sketches but will do almost anything to avoid doing his math homework. Yet Jay is one of the Gatewood Elementary School's premier computerniks and regularly helps teachers introduce fourth-graders to the machines. At West High School in Wausau, Wis., Chris Schumann, 16, a junior, has made a name for himself by translating musical notes into digital form and getting a computer to play Bach and Vivaldi through its loudspeaker. Originally, Chris regarded computers as remote and forbidding, but that changed when he was introduced to his first micro. "It looked real friendly," he says. "It didn't overpower you. It wasn't this ominous thing but something you could get close to." The closeness can be contagious. Explains Nick Newman, 15, Muller's chief disciple at Ridgewood: "The more you do on the machine, the more enjoyable it gets. It becomes habit-forming."

In Alpena, Mich., youngsters who had learned computer skills in junior high were devastated when they got to senior high school and found too few machines to go around. Says Alpena Elementary School principal Burt Wright: "I've got high school kids begging to come in after school and use our machine." The truly addicted—known half scornfully, half admiringly as computer nerds—may drop out almost entirely from the everyday world. In Lexington, Mass., one legendary 16-year-old nerd got so deeply immersed in computers that he talked to no one, headed straight to his terminal after school and barely sat down for meals. The only way his father could get him away from the terminal was to go down to the cellar and throw the house's main power switch, cutting off all electricity.

Barry Porter, 14, of San Francisco, is a computer-age truant, so attached to the machine that he often skips school, rarely reads anything other than computer manuals and hangs out with his pals in the Market Street computer store, often plotting some new electronic scam. Barry (not his real name) currently boasts an illicit library of about 1000 pirated (*i.e.* illegally copied) programs worth about $50,000 at retail prices, including such software gems as VisiCalc, the popular business management and planning program. Before security was tightened up, he regularly plugged his computer into such distant databanks as the Source (which provides news bulletins, stock prices, etc.) via telephone without paying a cent.

Computer Generation

No one can say exactly when the computer generation began—certainly not earlier than the 1960s, when computers began appearing in schools. But even computer whizzes in their twenties are acutely aware of how soon they are likely to be outstripped by today's grade schoolers. Says Steven jobs, 27, the multimillionaire co-founder of Apple Computer Inc.: "These kids know more about the new software than we do." New York computer executive Charles Lecht goes further: "If you were born before 1965, boy, you're going to be out of it." Where their parents fear to tread, the microkids plunge right in, no more worried about pushing incorrect buttons or making errors than adults are about dialling a wrong telephone number.

Says mathematician Louis Robinson, IBM's resident computer sage: "They know what computers can and cannot do, while adults still regard them as omnipotent." Says Hughes Aircraft Chairman Allen Puckett, who shares an Apple with son Jim, 12: "A lot of adults grew up in a slide-rule world and still reject computers. But computers are as natural to kids as milk and cookies." More and more members of the computer generation are tasting the heady pleasure of teaching their own teachers how to use the machines and, if they are lucky enough to have computers at home, instructing their parents as well. Says Ridgewood's Newman, a regular teacher of teachers: "It's a sort of mutual doorway.

The barriers between adult and child, between teacher and student, are broken, and it's person to person. Nobody's looking down on anyone; they're looking each other right in the eye." Often adults find it easier to ask a child how to do something than to ask another adult. Says University of Kansas education professor Mary Kay Corbitt: "One adult student of mine brought her son to computer class, and we discovered that he was doing her assignment while she watched. Two weeks later she overcame her anxieties and was participating fully." Confronted with the strange and unsettling world of the computer, teachers can get a useful perspective on what it is like to be a student again. After taking part in an elementary course in programming, Lois Brown, 54, a Wausau grade-school teacher, is thoroughly chastened. "Now we realize how little kids feel when there's a concept they don't understand.

We sat in that course not wanting anyone to know all the things we didn't understand." Despite their obvious wariness of computers, parents are taking the lead in getting them into the schools. In Florida, communities have staged cake and candy sales, carnivals and tree plantings, weekend car washes, even a bike-a-thon to raise funds to buy computers. Says Marilyn Neff of Miami: "We feel computers will be the new paper and pencil." Of the 250 computers in the schools of Utica, Mich., more than two-thirds have been purchased by parent-sponsored fund drives.

Says Utica Principal Paul Yelinsky: "Moms and dads are coming in and telling the counsellors they have to get their kids in computer classes because it's the wave of the future." So important is computer literacy that the Alfred P. Sloan Foundation is beginning a major program to get even such traditional liberal arts schools as St John's College in Maryland to begin giving courses in it. Though many schools began purchasing computers with federal aid budget cutbacks are drying up that well. Apple's jobs points out that other nations, especially Britain, France and the Soviet Union—though surprisingly not the electronics-minded Japanese—are paying far more attention to computer education than is the US. Earlier this year, jobs persuaded California Congressman Pete Stark and Missouri Senator John Danforth to introduce bills in Congress that would allow computer manufacturers to take a hefty tax write-off for any machines they donate to elementary and high schools. Under the present law, full deductions for such scientific equipment are allowed only if it is given to colleges and universities.

Computer Education

Jobs originally spoke of giving an Apple to every public elementary and secondary school in the country, more than 80,000 computers worth as much as $200 million retail. Now he thinks private schools should be included and is encouraging other manufacturers to join in the program as well. Meanwhile, Apple's archrival, the Tandy Corp., maker of the Radio Shack computer line, is taking a different tack: it has pledged $500,000 in equipment to spur development of educational programming, or courseware, for the classroom.

Many of the approximately 100,000 computers now in US schools—roughly one for every 400 students—are in affluent suburbs like Ridgewood, a national leader in computer education. But the machines are also found in the unlikeliest of places. On a Chippewa Indian reservation in Wisconsin, computers are being used by young members of the tribe to learn their ancient and nearly forgotten language. Alaska's small rural schools have been ordering computers to meet a special need: they allow students of different ages and abilities in the same small classrooms to learn at their own pace.

Dubuque, Iowa, where the *New Yorker* founding editor Harold Ross disdainfully located his provincial old lady, has 13 machines and another 20 on order. Bill

Holloway, a professor of computer education at the University of Kansas, calls the spread of small computers in the classroom nothing less than an avalanche. According to various industry studies, there may be from 300,000 to 650,000 computers in the schools by 1985. So far, the most common, and least interesting, way to use school computers is in direct drill and review.

The machine simply quizzes, prods and grades the student, very much like a robot teacher. Hundreds of programs of this type are available for popular computers like the Apple II Plus, Radio Shack's TRS-80 and the Commodore PET. But many of these programs are little more than computerized rehashes of the old classroom flash cards that go back to the days of McGuffey's readers. One notable difference: today when the student answers correctly, the screen will light up with WOWS, HOORAYS or smiling animals.

Wrong answers may produce sad or scowling faces, perhaps accompanied by a falling tear. Partly because of teachers' fears—of the machines and for their jobs—and partly because of the poor quality of software, the frequently heralded electronic revolution in the classroom has been slow to occur. Now, however, it is being pushed along by steady improvements in teaching programs, thanks to imaginative enterprises like the Minnesota Educational Computing Consortium. One of its more refreshing drills: a program called Wrong Note, which helps teach sight reading of musical scores.

As a simple tune emanates from the computer's loudspeaker, matching notes appear on the screen, but sometimes the quiz intentionally errs and obliges students to find the false note. In order to do so, they can order up a repetition of the tune as often as Bogie and company did in *Casablanca*. Says Kenneth Brumbaugh, director of the consortium's instructional services:

"Imagine asking a teacher to play it again and again!" Even very young children can profit from such exercises. At the Nordstom Elementary School in Morgan Hill, Calif., a suburb of San Jose, Colin Devenish, 7, is working with a classmate on the arithmetic drill, honing his skills in addition and subtraction. Unlike youngsters doing such drilling in the past, Colin seems to be enjoying himself enormously. Why? "Because," he replies mischievously within earshot of his teacher, "the computer doesn't yell."Computers, operated only by touching a few buttons, are also remarkably effective devices for educating the handicapped. At the California School for the Deaf in Fremont, Rhonda Revera, 16, has worked with computers for five years, studying every subject from fractions to spelling.

Rhonda offers a paean to the machine in sign language: "Computer makes me remember. It is fast, easy and better than writing on paper." Still another important use of computers is as a remedial tool. One is a spelling drill with a special incentive built into it: if all the answers are correct, a video game pops onto the screen as a reward. When one youngster worked his way through the drill, even classroom hecklers were impressed. Said one: "Hey, Old Wentworth's getting better."

More entertaining and demanding are think tank-type strategy games like Geography Search, which launches competing teams on a Columbus-like voyage of exploration. They must make their way across the Atlantic, taking into account currents and winds, finding their longitude and latitude by means of star patterns and the length of a shadow thrown by a stick at high noon (methods that worked for Columbus, after all), and coping with such unforeseen perils as an outbreak of scurvy, an attack by pirates and a tropical storm. Only shrewd planning, wise choices and cooperative action ensure survival. The simulated voyage becomes uncannily real to the participants. Says the game's creator, Thomas Snyder, 31, who heads Computer Learning Connection, Inc., of Cambridge, Mass.: "When they get near the end and the computer finally shows them another ship near by, they act as if they had actually spotted a ship at sea." Until a few years ago, the few computers available in secondary schools were essentially "dumb" terminals linked by telephone lines to a large, centrally located machine that served a variety of users through an arrangement called time-sharing. All the courseware was stored in the big computer's powerful memory, which could be tapped at will by students and teachers.

The most successful example of such a system—and the one still used by Wisconsin's Chippewa Indians—is PLATO (for Programmed Logic for Automatic Teaching Operations). Developed in the 1960s by the University of Illinois and Control Data Corp., PLATO is an exemplary teacher containing more than 8000 hours of courseware, much of it in a continuous curriculum. Thus, if a youngster forgets a point from an earlier lesson, PLATO will search its prodigious memory and patiently recapitulate. But such time-sharing schemes are extremely expensive, since they require open lines to the central computer.

They also can become backed up at peak hours, and do not always lend themselves readily to what is the most intellectually demanding use of the computer: learning how to program it. For this, the inexpensive, easy-to-operate personal computer, entirely self-contained and relying on equipment immediately at the student's side, is an ideal instrument—much more "user-friendly," as manufacturers like to say, than big machines. Yet even with a handy micro, programming can overwhelm the uninitiated. The programmer and computer must "speak" a common language. In the early days of the digital computer, this was extremely difficult. The machine reduces all the information it receives, whether it arrives as letters, numbers or graphic symbols, into the simplest possible electronic statements: either a yes or a no, represented by pulses of high or low voltage. To command the machine in its own internal language meant writing out endless strings of one or zeros, called bits and bytes, symbolizing those yes or no statements. But scientists soon began creating alternate languages for communicating with the machines that vaguely resemble everyday speech.

The most popular of these computer tongues is BASIC (for Beginner's All-purpose Symbolic Instruction Code). Developed at Dartmouth by mathematician John Kemeny and his colleague Thomas Kurtz to let even the least mathematically gifted student converse with the university's computers, it is "understood" by virtually all of today's personal computers. To show just how easy the language is, Kemeny offers this extremely simple lesson in programming: tell the computer to find the square roots (i.e., the numbers that, when multiplied by themselves, yield the original numbers) of eleven successive values, say 20 through 30.

The entire operation can be accomplished for a program of just four steps:

```
1  FOR N = 20 TO 30
2  PRINT N, SQR(N)
3  NEXT N
4  END
```

Translated into everyday language, the first line tells the computer to let N stand successively for 20 through 30.

The second instructs the machine to print the first value of N (that is, the number 20), compute its square root (SQR) and print out the result. The third tells the computer to go on to each of the succeeding values all the way through 30. Finally, the program tells the computer to call it a day, its job having been done.

Even the smallest machine can do such calculations in a flash, compared with the hours of work they might require of human computers. To preserve their creativity, the students can readily store their programs on magnetic tape or on a small, 45 rpm-size plastic record called a floppy disc—which is not, as some parents believe, a new form of back injury. Then when the occasion arises for using the program again, the computer operator merely loads the instructions back into the machine and punches in some new values for N. The same broad principles apply to the creation of all software, even complex simulations like Geography Search.

Literal-minded brutes that they are, computers do exactly what they are told. No more and no less. But youngsters of even the most tender age are surprising educators by showing they can master the beasts with startling ease. Computer software expert Leona Schauble of the Children's Television Workshop (producers of *Sesame Street)* recalls getting an eight-year-old boy at Manhattan's Little Red School House started on a simple computer game. The game generated an image of a frog that would leap up and catch a butterfly, provided the right buttons were hit.

After a few minutes, she checked back and found the frog jumping in slow motion. When she asked the youngster what happened, he replied, "Well, we wanted to make the frog catch more butterflies. So we got a listing of the variables and slowed him down." In other words, the youngster had broken into the game's program and changed it to suit himself. To instruct very young children, even Kemeny's BASIC is much too mathematical. Instead, more and more schools are turning to an innovative computer language called LOGO (from the Greek word for reason), developed by Seymour Papert and his colleagues at MIT.

A mathematician who studied with the Swiss psychologist jean Piaget, Papert has become something of a guru of the computer generation, preaicting that the machines will revolutionize learning by taking much of the mystery out of mathematics, science and technology. Says he: "The computer can make the most abstract things concrete." With a deceptively simple set of commands, LOGO enables youngsters who know nothing of geometry and algebra, and barely know how to read, to manipulate a triangular figure, dubbed the Turtle, on a computer screen and trace all manner of shapes with it. At the Lamplighter School in Dallas, teachers using LOGO get youngsters of three or four to write simple computer instructions.

In one game, they maneuver "cars" and "garages" on the computer screen in such a way that the cars are parked inside the garages. While playing with LOGO, the youngsters learn simple words, the difference between left and right, and geometric concepts that they would not ordinarily encounter until junior high. The machines crop up in the lives of youngsters even before they enter school—and sometimes before they learn to walk or talk—in the guise of such siliconised gadgetry as Little Professor and Speak & Spell. With a few presses of the button, these computerized games produce flashing lights, squealing sounds and disembodied voices that inculcate the rudiments of spelling and calculating.

A record of sorts may have been set by Corey Schou, a computer scientist at the University of Central Florida in Orlando: he rigged up a home computer so his five-month-old daughter could operate it by pressing buttons in her crib and changing the designs on a nearby screen. Says the proud papa: "Basically, it's an electronic kaleidoscope, another diversion, another learning device." Whatever it is, it prepares youngsters for all those buttons they will encounter soon enough in and out of school.

Parents and teachers may shudder at the thought, but it is only a short hop from skilful operation of a video game to learning fundamentals of programming. Says MIT Sociologist Sherry Turkle, 33, who has been studying the youthful computer culture for five years: "The line between game playing and programming is very thin. Programming takes what is powerful about games—this articulation of knowledge, this learning about strategy—and carries it to a higher level of power." By the time the youthful programmers reach the eighth or ninth grade, their skills may reach a marketable level.

In Chicago, Jonathan Dubman, 14, and Kay Borzsony, 13, have formed a company called Aristotle Software to sell their own computer games and graphics programs. Says Kay: "The nice thing about the computer business is that there is no real bias against children. In the computer magazines, you read articles by 12- and 13-year-olds." Laura Hyatt, 15, of Ridgewood, helps a stymied local insurance office figure out how to use its software. Says she: "It's better than babysitting." And, at $3.50 an hour, somewhat more profitable. The prodigy of prodigies may be Eugene Volokh, 14, of Los Angeles.

A Russian emigre, he earns $480 each week by doing 24 hours of programming for 20th Century-Fox, while carrying a full load of courses as a junior at UCLA. This year Greg Christensen, 18, of Anaheim, Calif., could make $100,000 in royalties from a video game he developed that was bought by Atari. Other youngsters are waiting at the sidelines in hopes of catching up with these young entrepreneurs. Every Tuesday night, Scott Whitfield, 13, and his brother Shawn, 11, appear at the Menlo Park, Calif., public library to get computer instruction. Says Scott: "We'll probably never get a job if we don't learn how to use a computer." Not all youngsters take equally to the machines.

In a typical computer class, only about one in five students becomes seriously involved. Says Steven Scott, 16, of Wausau's West High: "Either you get the hang of it or you don't." Even so dedicated a computernik as Ridgewood's Nick Newman finds programming interesting only for a purpose. His own goal is to apply his computer knowledge to a career in science or medicine. Whatever these youngsters make of their computer experiences, they will surely confront the world differently from their parents.

The precise, orderly steps of logic required to use and program the machines promise to shape—and sharpen—the thought processes of the computer generation. Indeed, the youngsters playing all those strategy games are doing precisely what corporations do when they plan to launch a new product, or what military leaders do when they devise strategies to confront a potential foe. Whether such abilities will change the world for the better is another matter.

Princeton psychologist George Miller, for one, has doubts that "a few years of thinking like a computer can change patterns of irrational thought that have persisted throughout recorded history." Other social critics ask if clear thinking is enough—if, in fact, there might not be a danger in raising a generation to believe that it has the analytical tools to contemplate any problem. Says MIT computer science professor Joseph Weizenbaum: "There's a whole world of real problems, of human problems, which is essentially being ignored." It is still impossible, after all, to reduce a human relationship to a printout or to solve a moral question by bits and bytes. Some critics predict a future not unlike that portrayed in Isaac Asimov's I, *Robot,* a science fiction novel set in a society so thoroughly computer-dominated that the people cannot do arithmetic. Humanist critic George Steiner acerbically calls the computer generation the advance guard of a breed of "computer-mutants." Says Steiner: "They will be out of touch with certain springs of human identity and creativity, which belong to the full use of language rather than mathematical and symbolical codes." Many others are much more sanguine.

University of Chicago philosopher of science Stephen Toulmin predicts that computers will "re-intellectualize" the television generation. "TV relieved people of the necessity to do anything," says Toulmin. "Computers depend on what you do yourself." Catholic theologian David Tracy argues that "using computers sharpens the mind's ability to deal with our world: the world of technology." The final word may be simpler, and not pronounced by elders who find a devilish soul in the new machine.

9

Personal Computers

A great variety of computers, large and small, are now available. A personal computer is a machine or system meeting all the major qualifications. The system is designed to accept secondary memory devices to supplement the primary, built-in memory, the user is expected to interact with the system continuously, not only at the beginning and end of a problem, at least one general language (BASIC, FORTRAN, COBOL, PASCAL, ADA, or C) is available for this interaction, the system is usable for a wide variety of problems and is not designed for any single application and the computer is distributed through mass-marketing channels, with the marketing emphasis on the first-time computer user. A typical modern personal computer consists of a circuit board with a silicon chip microprocessor and one or more memory chips attached.

The microprocessor can perform hundreds of thousands of calculations every second, and the memory chips provide the primary storage for instructions and data. External storage devices, such as cassette tape units or small recording disks (floppy disks), augment the memory capacity and provide a storage medium that can be physically transferred from one personal computer to another. (Typical users begin with cassette units but soon change to disks to gain the advantages of greater speed and capacity.) Input is through a typewriter-like keyboard unit. Output typically takes the form of words and numbers displayed either on a television screen or a similar specialized screen called a monitor. Most monitors are designed to display 24 lines of letters and figures, with each line containing a maximum of 80 characters. Adding a printer unit permits output in the form of a printed paper.

A special device, called a "modem" (for modulator/ demodulator), permits the computer to receive and transmit data over a conventional telephone line. But the significant factor in defining a personal computer is not its physical features but the characteristics of the operating system. Designers of personal computers and software attempt to provide a friendly human-machine interface, even at the expense of brute computing power.

Optional programs are also available so that the computer can be used for many different purposes. Although word processors and hobby computers have many characteristics of personal computers, they lack this flexibility. Recent trends in microelectronics, memories, input--output mechanisms, and software suggest that the trend in microprocessors is toward larger "words" and higher circuit speeds.

A computer capable of handling larger "words" is able to perform a complete operation in fewer machine cycles and to operate directly with larger memory. Both these assets enhance performance by increasing the speed of operations and the number that can be performed in a sequence without the operator's intervention. In addition to greater speed and memory access, these larger microprocessors have the advantage of greater accuracy. The first wave of personal computers used 8-bit microprocessors that is, microprocessors in which 8 binary digits (0 or 1) can be processed in parallel, giving the capacity to process in a single operation any number up to 256, or to address any of up to 256 points in the memory.

Processing larger numbers with an 8-bit microprocessor requires multiple operations, which take more time. Newer systems use 16-bit microprocessors, and 32-bit microprocessors are now available. The primary memory in personal computers is of two different types: read-only memory (ROM) and random-access memory (RAM). In the forme information is fixed in the memory at the time of manufacture and is not lost when computer power is switched off.

The role of such a ROM is to guide the computer through a fixed procedure, such as calculating square roots translating a user's program into machine language. In a RAM, information such as special programs and data files can be "written in" or "read out" a frequently as desired, with any storage location directly accessible. RAMS are of two types: dynamic RAMS, which are cheaper but lose their store information unless they are "refreshed" often, and static RAMS, which are costlier but do not need to be "refreshed." If power is lost, both types of RAM lose their stored information.

The number of memory circuits per unit of area on chip has increased by a factor of 64, and cost on a unit basis has been reduced by a factor of 50. Both these trends will continue. So-called 64K dynamic RAMs (each contains 65,536 bits of information [K = 2 10 = 1024; 64K = 64 x 10241) are expected to remain popular until about 1984, when the much larger memory capacity of 256K dynamic RAMs is expected to become standard. Most manufacturers supply system programs on ROMs, and this practice will continue because programs are secure against power failures and users are less able to duplicate programs in this form. Computers' main memories will be supplemented by secondary storage devices that offer larger and relatively inexpensive, though slower, capacity for long-term storage of program and data files.

The most popular of these is a so-called "floppy disk"—a disk of mylar coated with magnetic material on one or both sides. Data are stored in a series of spots—either magnetized or demagnetized—along the concentric tracks. Heads for reading or writing data can be moved radially across the disk to reach a specified segment of circular track. Storage capacity depends on the format used for the stored data, the quality of magnetic surface, and the design of the reading-writing head. Floppy disks in current use typically have capacities of 1 to 4 million bits, sufficient to store 20,000 to 80,000 words of English text.

During the next four years, higher-density floppy disks will be common. Indeed, disks offering capacities of 50 to 100 million bits are already becoming popular, but they are much costlier than floppy disks. The primary display device used in all personal computer systems is a cathode-ray tube (CRT), either standing alone or as part of a television receiver. This system will continue through the foreseeable future. Output is typically presented in alphanumeric form-letters and numbers. Charts and game boards can be presented, but the memory and software required to display such graphical images is often complex and expensive.

The letters and numbers in alphanumeric displays are patterns of dots programmed in special ROMs known as "character generators." The quality of the image depends on the number of points (or pixels) on the screen that can be addressed by the computer-that is, the number of points at which dots can be located. A typical low-resolution screen has a field of 6144 (128 times 48) pixels (picture elements-dots on the screen). High-resolution systems (100,000 pixels or more) allow sophisticated graphics for animation or detailed figures and may provide colour as well.

The market and the players

The personal computer industry has grown as a direct result of the evolution of the microprocessor. This evolution began when Intel in 1971 packaged a complete, if somewhat limited, processor with a 4-bit word size in a single integrated circuit. The company followed with the first 8-bit processor in 1972 and an improved version in 1974. One year later Micro Instrumentation and Telemetry Systems, Inc. (MITS), an Albuquerque firm, developed the first personal computer around Intel's 8-bit processor.

The basic system sold for $395 in kit form and $621 in assembled form, not including accessories (peripherals). Though the MITS system is no longer manufactured, its method for connecting peripherals and the main computer has become an industry standard. Within three years after it was introduced, Radio Shack, Apple, and Commodore had entered the market. Now makers of large computers such as IBM and Honeywell, as well as minicomputer leaders such as Digital Equipment Corp. and Data General Corp., are also making personal computers, having observed their traditional markets being eroded by the new low-priced products.

The results are rapid development of the market and growing popular interest and faith in personal computers. The pioneering manufacturers did not survive beyond the initial phase of personal computer development results from the preoccupation with the needs of hobbyists. New entrants such as Radio Shack, Commodore, and Apple captured a major share of the market in 1978 by promoting fully assembled, ready-to-operate systems that were easier to use. Though the success of the companies now in the competition will depend at least partly on their financial and technical resources, their products' ease of use (or "user-friendliness," in trade jargon) is a significant competitive feature. The personal computer market can be divided into four segments in terms of the computer's intended use: business, home, research-technical, and educational.

The business segment, by far the largest at present, accounted for 750,000 sales (retail value of $2 billion) in 1982, or 54 percent of the units sold and 65 percent of the dollar sales. This segment will continue to be a major factor, with more sales than all other segments put together. No wonder, then, that the leading makers of personal computers are concentrating their sales efforts on the business sector. The most visible segment of the personal computer "revolution" is in homes, where computers are used for entertainment and education, sending messages, and home finances.

The development of appropriate software will soon enable sophisticated users to pay bills, manage bank accounts, compute taxes, and even buy household items without written transactions. The potential market for personal computers in education has barely been tapped. Computer manufacturers recognize that schools are the logical environment in which to develop computer skills, and they have reason to expect that students will purchase the machine on which they first learn computing. So manufacturers are offering many price incentives to the educational sector. Yet the educational sector will continue to account for only about 15 percent of total sales of personal computers for the rest of this decade, as school funding will be limited. Although they want to serve all four segments, the industry leaders

(Apple, Radio Shack, Commodore, IBM, and Xerox) are focusing on the business market. Vector Graphics is also emphasizing this market by tailoring personal computer systems to the needs of particular industries. Atari (Warner), Intellivision (Mattel), and Texas Instruments are focusing on the home market.

Hewlett-Packard is offering a highly specialized compact product with built-in printer, tape memory, and video monitor especially for the scientific community. In general, both prices and manufacturers' profit margins are failing, and mass marketing is becoming the rule. The major competitors win each spend over $10 million in 1983 on advertising aimed at expanding the market and establishing their place in it.

The dynamics of the entire personal computer market may be changed substantially by new entrants by 1990. Traditional barriers to entry into this field have crumbled. For example, manufacturing capability is not essential: the IBM personal computer is assembled almost entirely from premanufactured components not of IBM origin. By contrast, strength in marketing and distribution is a significant advantage, and many organizations with this capability may seek to replicate IBM's strategy for rapid entry into the field. Organizations such as General Electric, Procter and Gamble, Phillip Morris, and Du Pont all have the ability to enter the personal computer market in this way.

Selling personal computers

Strategies for marketing mainframe computers are not appropriate for marketing personal computers-profit margins are not large enough to justify hiring internal sales forces to sell directly to end users. As a result, producers are now experimenting with a wide variety of distribution strategies.

Franchised retail chains constitute a major distribution channel. For example, the Computerland chain sold $200 million worth of computers and related accessories in 1981. These stores distribute the products of many vendors, and their volume is large enough to support a technical and maintenance staff.

Manufacturer-owned retailed stores have been used successfully by Radio Shack. IBM, Digital, and Xerox have also opened such stores but only to supplement existing distribution channels. Except for Xerox, each manufacturer's stores sell only that manufacturer's products, and a prospective buyer is thus obliged to visit several stores to compare equipment of different makes.

Department store outlets have generally been unsuccessful. Mass merchandisers depend for profits on fast-selling commodities. According to computer industry data, personal computer buyers make four shopping trip totalling as much as seven hours when selecting their machines. These buyer also expect sustained support and maintenance services that department stores are unaccustomed to providing.

Office equipment stores specializing in copiers, typewriters, word processors and other office equipment are well positioned to reach the most Promising future market for personal computers and auxiliary equipment. If these stores can provide adequate servicing, they will become very popular.

Consumer electronics stores such as Tech Hi-Fi have been marketing personal computers with some success, but the lack of expertise at the store level has been a constraint. Japanese manufacturers have also established ties with such stores as distributors of other Japanese products. These channels will become a major factor as the Japanese increase their share of the personal computer market.

Independent retailers often lack the capital required to compete vigorously and are therefore not gaining in numbers and importance as quickly as other retail channels.

Catalog showrooms have been used by Texas Instruments, but personal computers require follow-up support that such showrooms have been unable to provide.

Mail order firms offering discounts ranging up to 30 percent appeal to price-sensitive customers, but their total lack of continuing support disenchants users. Price-cutting penalizes the full-service dealers on which manufacturers want to rely as major sales outlets. Accordingly, major companies are trying to discourage sales through mail order firms.

Direct sales staffs are used for large-volume sales to government, educational institutions, and major corporations who prefer dealing directly with the manufacturer. But such direct sales tend to antagonize dealers by dipriving them of some of their most profitable opportunities, and profit margins are inadequate to support direct sales to small-volume and individual buyers.

Value-added houses serve specialized users with coordinated hardware and software, such as printing companies that need word-processing and typesetting capabilities but have little or no internal computing expertise. Though franchised retail outlets are the largest sellers of personal computers in the us, the one compelling characteristic of personal computer distribution today is diversity. No one form of vendor or market approach is dominant.

Selecting a personal computer

No one should select a personal computer system

without taking into account the tasks for which it will be used and the environment in which it will function. Even within a single business, personal computer users come from different areas-personnel, accounting, management, manufacturing, research, sales-and have different computing needs. Even within departments there are many possible uses.

The personnel department will run personnel files on a regular basis but also may want to study policy questions-the likely benefits in terms of increased revenue from a larger sales force, for example. Furthermore, different users have different strategies for using a computer for ad hoc applications. Thus, the person who will use a personal computer should-almost by definition-choose it, partly on the basis of the services it will provide and partly on the basis of its apparent user-friendliness. Indeed, the machine's responsiveness to its user's needs and style is the critical technological breakthrough. But it is not necessarily so simple.

Personal computers create and fill completely new needs that were not originally anticipated. Consider the example of a personal computer acquired to improve one lay worker's access to a main computer facility. While retrieving data from the main computer to run programs locally, this user finds that the personal computer can help evaluate alternative business strategies, answering, "what-if... ?" questions instantaneously.

The original application for which the personal computer was purchased becomes secondary. Given that the uses and benefits of personal computers are hard to predict, and that a wide range of systems and software are available, how should a potential buyer decide what and when to buy? And should such a buyer postpone action, expecting costs to decline in the future as they have in the past? There are two arguments against postponing purchase in anticipation of a lower future price. One is the high cost of waiting, based on the computer's great (and often unexpected) uses. The other is that prices are expected to decline less dramatically in the future than in the past: future systems will offer technological improvements that increase performance at unchanged cost. Prices seem likely to stabilize at around $1500 for a full personal computer system.

Future personal computers are likely to offer increased memory size, increased processor power (16-bit and even 32-bit instead of 8-bit microprocessors), improved printers, more powerful programming languages that give the user more compact and natural communication with the computer, improved user access (better keyboards supplemented or replaced by touch screen and voice systems), and greater flexibility (the computer will be able to intermix and manipulate text, numbers, and graphics more easily). Yet today's personal computers may rapidly become obsolete, reflecting the rapid pace of change in semiconductor technology. Changes in the microprocessor, the heart of any personal computer system, are most likely—and most serious.

A computer with a 16-bit microprocessor cannot operate on hardware and software designed for an 8-bit microprocessor. Though many vendors provide add-ons that enable a new microprocessor to support old software, there is never total compatibility. Software for a personal computer is expensive, and for most users new software development is impractical. So the amount and utility of the software available with a particular system is the key question in the buyer's choice of a personal computer.

The variation can be large: 11,000 programs are available for the Apple ii and Apple ii Plus computers, whereas fewer than 100 widely distributed programs exist for the IBM personal computer, a more recent introduction. Of course, the IBM programs may be just the ones the buyer needs, and more software will be developed for the IBM. Price is also an important variable, including not only the manufacturer's suggested price but the range of discounts offered by different retail computer sources. But discount alone does not tell the story.

The critical factor is the ability of the distributor to provide both routine hardware maintenance, usually at the retail outlet, and software support and maintenance. A company store is likely to offer very good service on that company's product line but not necessarily on any other line, while a retail computer store is likely to offer moderately qualified service and support for many different manufacturers' systems.

Mail order sales offer very little service but usually have the highest discounts. The ultimate question for the purchaser is that of system configuration: what combination of hardware and software is appropriate for a buyer's current and projected needs? Perhaps the most important options are off-the-shelf software. To be sure they buy what they need, buyers should gain some experience with available programs before making the purchase; otherwise they risk having to modify their needs to fit the software they've purchased or embarking on the costly and time-consuming route of software development. The programming tools on most personal computers are primitive compared with the equivalents available for mainframes, and the widespread dearth of good programmers is a complicating factor. Indeed, trying to develop special programming for a personal computer is inadvisable except under extraordinary circumstances.

Memory capacity is another important variable.

Most computers based on 8-bit microprocessors have no more than 48 or 64 kilobytes of built-in accessible memory (RAM), while the newer 16-bit processors can have 1, 4, or even 16 megabytes. (One byte is a string of 8 binary digits that represents one alphabetic character.) Additional memory can be inserted into most personal computers by plugging cards into slots or inserting extra chips directly onto the microprocessor board.

Storage capacity of the main memory for programs and instructions can also be supplemented by secondary devices, of which floppy disks are the most popular form. Disks with capacities ranging from 100,000 bytes to several megabytes now come in two standard sizes: 8 inches and 5¼ inches in diameter. But personal computer buyers should be aware that disks designed for one system will not generally operate in another maker's system because of different data-formatting conventions. The critical performance characteristic of a floppy disk is the response time to a read-write request, which may range from 200 to 500 milliseconds.

Though the response time for such a single file request is very short, a single compilation or word-processing command may involve 20 or more accesses to a floppy disk, and access time may account for 80 percent of the total command execution time. Where better performance and/or capacity are required, "hard" disks in the same format as the 5¼-inch and 8-inch floppy disks are useful. They offer storage capacities ranging from 5 to 50 megabytes and response time averaging 20 to 40 milliseconds, but their high cost (around $2000, including interfaces) can double a buyer's total investment in hardware. All personal computer systems use cathode-ray tubes as output devices. If "hard copy" is required, buyers have a choice of several printing devices.

A dot-matrix printer, costing from $500 to $1500, has a vertical array of 7 to 10 dot-printing elements. These are activated by the computer as the printing head passes across the paper, forming alphanumeric characters and also graphs and drawings. The limited number of elements results in a somewhat stylized character, but the process is as fast as thermal printing—50 characters per second. If letter-quality printing is required, a printing mechanism with precisely machined character matrices that strike the paper through a ribbon is required. Such printers cost $750 or more and print between 30 and 90 characters per second.

The IBM personal computer offers five such slots for peripherals such as printer, colour display, dual floppy-disk controller, communications channel, and memory module. All business-oriented personal computers offer text editing for word processing. Some permit use of a light pen to directly indicate on the screen the word to be edited, and a few check spelling against a mini-dictionary stored in the computer memory.

Business data manipulation is facilitated by "spreadsheet" packages such as VISICALC—a very popular package that enables users to see on the CRT the impact of altering one figure (say, retail price) on all other figures (profit margin, corporate profit, return of investment). Software is now becoming available for generating displays such as those accompanying this article with only a few minutes' effort. For example, ExecuVision permits displays combining information in numbers, text, and pictures. It also provides animation that can add emphasis to presentations. Though personal computers are today viewed primarily as stand-alone work stations for individual users, the ability to transmit and receive data and programs is an important attribute of most contemporary systems.

Personal computers are already serving as intelligent terminals for retrieving and manipulating files from large computers. These networking and communication capabilities are important considerations in selecting a personal computer. Unfortunately, no industry standard for communication protocols and interfaces exists. Different vendors use different protocols, so it is difficult to link various personal computers in a single network. Technological advances in communications are expanding the power of personal computers. For example, owners of personal computers can now receive current stock market quotations by telephone.

Personal computers can be connected with nationwide electronic funds transfer systems, so users have access to full banking facilities. They may transfer funds from one account to another and buy and sell financial instruments. In homes, personal computers are now primarily used for recreational activities such as computer games. But these applications should not be underrated.

Computer games test and develop mental capabilities while generating familiarity with computer operations. Home computers are also used for office work at home, and many other applications are--or soon will be-possible. For example, a tax return can be prepared with the aid Of VISICALC. The user can analyse which forms and deductions to use for paying the minimum taxes.

A personal computer can be used to balance checkbooks and plan investment strategies. And, of course, word-processing capabilities are useful in writing letters and professional papers. As commercial databases such as Dow Jones News/Retrieval and the Source are expanded and their subscription costs reduced, personal computers will be useful for locating stores and services, comparing prices, and placing orders. This would be especially appropriate for products or services whose prices fluctuate rapidly, such as those of the airline industry. Computers are being used increasingly for security applications.

Traditional home security systems are limited, often failing to distinguish between a natural event and an intrusion by an unwanted visitor. Computer-controlled home security systems can include a variety of routines to analyse the signals from sensors before generating an alarm. Such an analysis can distinguish, for example, between the entry of a cat and the entry of a human being, or between the noise of a telephone ringing and a door opening. Another home-oriented application is a medical information system that performs some of the diagnostics of a medical doctor. Perhaps the most useful application of this is a database for poison or first-aid: the user reports what substance the patient has ingested or the nature of an accident, and the computer responds with a step-by-step first aid plan.

Children turn out to be heavy users of home computers. They enjoy computer games and seem able to learn computer languages faster than their elders. They find personal computers intriguing for recreation, school assignments, and self-paced courses that are now becoming available. Even though today's personal computers are equivalent in basic computing power to the mainframes of the 1960s and the minicomputers of the 1970s, they should not be used as substitutes for the earlier machines. Rather, users should capitalize on the new technical developments, including the diminishing cost of computing, and the Englishlike languages that replace the cumbersome digital languages of early machines, to make personal computers supplement, not displace, mainframe computers.

Personal computers should be used to analyse more issues in greater detail than ever before-not to do the more routine work typically assigned to mainframes. In the 1960s and 1970s, computers were used principally for well-structured, periodic jobs such as payroll accounting.

Today's personal computers are especially useful for more casual, ad hoc analyses and problem solving, such as studies of the impact of cost of living increases, new tax regulations, or alternative hiring and layoff policies. Consider the stock analyst who uses data from company balance sheets to evaluate investment risks. The balance sheets contain detailed, current information on assets and liabilities. But interest rates fluctuate, markets rise and fall, taxes change, competition falters or gains. Each such change affects a company's current performance and future prospects. Using a central computing facility is an expensive way to analyse such problems, resulting in time delays and partial answers. But using a personal computer in the interactive mode linked to the central computer and a financial database makes it possible to understand the impact of changes quickly and accurately.

Psychology of personal computers

Home computers would teach us French, help us with financial planning, even do our taxes. For many Americans, the first thing that computers brought into their homes was not a more efficient medium for work but new worlds to conquer in play. "Space Invaders" became a household word for people with home computers or the machines' junior siblings, computerized video games.

The experience of the decade has resulted in a widely shared public rhetoric. When people talk about the computer and their futures, they tend to fall back on the two images they know best: the computer as tool and the computer as toy; objective instrumentality and engrossing play. But there is another dimension. What people do with computers weaves itself into the way they see the world. People use a discourse about computers for thinking and talking about other things, about politics, religion, education, and about themselves and other people. The subjective dimension of the computer presence is not merely a matter of discourse, of using the computer intellectually as a metaphor or model.

There is another, and more emotionally charged, aspect which does not engage *ideas* about computers as much as the immediate quality of an individual's *experience* when working with them. Working with computers can be a way of "working through" powerful feelings. In this essay we develop this idea by using as a case study a group of computer users for whom issues related to control are particularly salient. For a first generation of computer hobbyists, controlling the computer is a way to deal with frustrations and desires, both personal and political, that have nothing to do with the computer *per se.* The subjects of my study are men and women who bought personal computer systems in the four years that followed the 1975 announcement of the "Altair"—the first computer small enough to sit on a desktop, powerful enough to support high-level language programming, and that you could build for only $420.

My study began in 1978 with a questionnaire survey answered by 95 New England computer hobbyists (their names had been drawn from the roster of a home computer club and from the subscription list of a personal computer magazine), and continued during 1978 and 1979 with nearly 300 hours of conversation with 50 individuals who owned home computers. What we found can be read historically: a study of the pioneer users of an increasingly ubiquitous technology. But most central to the intent of this essay is to use the story of the early hobbyists as a window into the highly personal ways in which individuals appropriate technologies. It is a case study of the "subjective computer," the computer as a material for thinking, for feeling, for "working through." We are emphasis on the subjective is at odds with a widespread ideology that quickly grew up around the emergent computer hobbyist culture.

The Altair, aimed at a strictly hobby market, was followed by other small systems—the Pet, the Sol, and, most successfully, the Radio Shack TRS-80 and the Apple, marketed to less specialized audiences of small businessmen and curious householders. With this explosion of hardware came a lot of rhetoric about a personal computer revolution. Most of the talk, both from the companies that marketed the machines and from those who claimed to be the most visionary spokesmen for the people who bought them, was about all of the things that a home computer could do for you. The utilitarian, "genie in the bottle," ideology is expressed in the content of hobbyist conventions and magazines, filled with articles on how to make your home computer dim your lights, control your thermostat, run an inventory system for your kitchen or toolroom. And it is also found in writing on the personal computer from outside the hobbyist world.

The view from the "outside" was well illustrated when, on May 14, 1979, the *Wall Street Journal* reported on its own little "evaluation experiment." The paper had drafted one of its staff reporters, Mitchell Lynch, into the ranks of the "home computer revolution." It presented him with a TRS-80 and asked him to take it home. His assignment was to report back six months later on what it had been like. The terms of Lynch's evaluation are instrumental: what can the computer do? On these terms it fails, and when he goes to the experts for an explanation of what went wrong, he encounters an official "instrument" ideology from within: "Experts say that people like me have neither the technical training nor technical inclination to make a home computer strut its stuff." The point of having the computer, says the expert, is to make things happen. And, reassures the expert, they will happen with a better operator or a simpler computer.

This instrumental view is an important ingredient of the hobbyist ideology but it is not the whole story. In the course of my work I found a very different answer from within. Most hobbyists do make their computers "strut their stuff," but their sense of engagement and energy are found primarily in the non-instrumental uses of the technology. When asked in a questionnaire "What first attracted you to computers?" more than half the respondents gave reasons that were highly subjective. In response to an open-ended question, 26 percent said that they were first attracted to computers by an appeal that was intellectual, aesthetic, involved with the fun of what I would call "cognitive play." They wrote of "puzzle solving," of "the elegance of using computer techniques to handle problems," of the "beauty of understanding a system at many levels of complexity." They described what they did with their home computers with metaphors like "mind stretching" and "using the computer's software to understand my wetware."

Another 26 percent wrote of reasons for getting involved that seemed more emotional than intellectual. They wrote of the "ego boost" or "sense of power" that comes from knowing how to run a computer, of the "prestige of being a pioneer in a developing field," of the "feeling of control when I work in a safe environment of my own creation." The hobbyists who responded to my survey seemed familiar with Lynch's brand of scepticism, with people who ask them what they do with their computers and who won't take "cognitive play" for an answer. David, a 19 year-old undergraduate at a small engineering school, put it this way: "People come over and see my computer and they look at it, then they look at me, then they ask me what useful thing we do with it, like does it wash floors, clean laundry or do my income tax—when we respond no, they lose interest."

David said that when he started out, he was attracted to the computer because "we liked the idea of making a pile of hardware do something useful, like doing real time data processing ... like picking up morse code with an amateur radio and transcribing it automatically into text," but in his list of things that he currently does with his computer. Thirteen percent of those who responded to my questionnaire told a similar story. Like David, they began their relationship with personal computation for instrumental reasons (they had an image of a job to do, a specific task), but they became absorbed by the "holding power" of something else.

A full two-thirds of my survey sample either began with or ended up with a primary interest in what I have called the "subjective computer," the computer seen in its relationship to *personal meaning.* Clearly, to understand what people are doing with their home computers we must go beyond the "performance criteria" shared by the hobbyist magazines and the *Wall Street Journal.* The simplest way of thinking about the subjective computer is through the metaphor of "the computer as Rorschach"—that is, seeing the computer as a projective screen for other concerns. In the Rorschach test, one is presented with a set of ink blots and asked to make some sense of them.

Some people see the blots as threatening; others see them as benign. Some focus on small, complex details; others on global form. So too, the computer presents us with an ambiguous stimulus. For example, although most people think of the computer as an object without real intentionality, they accord computers enough autonomy in action to make "blaming the computer" a commonplace of daily life. The very fact that the computer is a machine that touches on a sphere—intelligence—that man has always considered uniquely his is enough to make many people experience the computer as an object "betwixt and between," hard to classify, hard to pin down.

Sometimes people deny the irreducibility of computation by asserting that, no matter how complex the computation "product," a move in a chess game for example, "all the computer really does is add." Of course in a certain sense this is correct. But saying that a computer "decided to move the Queen by adding" is a little bit like saying that Picasso "created Guernica by making brushstrokes." Reducing things to this level of localness gives no satisfying way to grasp the whole. Just as in theoretical psychology there is a tension between the gestalt and the atomic, so too in computation there is a pervasive tension between the local simplicity of the individual acts that comprise a program or a computation, and what one might call the "global complexity" that can emerge when it is run.

The elusiveness of computational processes and of simple descriptions of the computer's essential nature, the tension between local simplicity and global complexity, all contribute to making the computer an object of projective processes, and exemplary "constructed object." Different people apprehend it with very different descriptions and invest it with very different attributes. In views of the computer's internal process, individuals project their models of mind. In descriptions of the computer's powers, people express feelings about their own intellectual, social, and political power—or their lack of it. Looking at the computer as Rorschach, as projective, puts the emphasis on aspects of the individual—from cognitive style to personal fears—that are revealed through behaviour with the machine. But of course the computer is more than a Rorschach. The Rorschach ink blots are evocative, revealing, but they stay on the page. They do not enter the life of the individual. The computer does. It is a constructive as well as a projective medium. For readers who have not had the experience of programming a computer, this idea may be sharpened by an analogy with another technology. In my own studies of people's emotional relationships with technologies, airplanes emerge as startlingly like computers in respect to the issues they raise for their hobbyists. Specifically, both are powerful media for working through the issue of control.

There is always a compelling tension between local simplicity and global complexity in the working of a computer and in the appreciation of a computer program. Locally, each step in a program is easy to understand; its effects are well defined. But the evolution of the global pattern is often not graspable. You are dealing with a system that surprises. This play between simplicity and complexity allows programmers, as pilots do with flying, to make of computation very different experiences that provide a context for working through different needs in relation to issues of personal control.

Depending on how the programmer brings the computer's local simplicity and global complexity into focus, he or she will have a particular experience of the machine as completely understandable, under control, or as baffling, even as controlling. By focusing on the local, the line by line, you can feel in control. By focusing on the global, you can feel control slip away. In their style of programming a computer, people betray different levels of tolerance for temporary losses of control. Some will avoid it at all costs; but others will seek it out, and enjoy "playing" with sensations of risk and danger. And so different people end up with very different relationships to controls and power in their programming work. To illustrate this point, it is useful to begin with an example at one extreme. We see a first style in Howard, an ex-programmer, now a university professor, who describes himself as "having been a computer hacker." Howard was not in my sample of hobbyists.

He has a terminal at home which links to a large timesharing system, but when asked about home computers, he winced in distaste and said that he "wouldn't touch the stuff. It's too simple." His case, in which we see a love of programming for the feeling of "walking near the edge of a cliff," is meant as a contrast for what we found to be a prevalent and more conservative "hobbyist style." Howard described his longtime fantasy that he would walk up to any program, however complex, and "fix it, bend it to my will." As he described his intervention, he imitated the kind of hand gestures that a stage musician makes toward the hat before he pulls out the rabbit. Wizards use spells, a powerful kind of local magic.

Howard's magic was local too. He described his "hacker's approach" to any problem as a search for the "quick and dirty fix." For Howard, what was most thrilling about the experience of programming was "walking down a narrow line," using the program's flexibility (for him defined as the possibility of making a local fix) in a struggle to keep the whole under control. Weekends at the terminal with little to eat and little or no rest were frequent, as was the experience of not being able to leave the terminal while debugging a program, even when the obvious need was for sleep and looking at the whole in the morning, instead of trying to "fix it" by looking at it line by line all night.

For Howard, the urgency of these encounters was

tied to his sense that through them he was grappling with a computational essence—the struggle to exert control over global complexity by mastery of local simplicity. A second programmer, Bob, is a computer professional, a microprocessor engineer who works all day on the development of hardware for a large industrial data system.

He has recently built a small computer system for his home and devotes much of his leisure time to programming it. Whereas, for Howard, the excitement of programming is that of a high-risk venture, Bob likes it as a chance to be in complete control. Although Bob works all day with computers, his building and programming them at home is not more of the same. At work he sees himself as part of a process that he cannot see and over which he feels no mastery or ownership: "Like they say, we are just a cog." At home Bob works on well defined projects of his own choosing, projects whose beginning, middle, and end are all under his control.

He describes the home projects as a compensation for the alienation of his job. He works most intensively on his home system when he feels furthest away from any understanding of "how the whole thing fits together at work." Howard and Bob have very different opinions about what is most satisfying about programming. These translate into different choices of projects, into different choices of programming language and level to program at, and ultimately into what we might call different computational aesthetics.

Howard likes to work on large, "almost out of control" projects; Bob likes to work on very precisely defined ones. Howard finds documen-tation a burdensome and unwelcome constraint; Bob enjoys documentation, he likes to have a clear, unambiguous record of what he has mastered. Indeed, much of his sense of power over the program derives from its precise specifications and from his continual attempts to enlarge the sphere of the program's local simplicity. Hobbyist programmers mean different things when they say that machine language programming "puts them in control." For some, the reference seems objective. Given the primitive higher-level languages available on the first and second generation of hobby computers, machine-level programming seems to them the best instrumental solution. For others, the issue is more subjective.

Many hobbyists who said they felt uneasy using systems programs for which they didn't have the source code also admitted never looking at the source code listing which they felt they had to have. Having access to the code was symbolic. In other cases it was apparent that machine language programming was valued because the experi-ence of doing it was pleasing in itself. It meant that the programmer was writing instructions that acted directly on the machine, no "building on top of" somebody else's interpreter.

Most hobbyists have relationships with computation at work which involve sharing the machine with countless and nameless others. In personal computation they see a chance to be independent and alone. The machine comes to them virgin. They have full possession. Finally, there is the issue of asserting control over an inferior. Bob, like many of the other hobbyists I spoke with, is a middle-level worker in the computer industry. He does not feel very good about the importance of his job. Proving that he is "better than any dumb compiler" gives a sense of importance.

Using the computer to assert control was a central theme in my interviews with hobbyists. It was expressed directly, and also wove itself into four other issues that characterize the hobbyists' "subjective computer." These are using the computer to strengthen a sense of identity; to construct a completely intelligible piece of reality that is experienced as "transparent" and safe; to articulate a political ideology; and to experience a sense of wholeness that is absent in one's work life. It is these four issues to which I now turn.

Constructing reality

Hobbyist's descriptions of what it is like to work with their own computers frequently referred to the idea that the computer provides a safe corner of reality. Other hobbles can give a similar sense of security but often exact a price. For example, people can feel safe but limited. Alan, the French major, now "in love with his TRS-80," felt secure in his carpentry hobby, but he experienced it as a safety that came from refusing challenge. "It was an 'artsy' hobby. We couldn't see myself any other way."

The computer is more likely than most other media to allow the experience of playing worlds (let us call them "microworlds") that are secure and also adventurous enough to allow for mind- stretching explorations. Almost all of the hobbyists we interviewed described some version of a limited, safe, and transparent microworld that was embodied in their personal computer. For Alan just the fact of working with a computer created such a world. For others, it was more specific: a morse code microworld; a text editor microworld; and, most generally, the assembly language microworld. This use of the computer as a place to build a microworld is particularly salient for children when they are put in computational environments in which they have access to programming. Elsewhere I shall report on my study of elementary schoolchildren and adolescents who have gone through an experience with a LOGO computer system—a system designed to allow children to work in visually represented microworlds that are sufficiently constrained for a child to be able to understand and control them, yet sufficiently open-ended to give a child a real experience of intellectual power. Here I will mention only briefly one child and what she made of the computer as a medium for world building. Deborah at 11 years old was the baby of her family, the youngest of three children. Her childhood, had been spotted with illnesses which further exaggerated her "baby" position. The members of her family were always doing things for her, insisting that she was not old enough to do the things that she wanted to do most: take out the laundry, baby-sit, stay over at a friend's house, choose her own hair style and her own clothes.

Towards the end of her eleventh year a LOGO computer came into Deborah's classroom as part of an educational experiment. At first, she found the computer frightening and threatening: until one day she hit upon the idea of confining the designs she made with the computer to ones in which the lines always came together in multiples of 30 degrees. She called it her "30 degrees world." This restriction defined for her a space in which she felt safe but in which she was able to produce designs of great ingenuity and complexity. When I interviewed her two years later I found that she had used her experience with the "30 degrees world" as a kind of model, an experience-to-think-with.

In her mind it represented how you could take control and make things happen by the judicious use of constraint. In Deborah's words, it was the first time that she ever "laid down her own laws." It was a turning point in her ability to take control of other situations. She lost 20 pounds, has given up smoking and drugs, and says that she "only sometimes" has a drink. For Deborah and for many adult hobbyists the sense of safety with the computer derived from the feeling of working in a sphere of intelligibility and transparency, a sphere that is protected, much as the space of a psychotherapeutic or psychoanalytic relationship is set off, bracketed. People talked about feeling safe and secure in the world they had built with their home computers, a world where there were few surprises and "things didn't change unless you wanted them to." Of course, there was much talk of problems, of false starts, of frustrations.

There are "bugs" in hardware and in programs. Things don't work; things go wrong. But bugs, with time, are either fixed or become "known" bugs. Joe is an insurance salesman in a small North California suburb who owns a second-hand Commodore Pet "with a lot of hardware problems." To Joe the bugs in his system "have become almost like friends": "We turn on the machine and we systematically check for my 'old friends,' and we swear, finding them there has a certain reassuring element."

Alienation from work

The programmer is typically in a situation where he or she is in touch with only a very small part of the problem that is being worked on. Increasingly, programmers work in large teams where each individual has very little sense of the whole, of how it all fits together. Programmers have watched their opportunities to exercise their skill as a whole activity being taken away (for those who are too young, the story of the process remains alive in the collective mythology of the shop).

They have watched their work being routinized, being parcelled out into the well defined modules that make up the tasks of the structured programming team. They mythologize a golden age. This lived experience at work made programmers particularly sensitive to the parcellization of knowledge and to the alienation from a sense of wholeness in work. And they bring this sensitivity to their home computer hobbies. Hannah worked as a programming consultant for a large business system for ten years before starting her own consulting company through which she offers her services to other computer hobbyists. To her, nothing is more depressing than working on a tiny piece of a problem. In her old job, "most of the time we didn't even know what the whole problem was." She likes working with computers at home because she has more control of her time and can spend more time with her family. But she says that what is most important about working with a personal computer is that "we can finally think about a whole problem."

Hannah's feelings were widely shared among the hobbyists interviewed, most notably among programmers, ex-programmers, and "team engineers." Images of lack of intellectual balance, of fragmentation, of not being connected, came up often, with the computer at home usually placed in the role of righting what had been wrong at work. As Hannah put it: "With my computer at home we do everything, we see my whole self, all my kinds of thinking." For these people, having a computer at home meant "thinking experiences" where they could see what their real capacities were, where they had a chance to try things out. In the first half of an engineering project there is literally nothing coming together and that's when we find that we need to go home and put something together.

We used to make lamps like those in the living room out of glass bottles. But then towards the middle of an engineering project, things did start to come together and weI would lose the need for cutting glass. But if you never or rarely get to finish things at work, if your job is basically to make little pieces and it's somebody else's job to make them fit into a whole, then working with the computer at home can give you an experience of getting it all together. You do the whole thing—building up from machine code to finished project. It makes you feel in balance. When we spoke with Karl he was at a point where everything at work seemed "pretty disconnected." Or, as Karl put it, if he hadn't had his home computer, it would have been "glass cutting time."

Karl saw his current work with the computer as a corrective to fragmentation on the job. During our interview, he spoke to me about his current plans for revamping his computer system. Computer systems like his which have several components (keyboard, display screen, printer) have to be connected by using devices, usually simple circuits, called "interfaces." Karl's plan called for using a separate microprocessor as an interface for each component. He had conflicts about the "rationality" of his project. After all, he admitted, it was far from economical if one measures economy in terms of the cost of the hardware. Each interface circuit needed only a few specialized and inexpensive chips.

There was no need for a general-purpose microprocessor at each node. Specialized chips could do the job more cheaply, but could not satisfy his desire to experience the system as maximally coherent. By replacing the special-purpose circuits by separate, but identical, general-purpose microprocessors, the whole system, at least in Karl's eyes, became uniform, intelligible, and systematic.

Karl could not help concluding: "We guess you could say that my choice of projects is not always rational." But from the perspective of using a relationship with computation as a way of "working through" personal concerns, Karl's rationale was clear. For Karl the "inexpensive" solution, using a collection of opaque, *ad hoc* circuits, felt unintelligible. It felt to him like his work situation. His plans for his multiprocessor system were dictated by the logic of compensation rather than by the logic of material economy.

Body of the machine

In studying the hobbyist experience we have found people, largely people with technical backgrounds, in intense involvement with machines. They describe their work (or rather their leisure) with the computer as different from what they have done before with other hobbies. They describe it as an involvement with greater personal consequence.

Some of the sense of consequence comes from an historical moment: the computer hobby is seen as signifying a place in the "avant garde." Although in some circles "computer person" is a term of derision, the hobbyist experiences it with pride. Some of the sense of consequence comes from experiencing an individualistic and independent relation-ship with computation that can be mythologized as belonging to a now-past "golden age" of the pro-grammer. But most of the sense of consequence comes from the holding power and intensity of the time spent with the computer.

What is there about these people and these machines that makes possible relationships of such power and such intensity? For me, the relationships that hobbyists form with their home computers can be partially captured with a metaphor of the "mind" and the "body" of the machine. The "mind" of the computer is that side of compu-tation that involves thinking in terms of high-level programs. In this metaphor, relating to the "body" of the computer means not only working on hardware, but also, and indeed especially, working with programs in a way that is as close as possible to the machine code—that is to say, as close as possible to the core of the computer, its central processing unit (CPU). In terms of this metaphor I have found that the prototypical hobbyist is trying to get into a relationship with the body (rather than the mind) of the machine, to assert power and control in the relationship with the computer, and to create safe worlds of transparent understanding. In trying to find concepts for thinking more clearly about what draws the hobbyist to this kind of relationship with the CPU and about what its meaning might be, we find three issues particularly salient.

We think, moreover, that, although we formulate them here in terms of computers, they are relevant to understanding relationships with other technologies as well. The first issue goes back to control. The hobbyist complains of a work situation where everyone suffers from the constant presence of inter-mediaries. Bureaucracies stand between the programmer and the computer, a bureaucracy that schedules the computer, that decides its up and down time, that apportions the work for its software design and decides on priorities and procedures for access to it. At work, when something goes wrong with the system it is usually the fault of an intermediary person, one of the many "somebody elses" who deal with the machine.

Or it may be the fault of a technical intermediary, one of the many elements in the computer system that mediate between the user and the bare machine: a compiler, an interpreter, an operating system, someone else's program. At home, the hobbyists feel themselves as working directly with the CPU, in complete and direct control of the machine's power. And when something does blow up, the situation has a special immediacy. It is between them and the bare machine. When a FORTRAN program is run on a large IBM machine the events in the machine are far from being in one-to-one correspondence with the steps of code written by the programmer. Two factors contribute. First, it is in the nature of higher-level languages to work in a conceptual space different from that of the machine. FORTRAN works in a "formula" space, COBOL works in a "business" space, both very different from the space of bits and bytes.

Second, the sense of indirect relationship is exacerbated when the compiled code is run by an operating system which allocates memory, mediates control of peripheral devices, and even interleaves the program with other programs. At home hobbyists can follow machine-language programs step by step as their instructions pass through the CPU. They can envision the changes in state of the whole system as being produced by specific actions of the CPU. And if they suspect that there is a bug in the hardware they can pull out an oscilloscope and see whether the CPU is doing what it should in response to a given instruction. They can figure out where the signals should be going, they can collect their own evidence for what is going wrong, trap and fix the bug themselves.

Again and again in my interviewing I heard about the pleasures of debugging—of "going in with meters and scopes and tracking it down." The procedure exhilarates. With every successfully tracked bug comes an affirmation of direct control over the machine. The issue of control was often explicitly recognized by the hobbyists we interviewed. But they lacked a language for naming a second issue which has to do with a notion referred to as "syntonicity" within the psychoanalytic tradition.

Syntonicity implies that we should look for "body-to-body" identification in every powerful relationship with a technology—the body of the person and the body of the machine. It implies that we should understand the appeal of machine language in terms of people's ability to identify with what is happening inside the machine. The CPU of the hobbyist computer lends itself to personal identification with its primary action: moving something that is conceptually almost a physical object (a byte of information) in and out of some thing (a register) that is almost a physical place.

The metaphor is concrete and spatial. One can imagine finding the bytes, feeling them, doing something very simple to them, and passing them on. For many of the people that we met in the hobbyist culture, getting into this kind of identification feels safe. It makes the machine feet real. There is a third issue raised by the hobbyists' relationship to the CPU. It is an aesthetic one. The generation of hobby computers that was born in the 1970s are very primitive machines.

The hobbyist thinks of much about them as "klugey," a computerist's way of saying that one is dealing with a compromise, a collection of patches whose structure has been dictated by arbitrary corporate decisions, by economic necessities. The corner of the hobbyist machine that seems to them to have the greatest "intellectual integrity," that distills what they feel to be a tradition of some of the best ideas in computer science, that comes closest to being "clean," is the CPU. And so it is natural for the hobbyist to seek the closest possible contact with it.

10

Information Management

Information is important, we cannot operate without it. But more than this, we are discovering that our ability to process it by increasingly sophisticated technological means is fundamentally changing the way that employees perceive their organizational environment. The consequences of this could be either to break down established functional controls or indeed to enhance them by becoming super-efficient. Much will depend upon the characteristics of the organization before implementation. As firms become increasingly 'information dependent' we need to identify the perceptual relation-ship between ourselves and the information we use.

How, for instance, can we possibly design an adequate information system if we do not understand the nature of information? The answer to this lies, in part, with the conventional wisdom of the day. Managers, like everybody else, develop their views through exposure to established ideas. Thus the way in which they understand information will influence the way in which they treat it. Such conventional wisdom is coloured by the technicians on the one hand and the user's own experience on the other. Anecdotal prescriptions abound as guidelines to the way forward for all who care to listen. These arise from a blanket of professional and academic thinking which surrounds the business environment and provides remedies for action. We could categorize all these ideas into two bodies of thought, two paradigms.

The first could be termed the resource-driven paradigm. This is because its central theme in understanding information is the continuity and consistency of the information itself. It is very much in vogue at present. The second body of thought is the perception-driven paradigm. Information is seen as an abstract concept, the product of individual perception. It is a temporary phenomenon and as such belongs only to the receiver.

The difference is not merely one of academic debate. Managements adopting one or the other can affect the design of their organizations. If information is considered to be a resource then resulting systems are usually more centrally controlled, the assumption being that all information is corporate property. Whereas information considered to be personally owned is seen as being outside the formal structure. Within the framework of this paradigm the view of information is coloured by its use as a resource.

There is a range of propositions available which seeks to explain information. Each proposition has a consequence for organizational design. Listed below are those major themes and what their implications might be on business. Herbert A. Simon took the view that information, along with energy, constitute the two basic currencies of our society. We need energy to breathe, to move, to think, to live. But this alone is not enough. We need to know when to breathe, when to move and how to think. Information provides us with that knowledge. To adopt this perspective is to interpret information as an independent entity. It is all about us waiting to picked up and used. There may be minor variations in its interpretation by different individuals, but consistency can be easily achieved through better training. Specific sets of information, such as finance information, are given a unique value by organizations which is usually based upon departmental rather than individual need.

Information is then tied into that framework and cannot be used legitimately within any other context, thus guarding its consistency. What is excluded, therefore, is an important role for the individual receiver. This is not to suggest that information cannot be perceived by individuals. Psychologists such as Anderson and Bower have long been aware of the importance of information reception in determining an individual's behaviour. However, information can be received automatically without an individual having to understand it. For example, through training an employee could process production statistics without knowing what they mean. In this case it is the functional process (through its formal procedure) that is acting as the receiver rather than the individual. An accounting process, for instance, responds to specific inputs without anyone having to understand them.

A motor car responds to certain information transmitted through mechanisms such as the throttle, steering wheel or brake. Both of these examples are designed to act as receivers to specific information. By implication, information can be transmitted to any receiver that logs into the particular transmission. In the same way as a radio picks up a station when it is switched on, the right form will pick up the right information. And like radio waves, information is omnipresent, only needing the correct tuning. Such a view allows information the continuity and consistency required to be regarded as a resource. It also allows a further proposition. The design of any formal information system must assume that information does not change during transmission. It can, however, be transformed from data or other information sets before transmission. Within such a framework it is the transmitting functions (departments, processes, etc.) which are considered to be the main determinants.

The information receiving functions (also departments, processes, etc.) are designed to link into the operational needs of the transmitter functions. Each function, however, can be both transmitter and receiver of information, and together with other functions will form part of a integrated network. The functions are tied by their simultaneous roles as information receivers and transmitters, thereby being prevented as much as possible from deviancy in their information usage. Consequence. Business organizations are driven by those functions which transmit information.

The higher the value that a particular set of information is given, the more important will be its relating transmitter function. For example, the finance department could both transmit and receive information. Indeed, each job function within that department could also do the same. A cost clerk, for instance, receives information from the factory floor which he then processes into other information and transmits to some other source, perhaps management.

The value of the information he processes will depend upon the utility his organization has placed upon it. If the utility is high, then the prestige attached to the transmitting function will also be high irrespective of job complexity. In the same way, if a department has a great number of important information transmitters within its control, then it too will be prestigious and possess influence. Why certain sets of information are prestigious and others are not will depend, amongst other things, upon the organization's political processes. The perception-driven paradigm does not consider information to be a resource. Individuals or groups are seen to own their information. What belongs to the organization are the data sets, the facts and figures specific to certain functions. For instance, data on how an organization is performing in its market quite obviously belong to that firm.

How well that data is used is dependent upon the individual's own competence in interpreting it. Management can control this indirectly through training, but they cannot directly control the thought processes which turns data into information. Once again, there is a collection of propositions or ideas about information which formulate a general approach. Adherence to this paradigm, as in the previous paradigm, may not necessarily be by conviction but rather by default because people not treating information as a resource automatically form part of this group.

However, there are others who are members by conviction. Information is said to be receiver-dependent in that any set of information can be considered to be information only if it is recognised as having value by a particular individual. Thus a river flooding may be information to someone who lives on its banks but of no consequence to someone living several miles away. It would be difficult, therefore, to understand information as group or organization property since its determination is subjective.

Management teams have implemented computer technology and in so doing also developed their information sets into a resource. They experience problems, usually some time after a successful launch, and then abandon using their technology in an integrative manner, returning to the 'islands' approach (that is, a computer system, perhaps physically integrated through networks, etc. but perceptually segregated into different functional areas). Information is no longer seen as a resource; indeed its treatment as such is often seen as the culprit and not the technology itself. Both paradigms recognize a difference between data and information. Computer personnel, for example, have long known of the distinction. Information is seen by them as processed data.

The two are interrelated, data being the input to a process, and information the output. In the same way that an output of one system can form the input of another, information from one system can form the data of another. This is consistent with treating information as a resource. Perceptually-conceived information on the other hand is not the consequence of a formalized process. Data are a factor, but then so are other aspects such as individual traits, culture, structure and political processes. The relationship between data and information is, therefore, not so strong. This contradicts the objectives implied by the creation of management information systems and data processing.

The former allows the individual access to established information, whilst the latter converts data into information. Since the production of information cannot be formalized there is no point in trying to achieve it. Systems should, therefore, be designed to produce the most accurate and readable data in order to enhance easy conversion into information. When Ligomenides describes information as a fundamental force, he should be referring to data. Levitan, on the other hand, is correct in claiming information to be dynamic and continuously evolving.

The logic of these two views can be seen when data and information are differentiated. It is only data which is time-independent, and therefore unchanging and static—a fundamental force. By this we mean that data retains a constant empirical value: a fact is a fact and cannot be altered. Information, on the other hand, can be altered and changed. It is time-dependent and thus its value can alter from one moment to the next. It is dynamic and evolving because it is determined by an individual's perception. It is, indeed, time and utility which transform data into information. If at a particular time a set of data is useful to an individual then it can be described as information. Equally, at another time the same set of data may not have utility and therefore not be information.

The data themselves have not changed in any way, remaining always constant. What has changed is the individual's perception of those data. Information is in reality the consequence of a complex psychological process which transforms perceived data into usable thought inputs. It is, therefore, data which the individual receives from the environment, the brain which transforms these data into information. No formal system can directly pre-empt this stage; thus no formal system can transform data into information. Data can be transformed into different data, transmitted and received. For example, production data submitted to the cost department and processed into second generation costed production data, which are in turn submitted to the financial director.

Information is transformed, in part, from data; it can only be received and never transmitted. The financial director may attach value to costed production data and thus receive it as information. If he/she passes it on, it will once again be as data, perhaps refined into third generation data. There cannot be information systems because information is so transient. The individual's subjectivity, which can be developed by training and formal procedure, determines what is information. At another time that perception may be different. Information systems cannot work in this way. Their assumption must be that information is not transient but consistent. Quite obviously information systems do exist in one form or another. They may not be what they claim to be but they are nevertheless working. Is it worth arguing the difference?

The answer to that lies within ourselves. Our actions and behaviour, and consequently our organizations, are governed by our perceptions. If, therefore, we understand information to be permanent rather than transient then how we organize ourselves will be coloured by that. We will design systems which use information as a resource and expect it to be totally consistent.

Structural implications

The difference between these two paradigms may seem subtle, and in terms of information usage it may well be. However, NBS research indicates that the effects upon organizational design can be major. Structural characteristics consequent upon individually-owned information, for instance, can adopt two extremes. On the one hand they can be organic and informal (adhocracies) whereby all members are seen as contributing equally, each possessing a particular range of techniques to interpret data, whilst at the other extreme there are formal and mechanistic organizations (bureaucracies).

The rigidities of structure stifle any use of information as a resource, so by default such processes are left to the individual. These contrast with the resource-driven paradigm in which the structural characteristics of organizations are seen to be centrally orientated, with spheres of influence at the periphery, their importance dependent upon the perceived value of particular sets of information.

The wider implications of information

The development of an organization orientated toward the resource-driven concept of information is well known, and many large firms are aligned in that direction. A sophisticated network is established, more than likely computerized, accessing and distributing information. Particular attention is paid to ensuring standardization of information sets. For example, a piece of costing information is so devised that it can be used by accounts, marketing and production. These organizations treat all information as their property, attaching to it a value like any other asset.

This denies the employee any sense of ownership and tends to detach them from the work process with consequential inefficiencies evolving. It is asserted, that a motivated staff is a contented and efficient staff. One important way to motivate is to give the individual responsibility within their job. Such responsibility is manifest in how much ability a person will be given to determine the information need of their particular function. To standardize information in the way that many corporate systems do, takes away that fundamental element of responsibility.

Levitan, on the other hand, would claim this to be an inevitable consequence of increasingly sophisticated corporate structures. In addition, Karen Levitan and others imply that information which is not used as a resource is inferior. On the contrary, one could argue that giving the individual ownership could result in a greater entrepreneurial drive. Standardization is the killer of innovation. It is difficult to conceive of any substantial organization, however, where such a degree of individuality could be tolerated. Their size demands a need for cohesion through standardized practice. Therefore it is only in the smaller establishments where such freedom would work.

Large organizations which do not treat their information as a resource still exist. Their mechanisms of control, however, are not informal or organic. Indeed, the realities are the converse. Individuality is stifled by greater control, rather than less. No-one is trusted to use information for the organization's good without formal control procedures.

Classic examples of such organizations are to be found within the civil service or large quasi-government institutions such as the post office. It has been suggested that there is a relationship between the way in which a firm uses its information and its structure. A matrix can be established differentiating organizations in terms of how they treat their information and the consequential structural characteristics. If, for example, information is plotted against size (another important contingent of organization) four major structural types could be identified. Each is the outcome of the way a particular firm uses its information.

On the vertical axis of the matrix are the two extremes of information. On the horizontal axis are the two extremes of organizational size. Both information and size are considered to be contingents, that is variables which affect the characteristics of an organization.

The four possible combinations of these two variables determine four organizational structures. Thus each structure is an ideal for each of the four combinations. For example, a managerial structure is the appropriate structure for a large firm using information as a resource.

Structure parameters:
Managerial: larger in size with central/top control but with more departmental integration
Bureaucratic: larger in size with formal structure and a diversified control
Technical/professional: smaller in size with a professional body and formal structure
Entrepreneurial: centrally controlled but with less formal structure and smaller in size

Fig. 1. Information/structure matrix

Research into the validity of such a matrix is by no means complete. There is evidence from the NBS regional survey, for example, that such a correlation does indeed exist. In general, the more successful managerial-style firms tend to treat their information as a resource, whilst the more successful entrepreneurial organizations tend to treat their information as a perceptual phenomenon, and so on. It is not yet certain whether the matrix is predictive, that is implying combinations which are not successful.

There is sufficient evidence, however, to support the claim that information usage affects organizational structure. The issue of information is much more than whether or not it is a resource. Information is indeed the essence of an organization, shaping and determining its structure. For example, bureaucratic organizations could hot effectively treat information as a resource because their mechanisms could not control it that way.

A technical/professional organization, on the other hand, is better able to handle its information as a resource because of its structural characteristics. The implication is that there should be a natural balance between the design of an organization and its information structure. Where this has not been achieved it is because managers are not matching the structure of their organizations with an appropriate usage of information. NBS research has also shown that the implementation of computer technology can worsen any potential for imbalance. This is perhaps because of two factors.

— The characteristics of the technology itself do tend to enhance resource-driven rather than perception-driven information. Secondly, the greater volume of information generated makes the problem more apparent.

If the matrix in Figure 1 is valid then there is neither a right nor a wrong way to control information: much depends upon the individual circumstances. Resource-driven information and perception-driven information are opposite extremes of one continuum. Management teams were grasping eagerly at the new computer technology as a solution to their efficiency problems. There were at that time forces in the environment—market, political, social or economic—with which the traditional methods of organization could not cope; it was believed that the computer would provide all the answers. In the space of that time many colleagues began to discover that the impact of computer technology seemed to be contradictory.

On the one hand, it did tend to improve efficiency, whilst on the other it was not always so certain that an improvement in effectiveness followed. It seemed that underlying, and as yet not understood, forces were at work. Departments employing the same technology were more or less successful than others. Business organizations with all the ingredients of success and implementing computers to further fuel their growth quite often experienced failure a few years later.

Since those early days there has been considerable discussion and research on the impact of information technology. It seemed that the perceptual aspects of organization were not merely misunderstood but often ignored, and thus we were not able to understand fully the implications of introducing information technology. We now realize that not only does it have an impact on the way we run organizations, it also has an impact on our behaviour. There is a readily understood physical aspect of any firm and a more abstract, perceptual aspect which arises from the way that people behave as a collective. Information technology is not the only agent in this process, but because of its particular characteristics it can have an extraordinarily powerful effect on both these aspects.

One of two main objectives of this book, therefore, is to underline the importance of the relationship between information technology (and to a lesser extent general technology) and its organizational structure. The two are inseparable. Models that seek to understand either technology or organization must do so within the framework created by this relationship. Otherwise an essential factor leading to an appropriate analysis will be missed.

The other main objective is to produce a model which can do this. Unlike many of its predecessors, the model will not concentrate -on the functional or hierarchical nature of organizations but rather on the dichotomy between the physical and perceptual aspects. This exists whether or not there is information technology present, but in many cases the implementation of such technology can exacerbate potential dysfunctional forces existing between the two. In effect there are two organizations—a physical organization and a perceptual or virtual organization. The impact that information technology can have on the sometimes tenuous relationship existing between the two can be quite profound.

The model explores thoroughly this relationship. It proposes virtual organization as the antithesis of physical organization. That is abstract, unseeing and existing within the minds of those who form a particular organization. The point being that because the framework of virtual organization is often subjective and open to many different perceptual interpretations, it is difficult for anyone to establish an appropriate response to it. This makes it no less real; nor does it reduce the need to respond to it. Left unattended the effects of virtual organization can be quite catastrophic, especially if stimulated by the impact of information technology. This has considerable significance for the practitioner, especially those who have introduced, or are thinking of introducing, information technology.

The model suggests that for a firm to survive there would ideally exist a dynamic equilibrium between the two organisations which has been termed the organizational balance. Anything which upsets this balance, such as the introduction of information technology, has to be compensated for by proactive action of management. If managers do not understand, nor indeed perceive the existence of virtual organization, then they will not be able take the appropriate measures. Long-term structural weaknesses or even total failure of the business can result. Demonstrating the existence of virtual organization can be problematic. By definition it cannot be observed directly since it exists only in the mind. At best one could ask a selection of staff for their impressions and make certain deductions, but these are likely to be dubious and tainted with the researcher's own perceptions. As such there has deliberately been no direct empirical research to establish the foundations of this model. Support for its validity has been sought in three other areas.

Firstly, there is indirect empirical data gained from several research projects conducted at the Newcastle Business School. This comprises a study over two years by Stuart Maguire and myself into eighty-five small to large firms in all sectors of the North East. We examined particularly the strategy that firms employed to implement and control their information technology. The data were gathered through a series of observations, interviews and involvement in the process. The argument for using these data rather than dedicated data is that they should be less contrived.

Secondly, there is support to be gained from relevant personal experience. Although many would find this approach invalid because it does not comply with traditional or conventional ideas about research data, there is an increasing acceptance that such data can prove useful. In the social sciences, for example, Duke argued that such an approach (amongst others) would make a valuable contribution to the understanding of social experience. We return to a more traditional style in support of the main arguments.

That is, rather than gathering empirical evidence first and then developing a model, we should develop the model first from experiential instincts and then support it with data. This is put forward in the belief that to pursue the traditional methods of data-first research would not produce the generic model necessary to achieve the objectives set above. We have become unimaginative in our ideas about organization because we have been blinkered by too many sets of data.

How the book is structured in terms of presenting a logical argument takes on a greater significance than if it were based merely upon direct empirical data. It requires presentation of basic argument, counter-argument and a compromise position which leads the reader forward to the logical conclusion. This is the dialectic which involves thesis, antithesis and synthesis. This overview, therefore, should not only cover the background to the book's major arguments and supportive material, but also provide the reader with a basic chapter plan.

The importance of information is reflected in its ability, through the appropriate technology, to corrupt departmental boundaries. This chapter, therefore, proposes that it is better to understand an organization as a network of information flows, which is itself set within other network flows of region, market, industry and so on. Such a perspective is underlined by many firms accessing information beyond their established functional boundaries. Within the organization, this could involve different departments accessing a common pool of information from the company database.

Externally, employees can gain entrance to public databases such as Prestel, which are run by autonomous bodies. The drive is towards centralization and hence better management control. Paradoxically, the opposite is being encouraged, whereby every user has the potential to access information which enables them to operate more efficiently, and also to do so outside the control of their manager. Under these conditions it is difficult for managers to control not only who reads and writes what but also, and perhaps more importantly, who knows what. Large amounts of information can be processed and communicated via a network without managers ever being able to determine whether it runs contrary to their own policy.

Security has, as a consequence, become an extremely important issue. The more the dissemination of information is allowed, the more likely control mechanisms will become corrupted. In simple terms, data are facts, whilst information is the consequence of interpretation. What is information to some is not to others, and it is the subjective interpretation of what is and is not valuable which has caused managements considerable problems. The control parameters on the organization's database are based upon managers' own perceptions of its value as information which may not coincide with that of a potential intruder or misuser. But more than this, individual employees' perception of their information stock widens because of their greater accessibility to the information network. As a consequence, their perception of their own job parameters also widens beyond what management might think desirable.

What is information technology?

In so far as control over information forms the basis of managerial authority, the technologies which process it are inherently political. Indeed, business organizations are under pressure to change their decision-making structures as a direct consequence of information technology implementation. These 'subversive' effects on organizational structures are not immediately obvious to management. They arise as the new technology changes established work practices and consequently creates different relationships on the organization's information network. Management is then faced with a dual threat:

1. A new pool of knowledge outside its formal control structures. Employees are able to access information without hindrance.
2. Power is shifting from line managers to those who, control the information technology, such as the technicians in the DP departments or knowledgeable users.

Management's response has been weak and incremental. The control of information generated by computer technologies increasingly reflected the new power structures that these technologies established. On the one hand, functional control (allocation, budget, etc.) remains with general management. On the other, operational control (how and what is processed) is left to the technicians in the DP departments. The pervasive nature of the technology spreading through all levels of the organization established those who controlled it as important powerbrokers or gatekeepers.

Newcastle Business School research has shown that senior managers are often unwilling to become involved. They served their apprenticeship in computerless or, at best, early mainframe-driven organizations and therefore do not always fully understand or appreciate the new technologies. Despite the obvious need for new control structures the traditional methods are adhered to. The dichotomy between the established management structures and the changed (and changing) technological structures is therefore maintained and often worsened. Such opposing forces create a complex environment and place considerable constraints on management action.

The dichotomy quickly becomes institutionalized. Lack of management action causes other user employees to perceive themselves as powerless in any dealings with the new technologies. This serves to enhance the influence of the technicians and is built into the organization's structures. Business action then tends to become increasingly inflexible; user managers are reluctant to take risks in an environment they do not understand, and many operational decisions are left to the technicians. This area of decision-taking is also built into the firm's task structure. Meanwhile the new networked systems demand increasing flexibility in order to work but are instead being faced with increasingly inflexible and decision-shy managements. To appreciate the nature of this threat and how profound its impact can be on the organization, it is essential to grasp the characteristics of technology, in particular its integrative nature with any social entity whether it be an organization or something else.

The relationship between technology and an organization has, indeed, been thoroughly explored. It is obvious that a firm's structure is characterized by the many forces emanating from its operating environment. What is perhaps not so obvious is that technology is one of those forces. This is because it is quite often seen as a locally owned, physical resource.

The machine on the shopfloor is just that and not part of a more complex social process. Within the framework of this perspective technology is a tool, totally predictable and controllable by management. The physical technology alone (e.g. machinery or computers) will not explain how organizations are affected by it. As Weizenbaum suggested, a computer or telecommunication system (or any form of technology) is merely junk without the people to relate to them. It is how those people relate to their technology, how they use it, their perceptions of it and so on, that are important.

These aspects govern not only the technological process but also the characteristics of the organization structure. In the same way, structure should not be seen merely in a physical sense. The dividing of a firm into departments and functions, although of interest, does not capture the essence of an organization, which is to be found within the minds of its employees. The relationship between technology and structure is thus not physical but perceptual because it is within people's minds that the links are made. Our understanding of such techno- behavioural forces is not great. This is partly because of the hegemonic view of business organizations as hierarchies in organization theory. It would seem, therefore, that we have not as yet learnt to examine organizations in an appropriate dimension which can highlight the effects of information and its technology. The traditionalist's view of an organization is typically presented by Schein as a rational co-ordination of activities.

This emphasizes the hierarchical and functionally-bound aspects. Butler, on the other hand, discussed the lack of understanding of such models determining that all the interrelationships are not adequately identified. They tend to portray firms as static entities without the turbulence of opposing forces. In particular, technology is seen as a side issue, if at all, and not central to the fundamental mechanisms of an organization. A more appropriate model in Butler's mind is Udy's, which puts technology at the centre of an interactive environment of production objectives, social setting, physical exigencies and work organization.

Technology, not the structure, sets the constraints ('trade-offs' as Butler calls them) upon an organization. Thus a certain structure can be considered suitable for a given technology. For example, a company using mass production techniques, such as Ford, will best be structured to suit the needs of mass production technology. The relationship does not end there, however, as in Pugh's model, because he suggests that it is technology which drives the organization.

Where this model fails is in not identifying with sufficient clarity the perceptual aspects of an organization's technology. It is only within this domain that useful links can be established between technology and structure. The perceptual aspects of structure must also be emphasized for this to be successful since within any physical domain technology can only be seen as a resource and structure as a functional framework. It will then demonstrate that employees' perception of their structure determines the consequent structural characteristics. This chapter also suggests, however, that the relationship is two-way, in that an established structure can itself influence and change the perception of the employees.

The impact of information technology is then again introduced. Already have established that such technology can change the way that individuals perceive their environments. A link with the present chapter is that since an employee's perception of the environment can be changed through information technology, his/her perception of the firm's structure must also change. The post-implementation structure that emerges may be profoundly different from any previous structure. This control-theoretic view of information tech-nology's impact is particularly relevant to the devolution of management authority.

The impact of the new technology may radically affect the power structure or the political relationships between management and staff (but not the functional relationships) thus creating an imbalance between the perceptual and physical aspects of the organization. Through the perceptual domain, information technology has also infiltrated the cultural base of organizations and has thus had the potential to alter cultural objectives, which are the consequence of existing value systems. For example, it may be the formal objective of one firm to produce good quality products at the expense of higher profits. This objective has arisen from the organization's culture, but any form of technology, especially information technology, is not sensitive to cultural requirements. Managers may try to fit the technology into their companies but it is generally within a framework provided by the physical domain.

The objectives suitable for the technology do not always match existing cultural needs. To seek an explanation of the technological impact, therefore, we should no longer look at organizations in terms of departments and divisions. Any boundary established by such a definition may be rendered irrelevant. It is more sensible to consider an organization as a network of perceptual maps, dependent on an information network which is itself part of a wider network within the region, market, industry and so on. The need for such an outlook is underlined by the number of firms accessing information beyond their established functional boundaries. Internally, this involves different departments accessing a common pool from the company database; externally, employees gaining entrance to public databases such as Prestel. It is increasingly difficult to understand these organizations as physically controllable entities.

The problem, however, extends beyond management. If it is accepted that our models of organization are also too limiting because of their inability to highlight the dichotomy between the perceptual and the physical, then we must develop new models, which is one of the major proposals of the book. In order to do this we must first establish an appropriate methodology.

The analysis which must be pursued is wide-ranging. It extends beyond the convenient boundaries that traditional theory has established. The tidy logic of an organization reaches only into the physical domain, beyond that is a vast perceptual arena which can be understood only as a network of relationships.

The dynamic element

The point has already been made that an organization is a fluid and ever-changing entity. The components so far discussed form the framework of the organization but they are no more than boxes in an analyst's model. Other forces exist which breathe life into these concepts. They can be termed as the dynamics of an organization. People are the organization, and as such their perceptions, aspirations, alliances and conflicts form an important dynamic. For managers the issue is how such diverse forces can be controlled. They can only directly access the physical domain and therefore have to attempt to manipulate this in some way to have any impact upon the perceptual domain.

One area, however, which allows a controllable linkage between the two domains is the information network. The quality, quantity and content of information, amongst other factors such as historicity, will determine an individual or group perception. On the other hand, the network itself can be physically manipulated thus affecting the quality, quantity and content of information. Its control is therefore of considerable importance to management. Its particular emphasis is on the use of computer technology to generate information.

Other forms of generated information through manual methods can also be controlled as information management, but because of the computer's ability to generate so much information other important forces come into play which are not present in a manual system. The ways in which employees regard the characteristics of their information will determine in part the nature of their information network and ultimately the organization structure itself.

Management must be aware of this and develop strategies through training and computer technology implementation which are sensitive to this. Information, however, is only part of the process. On its own it is not particularly a dynamic of the organization. Individuals may receive information and do nothing with it. A firm, therefore, does not change because of information. Information must be used. Action or behaviour is the consequence of information being used in the physical domain. In the perceptual domain, information being used is manifest through the decision process.

There are no actions without decisions, no matter how minor or simple they may be, so that an organization, which can be analysed in terms of its actions, is driven by its decision processes. In any context there is no such thing as an individual decision, even if the person involved is on a deserted island. Especially within a complex social process such as an organization, a decision is based upon a range of perceptual and physical influences.

A person's experience coming to bear in a decision, for example, is the consequence of previous interactions with other people and institutions. Therefore one cannot fully control the decision process by controlling those individuals who are seen to own it. Their actions might be constrained but the source of their decisions is to be found in the perceptual domain. This is particularly important when such processes are affected by computer technology.

Managers tend to develop mechanisms around the physical aspects of the technology and ignore the wider perceptual impact. It then places these ideas in the context of the other major components of a firm, in particular the information network, by highlighting the close relationship between a decision and information. We have so far developed the framework of an organizational structure dominated by two domains: the physical and the perceptual. In a similar fashion to matter and anti-matter, their forces conflict and contradict one another. Management must maintain the narrow ground between the two, because it is only here that long-term stability is established. At this point the forces of both domains are in equilibrium, which for the purposes of the model has been termed balance.

The achievement of such a state is one of the key outcomes to be identified. The domination of one domain over another could lead to long-term instability, the degree of which depends upon a range of factors unique to specific organisations. For example, if there is no balance and an organization is dominated by its physical domain, then its short-term survival, at least, will depend upon how effective that domain is in dealing with the firm's particular environment.

In the longer term, however, all firms must achieve an equilibrium whether the dominant domain is in tune with the environment or not. This is because the cost of not achieving equilibrium will be manifest in the dysfunctional relationship between the two domains. Forces will come into play that will undermine stability. It shows a complex social entity driven by an abstract relationship between two sets of forces. Much of this arena exists within the minds of the employees, of course, but like other societal phenomena its logic extends beyond them.

The forces can exist independently of particular individuals in that they are perpetuated by culture, technology and training. Individuals may come and go, some people may contribute more than others, but the logic of the organization as a separate entity remains consistent. It is proposed that an, organization can pass a significant point, the virtuality point, whereby its survival does not depend upon a particular set of individuals. This is a different world from the one portrayed by established theory. It comprises many of the same elements, such as structure and technology, recognized by conventional wisdom, but it is the perspective, the way in which those elements are arranged, that is different. The emphasis is upon a force field relationship rather than the aspects of one domain or another. By having this different framework, we can also analyse the effects of change in other ways. In particular, the impact of information technology is shown to have a far wider effect upon organizations than the traditional models may lead us to suppose.

Information is one of those misunderstood concepts. Yet it is at the same time one of the most used. We go to the bus station to seek information from timetables. We obtain information from government offices, banks, supermarkets, leisure centres, libraries and even the police ply us with more. Newspapers, television and the radio present us with their own ideas of what information should be. We all understand and deal with this accordingly when extracting news from the media, for example. Yet many of our organisations consider information to be something more. They see it as a vital resource, to be managed like any other valuable resource. How it is used and disseminated through the available technology can determine how efficient, and indeed effective, an organisation is.

Information is important, we cannot operate without it. But more than this, we are discovering that our ability to process it by increasingly sophisticated technological means is fundamentally changing the way that employees perceive their organisational environment. The consequences of this could be either to break down established functional controls or indeed to enhance them by becoming super-efficient. As firms become increasingly 'information dependent' we need to identify the perceptual relationship between ourselves and the information we use. How, for instance, can we possibly design an adequate information system if we do not understand the nature of information? The answer to this lies, in part, with the conventional wisdom of the day. Managers, like everybody else, develop their views through exposure to established ideas. Thus the way in which they understand information will influence the way in which they treat it. Such conventional wisdom is coloured by the technicians on the one hand and the user's own experience on the other. Anecdotal prescriptions abound as guidelines to the way forward for all who care to listen. These arise from a blanket of professional and academic thinking which surrounds the business environment and provides remedies for action. We could categorise all these ideas into two bodies of thought, two paradigms. The first could be termed the resource-driven paradigm. This is because its central theme in understanding information is the continuity and consistency of the information itself. The second body of thought is the perception-driven paradigm. Information is seen as an abstract concept, the product of individual perception. It is a temporary phenomenon and as such belongs only to the receiver. The difference is not merely one of academic debate. Managements adopting one or the other can affect the design of their organisations.

Within the framework of resource-driven paradigm the view of information is coloured by its use as a resource. Like any other resource it can be tapped at any time with the certainty of achieving a predictable value from it. Information is regarded as unchanging, and therefore can be easily accommodated into a firm's formal procedure.

Herbert A. Simon took the view that information, along with energy, constitute the two basic currencies of our society. We need energy to breathe, to move, to think, to live. But this alone is not enough. We need to know when to breathe, when to move and how to think. Information provides us with that knowledge. To adopt this perspective is to interpret information as an independent entity. It is all about us waiting to be picked up and used. There may be minor variations in its interpretation by different individuals, but consistency can be easily achieved through better training.

Specific sets of information, such as finance information, are given a unique value by organisations which is usually based upon departmental rather than individual need. Particular information is thus attached to particular departments. This allows information to be generally accessible because perceptions of it are bound by the formal departmental framework. Information is then tied into that framework and cannot be used legitimately within any other context, thus guarding its consistency. What is excluded, therefore, is an important role for the individual receiver. This is not to suggest that information cannot be perceived by individuals. Information can be received automatically without an individual having to understand it. For example, through training an employee could process production statistics without knowing what they mean. In this case it is the functional process that is acting as the receiver rather than the individual.

An accounting process, for instance, responds to specific inputs without anyone having to understand them. A motor car responds to certain information transmitted through mechanisms such as the throttle, steering wheel or brake. Both of these examples are designed to act as receivers to specific information. By implication, information can be transmitted to any receiver that logs into the particular transmission. In the same way as a radio picks up a station when it is switched on, the right form will pick up the right information.

The design of any formal information system must assume that information does not change during transmission. It can, however, be transformed from data or other information sets before transmission. Within such a framework it is the transmitting functions which are considered to be the main determinants. The information receiving functions are designed to link into the operational needs of the transmitter functions. Each function, however, can be both transmitter and receiver of information, and together with other functions will form part of an integrated network. The functions are tied by their simultaneous roles as information receivers and transmitters, thereby being prevented as much as possible from deviancy in their information usage.

Business organisations are driven by those functions which transmit information. The higher the value that a particular set of information is given, the more important will be its relating transmitter function. For example, the finance department could both transmit and receive information. Indeed, each job function within that department could also do the same. A cost clerk, for instance, receives information from the factory floor which he then processes into other information and transmits to some other source, perhaps management.

The value of the information processes will depend upon the utility his organisation has placed upon it. If the utility is high, then the prestige attached to the transmitting function will also be high, irrespective of the job complexity.

In the same way, if a department has a great number of important information transmitters within its control, then it too will be prestigious and possess influence. Why certain sets of information are prestigious and others are not will depend, amongst other things, upon the organisation's political processes.

The perception-driven paradigm does not consider information to be a resource. Individuals or groups are seen to own their information. What belongs to the organisation are the data sets, the facts and figures specific to certain functions. For instance, data on how an organisation is performing in its market quite obviously belong to that firm. How well that data is used is dependent upon the individual's own competence in interpreting it. Management can control this indirectly through training, but they cannot directly control the thought processes which turns data into information. Once again, there is a collection of propositions or ideas about information which formulate a general approach. Adherence to this paradigm, as in the previous paradigm, may not necessarily be by conviction but rather by default because people not treating information as a resource automatically form part of this group. However, there are others who are members by conviction. Infor-mation is said to be receiver-dependent in that any set of information can be considered to be information only if it is recognised as having value by a particular individual. Thus a river flooding may be information to someone who lives on its banks but of no consequence to someone living several miles away.

It would be difficult, therefore, to understand information as group or organisation property since its determination is subjective. Management teams have implemented computer technology and in so doing have also developed their information sets into a resource. They experience problems, usually some time after a successful launch, and then abandon using their technology in an integrative manner, returning to the 'islands' approach (that is, a computer system, perhaps physically integrated through networks, etc. but perceptually segregated into different functional areas). Information is no longer seen as a resource; indeed its treatment as such is often seen as the culprit and not the technology itself.

Both paradigms recognise a difference between data and information. Computer personnel, for example, have long known of the distinction. Information is seen by them as processed data. The two are interrelated, data being the input to a process, and information the output. In the same way that an output of one system can form the input of another, information from one system can form the data of another. This is consistent with treating information as a resource. Perceptually-conceived information on the other hand is not the consequence of a formalised process. Data are a factor, but then so are other aspects such as individual traits, culture, structure and political processes.

The relationship between data and information is, therefore, not so strong. This contradicts the objectives implied by the creation of management information systems and data processing. The former allows the individual access to established information, whilst the latter converts data into information. Since the production of information cannot be formalised there is no point in trying to achieve it. Systems should, therefore, be designed to produce the most accurate and readable data in order to enhance easy conversion into information.

When Ligomenides describes information as a fundamental force, he should be referring to data. Levitan, on the other hand, is correct in claiming information to be dynamic and continuously evolving. The logic of these two views can be seen when data and information are differentiated. It is only data which is time-independent, and therefore unchanging and static—a fundamental force. By this we mean that data retains a constant empirical value: a fact is a fact and cannot be altered. Information, on the other hand, can be altered and changed. It is time- dependent and thus its value can alter from one moment to the next. It is dynamic and evolving because it is determined by an individual's perception.

It is, indeed, time and utility which transform data into information. If at a particular time a set of data is useful to an individual then it can be described as information. Equally, at another time the same set of data may not have utility and therefore not be information. The data themselves have not changed in any way, remaining always constant. What has changed is the individual's perception of those data. Information is in reality the consequence of a complex psychological process which transforms perceived data into usable thought inputs.

It is, therefore, data which the individual receives from the environment, the brain which transforms these data into information. No formal system can directly pre-empt this stage; thus no formal system can transform data into information.

Data can be transformed into different data, transmitted and received. For example, production data submitted to the cost department and processed into second generation costed production data, which are in turn submitted to the financial director. Information is transformed, in part, from data; it can only be received and never transmitted. The financial director may attach value to costed production data and thus receive it as information. If he/she passes it on, it will once again be as data, perhaps refined into third generation data. There cannot be information systems because information is so transient.

The individual's subjectivity, which can be developed by training and formal procedure, determines what is information. At another time that perception may be different. Information systems cannot work in this way. Their assumption must be that information is not transient but consistent.

Quite obviously information systems do exist in one form or another. They may not be what they claim to be but they are nevertheless working. Is it worth arguing the difference? The answer to that lies within ourselves. Our actions and behaviour, and consequently our organisations, are governed by our perceptions. If, therefore, we understand information to be permanent rather than transient then how we organise ourselves will be coloured by that. We will design systems which use information as a resource and expect it to be totally consistent.

The difference between the two paradigms may seem subtle, and in terms of information usage it may well be. However, NBS research indicates that the effects upon organisational design can be major.

Structural characteristics consequent upon individually- owned information, for instance, can adopt two extremes. On the one hand they can be organic and informal (adhocracies) whereby all members are seen as contributing equally, each possessing a particular range of techniques to interpret data, whilst at the other extreme there are formal and mechanistic organisations (bureaucracies). The rigidities of structure stifle any use of information as a resource, so by default such processes are left to the individual. These contrast with the resource-driven paradigm in which the structural characteristics of organisations are seen to be centrally orientated, with spheres of influence at the periphery, their importance dependent upon the perceived value of particular sets of information.

Wider Implications of Information

The development of an organisation orientated toward the resource-driven concept of information is well known, and many large firms are aligned in that direction.

A sophisticated network is established, more than likely computerised, accessing and distributing information. Particular attention is paid to ensuring standardisation of information sets. For example, a piece of costing information is so devised that it can be used by accounts, marketing and production. These organisations treat all information as their property, attaching to it a value like any other asset. This denies the employee any sense of ownership and tends to detach them from the work process with consequential inefficiencies evolving. It is asserted, that a motivated staff is a contented and efficient staff.

One important way to motivate is to give the individual responsibility within their job. Such responsibility is manifest in how much ability a person will be given to determine the information need of their particular function. To standardise information in the way that many corporate systems do, takes away that fundamental element of responsibility. Levitan, on the other hand, would claim this to be an inevitable consequence of increasingly sophisticated corporate structures. In addition, Karen Levitan and others imply that information which is not used as a resource is inferior. On the contrary, one could argue that giving the individual ownership could result in a greater entrepreneurial drive.

Standardisation is the killer of innovation. It is difficult to conceive of any substantial organisation, however, where such a degree of individuality could be tolerated. Their size demands a need for cohesion through standardised practice. Therefore it is only in the smaller establishments where such freedom would work. Large organisations which do not treat their information as a resource still exist. Their mechanisms of control, however, are not informal or organic. Indeed, the realities are the converse. Individuality is stifled by greater control, rather than less. No one is trusted to use information for the organisation's good without formal control procedures. Classic examples of such organisations are to be found within the civil service or large quasi-government institutions such as the post office.

A matrix of information control

It has been suggested that there is a relationship between the way in which a firm uses its information and its structure. A matrix can be established differentiating organisations in terms of how they treat their information and the consequential structural characteristics. If, for example, information is plotted against size four major structural types could be identified. Each is the outcome of the way a particular firm uses its information.

On the vertical axis of the matrix are the two extremes of information. On the horizontal axis are the two extremes of organisational size. Both information and size are considered to be contingents, that is, variables which affect the characteristics of an organisation. The four possible combinations of these two variables determine four organisational structures. Thus each structure is an ideal for each of the four combinations. For example, a managerial structure is the appropriate structure for a large firm using information as a resource.

Research into the validity of such a matrix is by no means complete. There is evidence from the NBS regional survey, for example, that such a correlation does indeed exist. In general, the more successful managerial-style firms tend to treat their information as a resource, whilst the more successful entrepreneurial organisations tend to treat their information as a perceptual phenomenon, and so on. It is not yet certain whether the matrix is predictive, that is, implying combinations which are not successful. There is sufficient evidence, however, to support the claim that information usage affects organisational structure.

The issue of information is much more than whether or not it is a resource. Information is indeed the essence of an organisation, shaping and determining its structure. For example, bureaucratic organisations could not effectively treat information as a resource because their mechanisms could not control it that way. A technical/professional organisation, on the other hand, is better able to handle its information as a resource because of its structural characteristics.

The implication is that there should be a natural balance between the design of an organisation and its information structure. Where this has not been achieved it is because managers are not matching the structure of their organisations with an appropriate usage of information. NBS research has also shown that the implementation of computer technology can worsen any potential for imbalance. This is perhaps because of two factors.

Firstly, the characteristics of the technology itself do tend to enhance resource-driven rather than perception-driven information. Secondly, the greater volume of information generated makes the problem more apparent.

As we increasingly complicate our information systems with computer technology, a gap develops between those who implement them and those who are expected to use them. But there is a definite perceptual gap between those who manage these systems and the staff who must use them.

The starting point for any organisational redesign should be its relational framework encompassing the information network, the political process and the structure. These will be affected by change which could in turn throw them out of balance. The introduction of a computerised system, then, will not only affect the information network of the firm but it will also have knock-on effects for the other two. The literature discussing this area is contradictory. There is a common belief in much of the 'management' literature that computerised systems reduce complexity, not increase it, by reducing the layers of administrators.

There are many changes which managers can implement which would upset the balance of their organisation. Generally, each has an obvious impact which is immediately addressed. A new work procedure should bring about new management procedures and hence new power relationships. The adjustment is immediate because its effect is obvious. There are, however, other, less obvious implications of those actions which are rarely addressed. Unfortunately they fester and sometimes grow within the body of the organisation, both perceptual and physical, preventing it from achieving a healthy equilibrium. The introduction of information technology is one such change, or, indeed the redesign of a system which is already supported by such technology is another.

In particular, traditional strategies are unable to recognise or manage the fundamental issues because they are based in the physical domain alone and do not recognise the interactive channels in the perceptual domain through which most of the computer technology impact is transmitted.

Every organisation possessing a computer system large enough to have a substantial impact is faced with a split in its task structure. This split is between the technicians (people knowledgeable about computing and information technology) and the user (people who use the facilities but generally do not fully understand them). Such a dichotomy, which is both perceptual and physical, has caused considerable problems for organisations because computer systems subvert the organisational structure by creating centres of power not in keeping with established control.

A particular firm is seen to be in disequilibrium because its three elements (structure, information network and political process) are not in balance. The consequences of this are often manifest in what has been termed the blackbox syndrome. Its symptoms, if not its nature, are well known throughout the business world. These are, briefly: the lack of management control over what is perhaps its most important technology; the creation of a three-way power dichotomy between management, user and technician, and an increasing alienation between employee and the work process. An example of this syndrome can usually be found in every firm with some form of data processing function.

The blackbox represents the point where the information is processed (normally in the data processing department). How it is done and the operation behind it is, in most cases, beyond the perception and control of management and user, hence the name. At one end of the overall process, of which the blackbox is a part, data are prepared for input to the blackbox and are generally understood by the user. At the other end, the output from the blackbox is received and, it is to be hoped, understood by the user. The middle area is, to both user and management, an unknown—a blackbox. For management there may be some political/line control but no understanding.

For the non-management user there may be some understanding but no political/line control. Any user audit trail tends to follow input data to the point of entry into the blackbox, stop there and then to pick it up as output at the other end. The blackbox itself is very much under the control of a specific set of personnel, the technicians. They are, in effect, gatekeepers to all information which passes through their domain.

The more an organisation computerises its information network the greater their control as gatekeepers and the greater their power. For example, financial data are produced by the finance department for processing. At that point the data are in control and possession of the originating department (finance). However, once they are received by the data processing department it is that department, acting as an agent, that gains temporary ownership of the data. This is because the originating department is not able to maintain control of it whilst it is in the DP department's domain. As such, the latter can process it in the way it thinks best, which may or may not coincide with the finance department's needs. Within this part of the process the data are, in effect, in a blackbox. When they reappear at the other end they have been transformed into financial information and once again pass back into the ownership of the finance department. But more than this the DP department, through its ability to change data to suit its perception of the environment, can influence the actions of its client departments.

The blackbox is a product of technological history. The way we organise information processes, even in a modern day micro-orientated business, has been determined by the mainframe applications of the late 1960s and early 1960s. These were not user friendly, requiring highly qualified specialists to run them, and very complex, almost indecipherable, programmes to make them work. Neither of these allowed for much interaction with the user. Indeed, it was debatable whether there were such things, as users in those days. They just seemed to be at the end of a complicated process and not considered at all. The machines themselves were bulky and their operation did not allow for flexible workflow. They were locked away in contamination-free, air conditioned rooms with restricted access so that any integration was negligible. Input was thus introduced in batches and returned to the user as output in batches. This was not a work methodology adopted out of choice.

The computers themselves could generally only run one programme at a time and therefore processing work had to be queued. Input devices were slow and cumbersome, more often than not comprising card readers which aggravated the batch nature of the system. Output devices were generally printers, chain driven and very slow. These were widely recognised as the bottlenecks in the system even though the computer itself (the central processing unit) was not particularly fast. Managers' response to this new technology was to create a shell around it, almost to protect themselves from its impact.

Data processing departments sprang up to house the technicians and the new technology and they quickly became something apart. Their jargon was not easily understood by outsiders; their culture was also not fully integrated into the rest of the company. In effect the manager of such a department had no immediate superior because none was able to understand its needs and objectives. As a consequence the data processing manager was placed in a powerful position because he became a gatekeeper to vital information sets.

The relationship between user and technician has to be developed if its computer implementations are to be a success. This chapter was written with latter-day information technology in mind, and more importantly with latter-day expertise in mind. During the early 1960s there was no user available who could act as implementor or developer alongside the technicians. Those in charge of the technology did not themselves see the need to develop such skills in the user and spent most of their energies in jealously guarding their newly founded domains. The responsibility for innovation, implementation and day-to-day running was given to them alone. The purpose of presenting the potted history of computer development is to demonstrate that the present organisational structures controlling information are derived from those of the early days.

Despite advancing beyond batch processing into real time processing we still quite often organise information as if it is to be batch processed. And despite the rise of the microcomputer and demise of the mainframe, we still have data processing departments attempting to control the work. Examples of such may not always be identifiable in the physical sense but rather in the perceptual sense.

To look at the computer magazines and management literature a casual observer could be forgiven in thinking that all our firms have reached fourth generation computing and possess nothing out of date. The reality is rather different. Even in those cases where this is so, it is quite often negated by staff attitudes. In many cases senior managers are not comfortable with the computer, let alone a networked system. Their learning experiences took place when the computer was still young, and they are now unwilling to learn anything new.

On the other hand, those technicians who are now themselves managers learnt their trade on the older style, batch processing computers, and although they are undoubtedly competent in the newer technologies their perceptions of the user and how their technology should be applied are based upon their early experiences. The net effect is that even today senior managers are willing to give up their control of what is an important resource, and the technicians/specialists managers are willing to accept such a responsibility.

Socialisation is the transmission of values and norms to individuals so that they develop an acceptable and standardised fit within their particular society. Children, for example, are socialised into being adults. It is a perceptual process rather than a physical one. Stories abound of where the mechanisms have gone wrong, for example the 'wolf children of Midnapore' where two children had been found in India in 1920 apparently brought up by wolves. They walked on all fours and preferred the diet of the wolf. They were in effect perceptual wolves, if not actually so physically. This example highlights an interesting learning experience permanently colouring an individual's perception and hence his actions. It is an extremely powerful process: the laying down of a perceptual veneer continuously updated by different experiences and social forces. However, it is not easily changed.

Individuals, as they get older, for example, tend to be increasingly reluctant to revise their established behaviour. Despite the aging influence it is a continual process that is with us all our lives. It is also a multi-dimensional process in that it relates to the different facets of our experiential framework. Thus we are socialised into roles within our family, gender, work and so on.

Individuals are, therefore, socialised into their places of work in just the same way as any other aspect of society. In so doing we develop a range of norms and values necessary to be accepted into a business organisation. Neither is it a one-off experience when we enter work for the first time. As our experience grows we may be able to develop techniques which can short-cut the process but when we change our jobs there will be new things to learn.

Cultures and norms vary from firm to firm so that during the first few weeks of any new job we have to modify our established perceptions accordingly. Schein, for example, is particularly keen to analyse organisations in terms of their differing cultures. There seem to be three relevant dimensions.

Firstly, there are societal norms and values. For example, it is the norm within our society not to steal. Any deviancy is not tolerated and formally punished. Being a member of a subgroup is generally not accepted as an argument for not complying.

Secondly, there are subset societal norms and values. These relate to specific groups or organisations within our society. The dos and don'ts of a business organisation are an example, or the codes of conduct of the legal or medical professions. They have been developed as a consequence of the wider societal norms and, although aimed at a specific body, are embraced by them.

Lastly, the structures of society and its subsets tend to be more abstract than the other two. They are ideas or general perceptions which cannot be regarded as societal or subset norms, which indeed possess their own socialisation process and thus their own particular norms and values. An example would be the general idea that firms are in business to make a profit. This is a convention arising from the 'Protestant ethic' of our culture. It is not a societal norm since many may not even be aware of it, and yet it is not solely a norm or value of a specific subset, such as management. It is, and can be adopted by many subsets, and this is what makes it different from norms themselves: consequential norms or values are transferred to those adopting it. In other words, by adopting such a conventional perception an individual is determined by acceptance of the associated norms to act in a certain way, to strive for a profit within a business organisation and so on.

Conventional Perception

Conventional perceptions become embodied within the accepted wisdom of many subsets. Ideas about information technology and its use are prone to becoming conventional perceptions. One such example is the idea that there is a need for a data processing department because of the technology's complexity. To be competitive, firms must computerise, is another example; manual systems cannot be as good as a computerised system is yet another.

The management literature is full of conventional perceptions about information technology. Neither are conventional perceptions easily changed. Societal norms can be changed by enactment of law or social pressure to alienate deviants. In a similar manner, subset norms are enforced by codes of conduct or peer action. Conventional perceptions, on the other hand, possess no such social framework through which to produce change. They come into being and change through a complex process of social historicism and thus cannot be easily altered by management decree for example.

The implication is that we cannot always directly control our technological environment because our perception of it is obscured by established ideas. We accept these ideas as being sound because we are comfortable with their familiarity. We justify them in terms of their historical continuity. That is, their persistence within the minds of people over the years ensures their increasing acceptance: the easy option is to do just that, accept them, and not to question them. In so doing we establish norms to enforce them into which newcomers have to be socialised. Such perceptions also have an important role in the development of the design of the organisation. We saw there that they are the consequence of our perceptions and the way we interact through the political process. These conventional perceptions form an important part of that, which ones we decide to adopt or reject have consequences which reach far beyond our attitudinal stance.

Computer systems are implemented within a certain perceptual framework. At that time they are themselves constrained by conventional perceptions, so that ideas established to that date influence the way the system is organised. In addition, however, the logic of the system itself, based upon those conventional perceptions, constrains future actions to within and around them. For example, a computerised information system controlled by a data processing department is implemented within a business organisation. The characteristics of that system are the consequence of the perception of its implementors. In other words, a conventional perception is that there must be a DP department, or that computer systems are better than manual ones, and so on. Once installed, then over a period of time the demands that the system makes upon individuals will itself alter their perceptions and generate new ones.

There is thus an interactive process which operates historically as well as in real time. That is the organisational framework for many of our activities has been inherited from the past. Organisations, therefore, are better seen as being time-independent, driven by interactions from the past and present, and creating the framework for future interaction. Tranfield thought this aspect vital in understanding new systems implementation. Individuals setting up systems brought with them a personal history of experience and conventional perceptions, which Tranfield described as their historicity. These then are built into the system.

Information Network

The development of a blackbox within any organisation encourages information to be used as a resource. The necessity of a balance within a firm is identified between how its information is treated (thus determining the characteristic of its network) and the corresponding organisational structure. If the two are not in sympathy then problems could arise and the host firm may not be effective. The implication of this is that the maintenance of a blackbox control mechanism could force an imbalance between the information network and its organisational structure.

Whether an information network and its organisational structure match and are balanced depends quite often on something akin to a managerial lottery. Before computeri-sation the information network is in many cases in harmony with its host firm. Subsequent to computerisation, whether the information network remains in harmony will depend upon two factors:

1) *The nature of information control implemented.* According to Mowshowitz managers have high expectations when deciding for the first time to implement a computerised information network.

However, such expectations are fuelled by more than hope: they are developed within the culture of management itself and linked to the established ideas on control which are themselves based upon experiential assessment from the existing environment. NBS research seems to suggest that managers do not link, in policy formulation or perception, the nature of their information network with the implementation of computer technology. The existence of the blackbox within organisations is encouraging this misconception.

2) *The nature of the organisational structure already in place*. This aspect is the outcome of a historical process. Managers can at times set out to change their structures, but generally the timescale of computer implementation does not permit considerable change. When computer systems are installed management do not therefore consider the needs of their organisation structure. Indeed, in parallel with the upgrading of their information network they generally, and artificially, implement totally inappropriate mechanisms of control.

Political Process

Efficiency is a physical domain based concept in that it refers to a productive entity's (firm, department, individual's) capability of meeting pre-set targets. Effectiveness, on the other hand, is more perceptual domain-based and relates to the productive entity's capability to fit into its environment. Thus a firm may produce widgets efficiently but it is not effective in its market because the widget has no demand. The contention of this section is that, in the final analysis, computer technology is not very suitable for the information networks of our organisations because of the way management is currently implementing it.

There can be no doubt that such technology increases efficiency, but it is doubtful whether it increases effectiveness. This is because the blackbox creates anomalies within the organisational structure which makes it difficult to achieve a balance between the political process of the organisation and its information network, and hence could threaten long-term effectiveness.

The balance between the political process of an organisation and its information network is a functional relationship which includes the organisation's structure as well. The information network and the structure together create the inherent characteristics of an organisation. One or the other could be the dominant determinant depending upon circumstance; and one or the other could be affected by variables, such as technology affecting the structure of the organisation.

The political process moulds itself to the needs of that relationship acting as a transmission mechanism between the two. The relationship between the information network and the political process is particularly close. Within this context the structure merely provides a framework or an arena. The way that individuals are allowed to control information and how much it belongs to them will determine to a great extent how much they will act politically. Conversely, how politically aware the individuals are within any organisation will also determine the nature of the information network. The two cannot be separate. For example, if an individual has knowledge which others do not have or do not understand then that person is more likely to use it to his/her benefit, to promote themselves within the organisation or to resist the action of others detrimental to their aims and aspirations. They have this power through the nature of the information network and thus have the ability to express such power through the political process. Both are therefore affected by the characteristics of the other.

It is when interference happens that problems arise because changes could well be implemented the consequences of which are not readily understood. As such, no corrective action will be taken to offset any imbalance. A classic example of this is a post-computer environment: the relationship between the particular information network and the political process can be affected in two ways. Firstly, the computer technology itself drives the information network out of balance with the political process destroying the established mechanisms within the network, thus making established political relationships inappro-priate. One obvious example is the relationship between a department manager and his employees.

The installation of a computer network could short-cut such a functional framework. No longer in control of the department's information the manager's relationship with the employees could change. For instance, power could go to that member who understands the new information system or who can access the most valuable information. Secondly, the management response to computer installation by creating a blackbox splits the company into a power dichotomy. The forces of change which this can produce are more easily accommodated by a managerially structured organisation since the political processes of such a structure are more akin to this type of impact.

Nevertheless this may be more theoretical than actual. The tearing apart of the information network and the political process in this manner can do no firm any good, and if its structures are not in any way prepared, such an impact could prove disastrous.

Pettigrew's model of an organisational network emphasises the political aspects and impacts which NBS research identified. Within the political process all information is a resource. How an individual obtains information is dependent upon the information network; how it is then manipulated depends upon the political process. The expression or manifestation of this is in terms of power relationships. These are natural to an organisation.

Structure

The structure of a firm, both physically and perceptually, is the framework in which the other two aspects—the information network and the political process—operate. They are dependent upon it just as much as it is dependent upon them. And yet we find once again that management policy after computer installation is tending to indeed drive them apart. Simon defined an organisation as a complex pattern of communications and relationships between groupings. His model emphasises how delicate an organisational structure is; how sensitive it is to the perceptions and actions of those within it; how in many instances, therefore, it is very much an abstract concept. The actions of managers, then, after computer installation may have a bigger impact upon their firm's structure than they perhaps realise.

The methods of work, control and interaction are in place because the previous way of doing things has determined them to be so. Thus any form of quantum, as opposed to incremental, change brings forth structural problems simply because the balance between the three forces is upset and not given time to adjust and reassert itself.

In many cases, after a short period equilibrium is established and the firm is once again on an even keel. The problem, however, with the existence of a blackbox within a firm is that the new equilibrium is rarely achieved. The blackbox is not a natural development but has been artificially implemented by conventional wisdom. The rigid dichotomy created by such an approach therefore may not suit or be in sympathy with the existing structure.

The firm relies upon flexibility in its management and control processes. Employees can approach other employees directly and without too many gatekeepers blocking their way. This allows for an entrepreneurial and innovative drive within the organisation. It has developed naturally and thus the structure, along with the other two major components of information network and political process, is in harmony with it. The implementation of a computer system into this firm would create unnatural barriers and thus force it out of equilibrium. The information network would be treating information as if it were a resource, whilst the structure of the firm was developed to treat information as a perceptual phenomenon. The consequence is a confused political process which no longer aids the organisation but acts as a hindrance, almost a catalyst to dysfunctional change.

While mankind has developed a myriad ways of applying and controlling power to dominate and shape our environment through the use of tools, weapons, machines, fuels, vehicles, instruments, clothing, buildings and roads, metals, plastics and drugs, agriculture, and electricity, the handling of information has lagged considerably, perhaps because the human brain is itself so remarkably powerful. Until recently, there have been only three major developments in this area: the invention of written language, some five or six thousand years ago; that of simple arithmetic operations, using what would now be called a digital representation of numbers, about a thousand years later; and that of printing, about five hundred years ago. With written language, we get the capacity to make a permanent record of information and also to convey messages across space and time: storage, retrieval, and communication.

With digital arithmetic, we get the ability to perform accurate, repeatable manipulations of quantitative data. With printing, we can make many identical copies of the same record and so broadcast a single message to a wide and continuing audience.

Beyond these outstanding advances, until the last hundred years or so, the only progress has been in the engineering and increasingly plentiful production of more powerful and reliable and efficient, faster and cheaper devices to implement these concepts. In the last hundred years, we see the rapidly accelerating advent of a technology so powerful, novel, widespread, and influential that we may indeed call it the Second Industrial Revolution. Its basis is electromagnetic, in many interconnected forms: photography, photocopying, cinematography, and holography; telegraphy, telephony, radio communication, radar, sonar, and telemetry; sound and video recording and reproduction; vacuum tubes, transistors, printed circuits, masers, lasers, fibre optics, and (in rapid succession) integrated circuits (IC), large-scale integration (LSI), and very large-scale integration (VLSI) of circuitry on a tiny semi-conducting 'chip'; and, finally, the bewildering variety of electronic digital computers.

The progress has been truly amazing. In only about 40 years, electronic communications and news media have become commonplace and indispensable; computers have proliferated, becoming increasingly fast, powerful, small, and cheap, so that now there is scarcely a human activity in which they are not to be found, bearing an increasing share of the burden of repetitive information processing, just as the machines of the First Industrial Revolution have taken over the majority of heavy and unpleasant physical labour. Now, information cannot only be stored, retrieved, communicated, and broadcast in enormous quantities and at phenomenal speeds, but it can also be rearranged, selected, marshalled, and transformed.

Until recently, these activities were the sole province of the human brain. While creative, judicious, moral, and esthetic choices are still best left to people, all the tedious and mechanical mental processes can now be relegated to the accurate, fast, and tireless machines. Any sequence of operations on information that can be precisely specified can be carried out without further human intervention or supervision.

At first, computers were the experimental toys of university researchers; then they became the tools of government establishments and giant corporations, huge, expensive, individually designed and manufactured, and beyond the reach of any but the wealthiest organisations.

People thought of the future in terms of machines of ever-greater speed and capacity; centralised behemoths would hold all the world's information in gigantic data banks, whence major decisions would issue to be imposed upon the populations at their mercy.

With the emergence of powerful, cheap, mass-produced computers-on-a-chip, the picture has changed radically. Now we see tiny computers everywhere: in wrist-watches, microwave ovens, electronic games, pocket calculators, cameras, typewriters, musical instruments, etc.

What used to be done, with few options, by intricate mechanical devices is now performed, with great flexibility and convenience and at much less expense, by the ubiquitous preprogrammed microcomputer.

The probable future has become one of millions of small yet powerful computers, controlling virtually every machine and appliance, distributed in every home, on every desk, in every workshop; many of them connected in a maze of small and large networks, much like the present telephone network, so that individual computers could communicate, sharing information in a gigantic distributed database, and gaining, through distributed processing, computational power whose extent is yet difficult to gauge; all this following the individual requirements and choices of the owner or operator of each machine. Increasingly, we are confronted, not only with the results of the use of computers throughout industry, commerce, banking, advertising, science, the communications industry, newspapers, airlines, and hospitals, but also with the realistic possibility of purchasing computer power for our own small enterprises, offices, and homes. This may be done in a variety of ways, but in all of them, the real cost of computation is constantly diminishing.

It is probably fair to say that the question of computerisation is not "whether", but "when" and "how". We must choose whether to lease equipment or to buy it; whether to install terminals, connected to a computerised "service bureau", or a complete local computer system; whether to get a package of standard programmes directed towards our kind of work, to commission new programmes tailored to our special needs, or to learn programming and write our own; whether to go it alone or to share a system with a number of similar users (especially if they are in the same building); how far to take our first efforts at computerisation; what to include and what to continue doing by hand. Computer programming is likely to become the literacy of the third millennium A.D.

Elementary schools may well be teaching it before long, and we might be well advised to gain at least a smattering of knowledge of computers and of programming competence, especially since computer languages and programming environments are becoming increasingly helpful and friendly to the uninitiated user.

A computer is a machine for the automatic processing of information. Historically, this information was numerical, and computers were machines for doing arithmetic. Unlike the simpler calculating machines, which can perform only one elementary arithmetic operation at a time, they need to be told what to do next (usually, by suitable button-pushes); computers can be given a list of operations to perform (often with branching and repetitions, depending on tests of sign or value included among the operations), and will then execute these in proper sequence without further intervention. This sequence of instructions is called a programme.

A digital computer stores its information in the form of words, finite ordered sets of digits, each of which can have only one of a finite set of values.

Considerations of simplicity, reliability, and economy dictate that electrical engineers should design computers to consist of a great number of similar pieces of circuitry, each of which can only be in one of two states, usually denoted by 0 and 1.

Such binary digits (or bits) are the elements of which computer digital representation is built. A row of eight bits is called a *byte,* and the majority of computers have their storage of information organised in words of one, two, four, or eight bytes (8, 16, 32, or 64 bits).

The number of bits in a word is termed its length; if this is k, then the number of possible distinct pieces of information that can be stored in such a word is two. In particular, four bits together can have 16 different contents, and these are standard binary representations of the numbers 0-15:

0000 = 0 0001 = 1 0010 = 2 0011 = 3

0100 = 4 0101 = 5 0110 = 6 0111 = 7

1000 = 8 1001 = 9 1010 = A 1011 = B

1100 = C 1101 = D 1110 = E 1111 = F

with A = 10, B = 11, C = 12, D 13, E 14, and F = 15. These may now be viewed as the 16 possible digits of a represen-tation (the hexadecimal, or hex), which is much more compact and humanly intelligible than a long string of zeros and ones. The byte 10110010 becomes "132", and the four-byte computer word 01001100011100101101000110001110 becomes the eight-digit hex word "4C72D18E".

The following are various parts of which any computer is composed. These are, essentially:

— a *central processing unit* (CPU), which is the controlling and computing centre of the machine;

— a *memory*, possibly of different levels, in which both data and instructions are stored;

— a variety of *input* and *output (I/O)* devices, through which the machine communicates with the world outside it.

The CPU consists of an *Operation Control Unit* (OCU), an *arithmetic/logical unit* (ALU), and a relatively small, very-fast accessible *Local Memory* (LM). The OCU keeps track of the memory location of the next instruction to be executed, and analyses the current instruction, so as to activate the proper operation of a memory transfer, non-sequential jump (by appropriately changing the address of the next instruction), input or output of information, or computation (performed by the ALU), as is indicated by the instruction code.

The ALU actually carries out the elementary arithmetic operations (addition, subtraction or negation, multiplication, division or reciprocation) and logical operations (these being bit-by-bit operations, without carry, such as not, and, and XOr; e.g., not 1010 = 0010, 1100 and 0101 = 0100, 0110 XOr 1010 = 1100) on the data given to it by the OCU. The LM receives the operands called for by the OCU and also the results of the ALU'S operations upon them. For example, the OCU may retrieve the factors of a multiplication from the main memory into a pair of LM registers and instruct the ALU to multiply them and place their product in another LM register. Such registers are usually called accumulators, and they are normally double-length (since the product of two k-bit numbers is a 2k-bit number). Other LM registers are used for counting (e.g., repetitions) and are called index registers; others hold intermediate values and are called buffers; and, finally, there are one-bit or two-bit registers which reflect the information on which tests are made by the OCU (for example, the occurrence of a carry, the vanishing or positivity of an answer, or the occurrence of an arithmetic overflow): these are termed flags.

Originally, the CPU was a sizable piece of electronics, hand-assembled and highly complex. With the advent of micro-miniaturisation of circuitry, printing, and photographic techniques, and the mass production of components only the largest computers (mainframes) are built in the old way. Smaller systems generally have the entire CPU on a single chip. Among these, the name microcomputer is now applied to those with less than a million words of memory and a word length of one or two bytes; the name minicomputer applies to the larger machines, with two-to four-byte words and one to a hundred million words of memory.

The *main memory* (MM) consists of magnetic or electronic components which store the information (both data and instructions) needed by the computer. The individual words are directly addressable from the CPU by number (rather like houses in a street), and their contents are retrievable in very short times, of the order of the operation time of the CPU (ranging from fractions of a nanosecond, 10^{-9} or one billionth of a second, for the fastest mainframes to several microseconds, 10^{-6} or millionths of a second, for the slower micros). This is often referred to as high-speed storage or *Random Access Memory* (RAM). While most of the MM is erasable and may be changed at will, some memory is used to store constants and often-used utility programmes and is not erasable by the CPU: such memory is called *read-only memory* (ROM). Sometimes this is optional and can be plugged into the computer: this is called *firmware*.

Note that a computer with one-byte-long addresses can have at most 28 = 256 words of mm; a two-byte address can reach 256^2 = 65536 words; a three-byte address can select any of 16777216 words of MM; and so on. In practice, most micros and minis have MM ranging in size from 214 = 16384 to 218 = 262144 words. It should be noted that 10^3 = 1000 and 2^{10} = 1024. Since computers are so heavily slanted towards base-2 representation, it has become almost universal computer parlance to use the prefix *kilo* or K (which usually denotes a thousand units) to denote 1024 and the prefix *mega* or M (which usually denotes a million units) to denote $2^{20} = 1024^2$ = 1048576. Thus, we write 16K for 2^{14} and ¼M for 2^{18}. Perhaps the commonest size of MM consists of 64K = 65536 words.

Almost all computer instructions comprise an operation code (usually one byte long, allowing 256 possible operations to be specified), followed by an operand reference (number, index, or address) of variable length (since some operations require more data than others; for instance, the STOP instruction needs no operand, so it is one byte long).

The *extended memory* (EM) is sometimes considered under I/O devices, both because it is often physically located outside the computer (while the CPU and the MM are usually in the same enclosure), and because its speed of access is much slower than the speed of operation of the CPU and is comparable with the range of speeds of I/O devices.

Most read/write memory is magnetic (optical memory is read-only, and fast RAM is either magnetic or electronic), either in the form of tape, drum, or disk, coated with magnetic material, much like sound-recording equipment; it is similarly erased, read, and recorded upon by "heads" which contain electromagnetic sensors/polarisers. The cheapest (and most limited, in both speed and capacity) device is a common portable cassette recorder, with ¼" tape cassettes. From this, one moves to specially engineered cassettes and recorders and thence to high-speed ½" or 1" reel-to-reel drives carrying thousands of feet of tape at very high speeds. Access times can be quite good for sequential access, along the tape, but random access time is poor at best, running to seconds or even minutes.

When we wish for practically useful EM, combining large capacity with relative economy and speed of random access, we must turn to drum or disk memory and, nowadays, the former have been practically replaced by the latter. Disk memory is of two types: floppy disk and hard disk, the first being the cheaper, slower, smaller-capacity option. Floppy disks are flexible, have diameters of 5¼" or 8" generally, and are removable from the disk-drive, so allowing one to build up an unlimited library of stored data. The information is stored on concentric circular tracks (not on a single spiral track, as on a sound record), on one or both sides of the disk.

The number of tracks and the number of bytes per track vary (the density increasing with precision of engineering, and so with cost of the drive), but the total capacity of a floppy disk is in the range of 50KB to 1MB. The disks rotate at, typically, 300 rpm, and access time is governed by the time required to place the movable head on the right track, a fraction of a second, plus the fifth of a second taken by the head to traverse the circumference of the track, in search of a record; thereafter, consecutive bytes are accessed at some thousands per second.

Hard disks are rigid and have larger diameters. There are drives with anything from one to a dozen disks, rotating at about ten times the speed of floppy-disk drives (and so diminishing the access time of records in a track) with one or several heads.

Fixed-head drives naturally must have a head for each track (which costs more), but save head-movement time in random access. Winchester disks are movable-head drives with sealed-in disks, which the heads ride very close to the disk, cushioned by the layer of air between. In floppy-disk drives, the head actually rides on the disk, eventually wearing it out. The capacity of hard-disk drive ranges from 10 MB to 100 MB in a single drive. Some movable-head hard-disk drives have removable disks or disk-packs, allowing for greater library storage.

The I/O devices are the computer's link with the outside world. In large mainframe computers, we see paper card (as in Hollerith or "IBM" cards) and paper tape readers and punches: the perforations in the paper carry the information. Increasingly in large computers, and almost universally in small ones, the main input is from the keyboard of a terminal. This is much like a typewriter keyboard, and depressing any key sends an 8-bit code to the computer.

When the computer is waiting for input from this terminal, it reads the code and interprets it as a datum; when it is busy, either the message is lost or it is held in a "buffer" for subsequent input (this depends on how the connection is made and what the computer is made to do). It is quite common for the computer to be connected to several terminals, all competing for its attention. This is called time-sharing. The computer cycles around the terminals, looking for their several inputs and dividing its CPU time among them. The main output of the computer is to the display devices of the terminals; these are either video displays (cathode ray tubes, CRT, just like the screens of black-and-white or colour TV sets; indeed, simple micros sometimes use ordinary television sets as display devices) or printers (in so-called hard-copy terminals). Of course, the computer may be connected to additional video displays and printers, of different qualities, as well as to plotters, a kind of printer for drawing graphs and diagrams. Many types and speeds of printers exist. Other input devices, such as audio amplifiers (receiving signals from radio tuners, record players, etc.), video receivers and recorders, laser disk drives and a variety of scientific instruments, can all be classified as transducers (devices that transform physical quantities, such as position, conductivity, pressure, temperature, vibration frequency, or amplitude, into electro-magnetic impulses) linked to digitisers (which convert such impulses into sequences of zero/one pulses). Output from the computer can similarly follow the reverse process, yielding visible or audible results, or the control of mechanical or electrical equipment. Thus computers can draw pictures (often, moving pictures), make music and other sounds, and can control appliances, machinery and whole manufacturing processes.

Beyond the programmes, there lies an endless variety of unquestionable applications programmes. There are programmes for ballistics, boat design, analysis of molecular structure from x-ray diffraction data, tabulation of Bessel functions, simulation of naval battles and economic cycles, etc. Most of these are not on the market and only work on one machine; but there are very many programmes available on the open market, produced or distributed by software houses, with various levels of efficiency, sophistication, and reliability.

Index